Fostering on the Farm

Fostering on the Farm

*Child Placement
in the Rural Midwest*

MEGAN BIRK

UNIVERSITY OF
ILLINOIS PRESS
Urbana, Chicago, and Springfield

First Illinois paperback, 2019
© 2015 by the Board of Trustees
of the University of Illinois
All rights reserved
1 2 3 4 5 C P 5 4 3 2 1
♾ This book is printed on acid-free paper.

The Library of Congress cataloged the cloth
edition as follows:
Birk, Megan, 1979–
Fostering on the farm : child placement in the rural
Midwest / Megan Birk.
pages   cm
Includes bibliographical references and index.
ISBN 978-0-252-03924-9 (cloth : alk. paper)
ISBN 978-0-252-09729-4 (e-book)
1. Foster children—Middle West—History—19th
century. 2. Foster home care—Middle West—History—
19th century. 3. Rural families—Middle West—
History—19th century. 4. Farm life—Middle West—
History—19th century.
I. Title.
HV875.56.M54B57   2015
362.73′3097709034—dc23   2014046098

Paperback ISBN 978-0-525-08436-2

Contents

Acknowledgments vii

Introduction: The Search for a Home 1

1. The Rural Ideal: Constructing a Myth 17
2. "Qualify them for the duties of life" 43
3. "The hideous consequences" 78
4. "The right of the state to interfere is unquestioned" 105
5. The Farm, the Federal Government, and the Decline of Placement 143

Epilogue: "The great drama of childhood" 178

Notes 184

Bibliography 214

Index 229

Illustrations follow page 104

Acknowledgments

In an effort at brevity, let me first extend my thanks to all those not specifically named here but who provided friendship, support, or suggestions as the process of research and writing took place. Uncovering the challenges of these children and their families makes me endlessly appreciative for my own modern family, which includes my sisters, Dana and Sara; my sister, Abbey, who skillfully edited early chapter drafts; and my parents, Jim and Maryjo. Historians often refer to everyone who is like family, but not related, as "fictive kin." There is nothing fictive about my extended family, including Patty and Ken Cramer, Eowyn Powell Ford, Michelle Degler Adams, and Betsy Knott, who all gave me housing, meals, and company—the trinity for historians working away from home. My colleagues at the University of Texas–Pan American, Brent M. S. Campney and Linda English, provided friendship and camaraderie. South Texas friends Moriah McCracken, Robert Ruetz, and David and Lillian Renner have made living here fun, and for that my entire household thanks you. Sara Morris, Erin Kempker, Eric Hall, Christina Abreu, and Kara Kvaran, all talented historians in their own right, have been professionally and personally supportive. Sara's unflappable research skills have earned her my unyielding appreciation.

Pamela Riney-Kehrberg of Iowa State University deserves a special mention for thoughtfully engaging my ideas, reading a copy of this manuscript and helping with the introduction, and sharing with me some of her own unpublished research from her excellent book about rural childhood. Pam's mentorship skills can be seen in the success of many of her former students, of whom I am only one. Members of my writing across the curriculum group at UTPA read portions of chapters 1 and 3, and I thank them for their thoughtful suggestions. R. Douglas Hurt oversaw the beginnings of this project in its dissertation stage. This is also a good time to recognize the influence of Jon C. Teaford, professor emeritus at Purdue University, who served on my committee and who showed me what a good teacher-scholar looks like. Portions of this book have been featured as articles in *Agricultural History*, *The Journal of the Gilded Age and Progressive Era*, and the *Indiana Magazine of History*. I thank the editors of those journals and the readers who reviewed the articles for their constructive and thoughtful feedback from which this book has benefited.

In the earliest stage this project benefited financially from a King V. Hostick dissertation award from the Illinois Historical Society and funding from the Purdue University Department of History. At UTPA I received assistance from a Faculty Research Grant, the office of the Vice Provost for Faculty Development, and the Dean's Office for the College of Arts and Humanities. The staff at the University of Illinois Press, particularly Laurie Matheson, have been wonderful to work with and patiently provided guidance. Additionally, archivists at the Ohio and Indiana Historical Societies, the Bowling Green State University Center for Archival Studies, the Troy County Historical and Genealogical Society, the Vigo County Public Library, and the Interlibrary Loan Staff at the University of Texas Pan American helped with materials and images. Without the work of local historians and genealogists, many of whom are specifically interested in the institutional history of their areas, the research for this book would have been less fruitful. These groups and individuals are saving documents, images, and in some cases the very buildings of this story. An additional note of thanks to Robert Beireis, who offered his family's story of placement in Ohio that enriched the manuscript.

This project would not be the same without the two guys who loved and supported me while I worked. This book is dedicated to Joe, who is a true partner, and to the memory of Rupert, my writing companion and sidekick.

Fostering on the Farm

Introduction

The Search for a Home

"This is not my home. It does not seem like home to me, and I would rather have a home of my own."
—*Sixth Triennial Report*, Rose Orphan Home, 20

In 1870, the superintendent of the Montgomery County, Ohio, children's home placed three-year-old James in the home of an area farmer. Despite the young age of his ward, the superintendent drew up an indenture contract in which the farmer promised care, a place in his family, and a payment to James when he reached majority age. While the details of James's childhood remain unknown, he probably grew up learning how to handle farm tools, animals, and related chores and attending a few months of school each year. At the age of seventeen, James wrote to the superintendent explaining his unhappiness. In his letter requesting an early release from his indenture, he expressed displeasure with his placement family; they did not treat him as a family member and he felt undercompensated for his work. After spending his entire childhood on the farm, James left with $50.[1]

This arrangement for James reflected the practices of the time, when institutions individually decided what to do with dependent children and the managers of those facilities were responsible for any oversight of children. Twenty years later, assigning children like James to a farm home continued to take place in states across the country and the popularity of such an idea was reflected on a national level through recommendations by professional child welfare workers who desperately wanted to find suitable homes for institutionalized children. In an increasingly urbanized, industrialized nation, the draw of the farm and the nostalgia attached to perceptions about simple, healthy, family-based labor created the illusion that the environment made the farm family good and masked the reality that morality came not from the land but from the family itself. Changes during the Progressive Era not only increased the amount of farm placement through more professionalized placement services but responded to the need for more supervision with a growing system of institutional oversight by the states.

Between 1870 and 1890, farm placement as a goal for dependent children transitioned from practice to policy through an emphasis on institutional removal by experts and officials. Reformers, convinced that family life could not be manufactured in an institutional setting, lobbied to get all able-bodied children placed out. The farm home potentially countered all that was wrong with an institution: if an institution stunted individualism, the farm fostered it; if an institution failed to teach work ethic and skills, the farm required them; if an institution lacked family relationships, the farm depended on them. During that period, not everyone agreed that finding new homes for children should be a priority, but those who argued in favor of the institution and its benefits found themselves outnumbered. As Progressive-minded reformers tried to gain control of child welfare care through private and public charities, supervision, and casework, these same reformers encountered issues with children being overworked, underloved, and separated from their parents simply because of poverty. Additionally, workers in both child welfare and the new field of rural studies took note of the decline in the prosperity and quality of farm life. What began in the 1890s and early 1900s as an effort at the local, state, and national levels to improve placements actually resulted by the 1920s in the transition to paid foster homes off the farm. The rise and fall of farm placements signifies an important series of changes in dependent child care; between the 1870s and 1920s, farm placements for dependent children increased alongside the number of children institutionalized, but problems with farms and farm placements saw this method exchanged in favor of paid foster care, adoptions, and family preservation. This book explains these transitions while stressing the foremost position of the farm home throughout. Policy about children's welfare did not move from institutional planning directly to paid foster care. Instead, the opportunity for free placements on farms bridged the two care methods and eventually recommended the latter.[2]

Historians have not neglected the importance of placing out children as a component of child welfare policy, noting the popularity of farms and the general lack of supervision. However, the popularity of the orphan trains, highlighted in studies such as those done by Marilyn Irvin Holt and Stephen O'Conner, concentrate the scholarship on the long-distance emigration practices of groups such as the Children's Aid Society of New York (CASNY). As Holt and O'Conner both show, the CASNY and others gained national repute for moving urban children into farm homes across the country, although the Midwest took the majority of the children. These emigration practices involved issues of Americanization and assimilation, nativism, and religious conflict such as those discussed by Linda Gordon in her study about the failed placements of white Catholic children moved to Catholic Hispanic families in Arizona.[3] However, children not moved from east to west in this manner did more in the long run to shape state policies and influence federal policies about child welfare. The practice of shipping children gained notoriety, but on a more local level the problematic power sharing between institutional workers and government officials, the endemic abuse, and the decades without proper supervision actually spurred states forward to develop agencies as a way to help their own children. Additionally, the perceived problems with orphan train children prompted calls to ban or restrict their importation in many Midwestern states, perhaps not coincidentally around the same time these states shaped their own methods for child placement onto farms. As states identified their own child welfare problems, they were less likely to be tolerant of other dependent children being brought in as competition for homes.[4]

The problem with understanding placement through emigration is that it overshadows the significance of farm placement from other institutions. These practices have ignited less attention historically but affected long-term child welfare policies in a more substantial way. The efforts to systematize placing led to more supervision, a challenge for underfunded agencies needing to travel hundreds of miles a week to find children. Not only was the farm discovered to be less than ideal; suburban and paid foster care made supervision easier. Those efforts began because of flaws with farm placements across the Midwest, and not from orphan trains.

To demonstrate the significance of farm placement separately from emigration societies, this study pursues a variation of what historian Kenneth Cmiel calls "social welfare history at the grassroots level."[5] While studying a single institution or place can provide valuable information, so can research at the regional level. The Midwest was believed by many to be the best place to find farm placements: it was the place where other regions wanted to send their children, it had a stable agricultural economy, and it typified agrarian America. The practice of placing children with farmers became so widespread that between 1850 and 1900 one-fifth to one-third of farm homes contained children who were not the biological children of adults in the home. Obviously, some of these children belonged to relatives or neighbors, but others were dependent children sent to the farm.[6] The region's institutions and charities not only participated in farm placement; their methods informed the national discussions that helped shape decades of child welfare policy. State leaders in the Midwest emerged as national experts on child placement.

For its part, the CASNY and its founder, Charles Loring Brace, play an important role in the story of placements, not for the distances traveled but for the insistence on farm homes for dependent children. Beginning in the 1850s, Brace specifically singled out farm families, particularly those in the Midwest, for placements. However, it should be pointed out that he popularized, but did not invent, the idea to send children to the homes of farmers. English Poor Law traditionally moved children into the homes of farmers and tradespeople, and was one of the provisions adopted by Americans. According to historian Michael Katz, only people who needed cheap labor took in pauper children, a trend that continued for some, but not all, placements during the 1800s.[7] In the United States, Benjamin Franklin noted that children placed out as farm laborers became a popular option in labor-barren colonial Georgia.[8] As early as 1810, cities such as Boston wanted to send children to local farms for two main reasons: first, they hoped to reduce the cost of their care; second, they hoped to use children to replace the laborers who had migrated to cities or the West.[9] The transportation of children onto farms took place in the British Empire as well, with children moving to Canada and Australia as parts of various emigration programs designed to match children to farms.[10]

The placing out of children increased as counties and townships formulated their own poor laws in the early decades of the 1800s. In a period lacking "social insurance," children who lacked family to care for them needed "charitable insurance."[11] In the Midwest, counties and townships formed the foundations of charitable insurance, sometimes through direct aid and other times through institutions such as poor farms, which were also known as county infirmaries. Local officials bore the responsibility of indenturing children, which became increasingly important as the amount of direct aid to families declined after the Civil War. The Midwest had no shortage of farmers to accept able-bodied children. Free of the stigma of the South, where labor practices kept many in crippling poverty and debt peonage, settled before the rigors and hazards of homesteading on the plains, and away from the crowded blight of eastern cities, the farms of the region were, as historian Kathleen Mapes notes, "supposed to be that place where those who worked hard would be rewarded with economic independence." The notion of working hard for economic self-sufficiency was particularly important for children dependent on charity.[12]

The farm did not rise to the top of preferred care methods without discussion, nor did sending children to country homes strike everyone as a wise choice. Experts specifically debated the propriety of using the farm as an alternative for institutional care. Among those challenging the idea was Lyman Alden, who from 1874 until 1883 was the superintendent of the

Michigan State Public School for Dependent Children. Alden became one of the leading spokespeople against placement practices. Unlike advocates like Brace, Alden actually did the placing and then supervised children where he saw problems firsthand. By the 1870s, Midwestern child welfare workers like Alden used the National Conference of Charities and Corrections (NCCC) to express their angst over the emigration system and the methods of farm placement being employed by institutions.[13] Midwesterners complained about orphan train practices, including shoddy supervision, the cost to local areas when long-distance placements failed, and charges that these children brought crime and bad habits into peaceful rural areas. However, many of those protesting Brace's methods could not throw stones because placing inside the Midwest involved a growing number of institutions that often did not prepare children for new homes, nor did they always do a good job of supervising children once they left the institutions. The desire to place children on farms paired with the increase in institutions meant that by the late 1880s, farmers had choices about where their dependent children came from. An institutional manager in Indiana complained that people in his area of the state "prefer[red] the waifs from Massachusetts or Ohio to those from the county home in their own neighborhood."[14] While many voiced their displeasure with some of the practices, the NCCC participants generally sided with the basic point of Brace's work, which was that children needed to be removed from institutions and placed with families.

However, the minority played an important albeit less popular role in specifying their concerns about using farm homes for placements. Lyman Alden used the national conferences as a platform to publicize the poor treatment of children in placement homes. In 1884, after leaving the state school for a job at the privately endowed Rose Orphan Home in Terre Haute, Indiana, he presented a paper entitled "The Shady Side of Placing Out." His missive undercut the notions supporting farm placement homes. Alden recited a catalogue of problems occurring because placers put too much confidence in farmers. He charged that bad techniques endangered children and ruined their chances for future success, claiming, "The humblest country home has been glorified into a child-saving instrument of wonderful efficiency . . . If these postulates are true, the logical sequence would be that no more institutions should be established."[15] Alden refuted the idea that farm families could be trusted because of their reputation, warning, "Many people are not qualified to care for and train their own, to say nothing of other children."[16] He had the support of a few other superintendents, but his talk did little to convince his colleagues that farms were not the answer. The prevailing ideas about the importance of building a good work ethic among the dependent, and providing children with a family environment that the middle class would find acceptable, carried the day.

For their part, farmers stood to benefit a great deal from participating in placement. There were two main reasons for farmers and their wives to take in children: financial gain or the emotional satisfaction of helping a child in need. These motivations were not mutually exclusive, nor were both always present. As a result, some children benefited from their placements and gained a family that provided both emotional and financial support while the family, in turn, gained a child in their home, bringing joy and companionship. Far too often, though, for James and others who followed him into placement homes, the reputation of farm homes was not borne out in the treatment given to placed-out children. Using farm families did not guarantee that children would gain the emotional bonds of parent and child. The need for affordable labor drove many placements.[17] Historian Pamela Riney-Kehrberg calls the Wisconsin State Public School, from which thousands of children were placed, "one of the largest employment agencies in the state."[18] Not only does her research prove that farmers took a majority of the placed-out children from the school, her statement also applies to an even larger number of children's institutions across the region. From the beginning, the ability to get farmers to accept dependent children relied on the understanding that most children would earn their keep by performing varying degrees of work.

Children working on farms were a routine aspect of American life. Although the overall percentage of children engaged in nonfarm work increased between 1870 and 1930, children who worked on farms still constituted a significant portion of the child workforce. Those considered workers on farms represented 53 percent of the child workforce in 1870, 43 percent in 1890, and 27 percent by 1910.[19] The decline does not tell the whole story though, as only children between the ages of ten and fourteen were included, and children who worked on a family farm while attending school were more likely to be uncounted as farm workers, helping to drive their numbers down as school attendance was more rigorously enforced. The work of dependent children was not necessarily different from that of farm children laboring for their own parents, but a biological child might be the first to attend school while a dependent child focused on work. In emphasizing an exchange of labor for care, we should not automatically infer that all farmers were brutal opportunists—it does not make all placed-out children victims, but it also does not make farm life glamorous.

Part of the romanticism of farm life centered on the family-based labor and the seeming partnership of children and parents in their work, but as

Riney-Kehrberg points out, in reality children spent many hours on farms working alone or without parental supervision. Despite how farm work really happened, the notion of family labor supported the increasingly popular idea of the late 1800s that parental bonding and childhood were a special and unique time. When paired with the popular belief that work on a farm connected children to nature in a special and beneficial way, the farm appeared to be an ideal locus for family relationships and healthy living. The focus on environmental determinism made the farm look particularly good in an era of urbanization and industrialization, but it also affected how struggling parents were viewed since it was believed that bad parents could create bad children by surrounding them with poverty.[20] This was significant for dependent children because most were not orphans without any parents to shape their destiny; in fact, most of them had at least one living parent. In the late 1800s, however, many believed that if parents were insolvent in some way, they could negatively influence the trajectory of their children.[21]

Nineteenth-century causes of child dependency were as varied then as they are today. Parents died, became chronically ill, went to prison, split up, abandoned their children, or needed temporary aid while they recovered from injury or financial setback. Institutional management and local officials determined which categories of dependents to accept and decided whether or not to find homes for children. Even though so many of these children had surviving family members, placements were intended to ensure that they got a better family than the one that had failed to provide them with care. Placements also helped remove children from the environment of an institution, which reformers seized on as a poor place to shape children. The emphasis on good families providing a stable platform for childhood growth and learning increased the desire to substitute biological families with better examples of self-sufficiency and replace institutions in favor of homes with a healthier environment. The policy of using free farm placement homes for children seemed a solution for these two issues by providing a good family and beneficial surroundings.[22]

Those who believed that good families could be found to provide healthy environments for children saw few merits in keeping children in institutions. Evidence of this attitude can be found at most of the NCCC meetings, including in 1892, when F. M. Gregg of the Children's Home Society in Illinois pronounced in his talk about child placing that "there are enough childless homes for all the homeless children."[23] The notion of paying for a child's care was initially seen as unnecessary, particularly for healthy children, thanks to the number of people presumed to want children. Despite the assertions of Gregg and others, there were not, in fact, enough childless homes for all the homeless children. As it turned out, there were not even enough "good" homes willing to take in children, a point Lyman Alden made during the early 1880s. As a result, the exchange of labor for care was used to entice farmers, but when that idea no longer agreed with larger notions of childhood, financial rewards were used to diminish the need for labor, creating a modern system of foster care. Neither working for care nor the exchange of money for care gave all children the type of home envisioned for them by those making a case for institutional removal.

The dilemma of how to categorize children who worked in their placements versus those who did not, or those who had placements paid for, has generated some scholarly confusion that de-emphasizes the longevity of free placements. Often the synonyms used by institutions, agencies, and caseworkers masks the popularity of unpaid placements. The assertion by Brace and historian Marilyn Irvin Holt that placing children without indenture papers somehow gained children a more permanent or familial home is not reflected in the experiences of the CASNY, nor is it borne out in other placements. It has, unintentionally however, prompted a misunderstanding about the duration of the use of indenturing in the United States. Indenturing did not stop when the CASNY decided not to use formal contracts; it continued to be used as one of a variety of options for placements by superintendents, county trustees, matrons, and others working to place out children to farms.[24] Indenturing and placement share so few actual differences that they can be, and were, used synonymously to describe a free placement. The placements done by the CASNY were often indentures without the paperwork; the distinction of paperwork could sometimes guarantee a child certain benefits on completion, like a payment, but even without a formal indenture most children were guaranteed some clothing and/or money once they reached majority. The existence of an indenture did not exclude the possibility that a child would be made a family member, nor did the absence of an indenture equate to familial membership; the treatment of the child was more often a better indicator of the relationship. The lack of an indenture at some institutions appears to have been a matter of convenience because the high rate of placement failures would have required a massive drafting and continual signing and rescinding of documents. Findings in this study indicate that between one-fourth and one-half of all placed-out children were re-placed at least once, and those figures are conservative for some institutions. Using the term "indenture" gradually fell out of favor nationally in the late 1890s and early 1900s because reformers came to associate the term with a relationship of servitude, but even with that new connotation some places continued to use "indenture" through the 1920s and 1930s.[25]

"Apprenticeship" was also used to describe free placements until the 1870s or so, making it appear to be similar to an arrangement for training organized or consented to by a parent. An example of how an apprenticeship and placement were blurred can be seen in the 1850 indenture of Aaron Porter from Huron County, Ohio, to learn the "art of farming" with Josiah Sutherland. Aaron, who was ten at the time and living at the county poor farm with no parents, signed his own consent. This placement did not last for the duration, and in 1860, two years short of completion, Aaron no longer lived with the Sutherlands. They owned more than four hundred acres, making Josiah one of the largest farmers in the area and making it obvious why extra help would have been appealing. Ten years later the Sutherlands had nine children at home, two hired men, and one fifteen-year-old "farm laborer." Aaron signed an apprenticeship and may have learned about farming, but it was really a placement for a dependent child.[26]

The language of placements includes "binding" as another synonym for indenture. In 1884, the *Michigan Farmer* published a response to a question about properly drawing up binding papers. But the resulting discussion demonstrated that the term could carry multiple meanings. The question, "What steps should be taken to bind out a boy upon a farm?" indicated an indenture arrangement, but provoked a response about the role parents played in the process, which included defending the child against abuse and cruelty, and highlighted the consent of both the apprentice and master for faithful treatment of one another.[27] If the parents were involved, this would be properly considered an apprenticeship or a parental indenture, but if it was between a farmer and an institution, it was a placement. Like "binding," "boarding" was also used as a term to cover a multitude of arrangements. Boarding in the late 1800s invokes ideas about paying for housing, laundry, and meals, but generally when children were referred to as "boarders," it reflected a work-for-care relationship and not a payment on behalf of the child. In general, the distinct absence of a payment for care is the defining feature of a placement arrangement and helps distinguish it from the practice that followed, paid foster homes.[28] Boarding payments, when used for children, were usually specified as such and were first used in Massachusetts as a way to place children not able to provide useful labor.

"Foster home" is perhaps the most confusing term of placement because it referred to free homes during the late 1800s and early 1900s and then transitioned to mean paying for care during the twentieth century. For example, historian Susan Tiffin's *In Whose Best Interest? Child Welfare Reform in the Progressive Era* contains an entire chapter dedicated to placements entitled "Foster Care," and the two terms are used interchangeably to discuss both free and paid homes. Tiffin notes that "foster parents were normally interested in taking children on a permanent basis." However, since in this capacity fostering, placements, and boarding payments are categorized together, it is unclear which type of foster parent was believed to have this interest or how this might be proven.[29] Long-term care was still placement, and in fact most placers hoped for a long-term successful placement. The term "foster home" as used during the twentieth century came to specifically and optimistically refer to short-term arrangements.

In other examples, what is being described as an adoption or a foster home is technically a placement home. Scholar Patricia Hart shows the trajectory of change in adoptions, but in so doing demonstrates the increasing popularity of the term "adoption" as a synonym for permanent placement.[30] These arrangements, while perhaps containing meaningful affection, were still placements unless a child was legally made a member of the household. Adoption, while legally available in most Midwestern states by the 1880s, was rare, especially for children over the age of five. As historian E. Wayne Carp demonstrates in his work on adoption, some Americans continued to believe that adoption carried a stigma and created "second rate families." Kinship of blood ties remained the legitimate way to define a family.[31] This attitude helps explain why many so-called adoptions of placement children were actually long-term placements. Informal, or nonlegal, adoptions were much more common than legal ones, allowing some parents to back out at a later date. Placement examples demonstrate this situation did happen. Marie Reeder's case file does not mention adoption on the part of her placement parents, but after five years with the Reeder family she was listed as their adopted daughter in the census.[32] Four-year-old William Schnell started life as a Peterson, but was adopted in 1903 by a childless couple with whom he stayed at least through 1920. Even his name change does not mean legal papers were filed. Often the children listed as adopted from the Miami County Children's Home had at least one living parent; William had two, Marie had one. In 1915, four-year-old Roy Gephart's parents were living in a tent beside a canal before being sent to the workhouse and insane asylum. He became Roy Crowell and remained with the Crowells through at least 1930. No records indicate whether Roy's biological parents signed over custody to the institution or consented to a legal adoption. Ruth May Ellis's case file indicated that she was intended for adoption but ended up back with her mother. Likewise, Nonie Silbert's placement parents told the superintendent they intended to adopt her, but instead returned her to the institution. "Adoption," like many of the terms used for placements, varied in meaning and permanence.[33]

This use of multiple terms to describe free placement homes for dependent children has made developing a reasonable time line for changes and transitions in welfare policy challenging. "Indenture," "foster home," and "adoption" were all, at varying times and locations, used to describe the same thing. By the 1920s, there were clear indicators of specific actions tied to these terms. Foster parents were more likely to be located in urban or suburban areas, and social workers maintained case files and visited their homes; foster parents often received payment for their services and were intended to provide temporary shelter for children whose parents were in distress. Adoptions, particularly for younger children, involved formal documentation and court proceedings. Placements referred to as foster homes but with no payment continued to be used, but less often, and were more likely for older children who were expected to help in the home. However, the confusion about terminology lingered, as illustrated in a 1940s application to become foster parents in Lucas County, Ohio: "Due to the nature of the application form, I thought perhaps you misunderstood my request for a girl. We don't wish to adopt a girl, however, we would appreciate having someone to live with us and help with the housework." This teenager would not be working on a farm, but instead inside someone's home.[34]

The farm is a critical factor in the changes that began to affect dependent children in the United States, especially between 1900 and 1920, when the farm itself became a target of reforms at the federal level. This marked a fairly drastic change in the perception of the family-operated farm in the American ethos. Traditionally the farm had served as a foil for the negatives of urbanization, industrialization, poverty, and blight. These strongly held beliefs about the farm encouraged Brace and others to pose the farm home as the best place for dependent children to embrace and learn American values. However, as Progressives examined the nation's problems, they fixed on the slipping quality of life and health on farms. They wanted to improve on them as a way to stabilize the rural population and the American food supply, and to preserve the classic American farming establishment. But as the farm declined, so did its hold on the dominant cultural normatives. This is seen not only in reform efforts targeting the farm but also in the role of middle-class suburban and urban Americans who claimed cultural superiority in the country during the latter half of the nineteenth century. The middle class not only supplanted the farm as the standard of living, it also altered the perceptions of childhood. Like the changes to farm reputation, the evolving notions about what childhood should look like began to embrace middle-class ideas that involved more schooling, less work, and an appreciation for childhood as a special and in fact sacred time in life.

Historians such as Steven Mintz and Viviana Zelizer mark this transition by demonstrating that middle-class Americans re-formed the nation in their own likeness by legislating truancy laws; restricting industrial work; investing in toys, playgrounds, and early childhood education; and even in the way they memorialized children.[35] As these ideas were accepted as part of American life, farm children, and by extension placed-out children living on farms, were behind the curve of their counterparts off the farm. On the farm, children went to school less, worked more, and were depended on, not to bring simple joys to their parents, but also to contribute to the greater financial stability of their homes. During the Progressive Era policies about dependent children were shaped by middle-class reformers, so it is significant that these people saw their own vision of childhood altered on the farm and sought to remove dependent children from that environment in favor of something they recognized to be more suitable. In this way, the decline of the farm reputation plays a role not only in discouraging farm placements because of conditions but also in forcing child welfare workers to act on their own ideas about what an acceptable childhood looked like. By the early decades of the twentieth century, acceptable childhood looked more like a school classroom and a playground and less like a one-room class and a barn that needed to be mucked.

Chapter 1 presents the ways that the rural ideal, or the beliefs about the prestige of farm homes and families, developed in the United States and how it in turn influenced the placement of dependent children. Historian Anne Effland describes the rural ideal as "the values that we as a society have ascribed to the rural life: close knit families, a sense of community, intergenerational enterprise, and a strong work ethic." These notions encouraged the movement of dependent children onto farms.[36] Although the farm and rural areas do not always reflect the same interests, during the period in which child placement prevailed, rural towns reflected the interests of agriculture and were thus also suited to placements. The dominance of these beliefs on the part of politicians, child welfare workers and reformers, and farmers themselves all contributed to the goals of child placement. The Midwest, which is the focus of this book, proved to be not only the most popular place for placements onto farms but also in many ways best represented the farm environment that reformers and placers sought to give children. As states such as New York and Massachusetts tested out options, including private institutional care and boarding homes, Midwestern institutions tended to embrace the notions of farm home placements. Potentially, the farm environment provided social uplift, improvement, and a family for dependent children. The farm home complemented the popular notion that changing the environment in which children lived could alter their destiny. Moving children to the country removed them from perceived vices and isolated them from trouble, while encouraging their long-term improvement by introducing the good influence of a family.[37] The reputation of the farm was magnified by the notion that family farms grew food for an industrializing nation as well as the seeds of democratic citizenship. Dependent children did not necessarily need Americanization because they were immigrants; indeed most in the Midwest were native born. What they did need were lessons in industriousness and self-sufficiency, two particularly favorable traits attributed to farm families. Had advocates of farm placement understood the changing nature of farming in the United States, they may have noticed that some farmers were also struggling to keep up, as indicated by increasing land values and tenancy, stagnant labor compensation, struggles with monopolies, and a lack of services in rural communities.[38]

Chapter 2 explains the child welfare situation in the Midwest, including the transition of care from poor farms to children-only institutions. In the Midwest, where placing out to farms was most successful, counties and townships formed the foundations of charitable insurance, sometimes through direct aid and other times through institutions such as poor farms. Local officials bore the responsibility of indenturing children, and in the primarily rural region this meant that children went almost exclusively to farmers. James lived in the second oldest of Ohio's fifty-five public county children's homes intended to remove children from the squalid environment of poor farms.[39] By the 1870s and 1880s, when a wider variety of institutions opened, the region already had a pattern of using farm homes as an outlet for the care and training of dependent children. At the same time, new ideas about charity and reform discouraged the use of direct aid, which provided supplies or money to needy families, and Americans increasingly believed that direct aid encouraged laziness and immoral behavior. The reduction of direct aid in the Midwest, which often came from counties, followed the national trend away from providing outdoor relief. When men and women could no longer get enough direct aid to maintain their household, children stood a better chance of ending up in an institution. Some of the new children-only institutions relied on placements.

Larger issues of religion and race, which heavily influenced urban child welfare practices, played a less significant role in Midwestern placements, in part because of a lack of racial diversity in rural areas and a lack of strong religiously affiliated groups to interfere with local placement practices. Placement was instead fueled by a belief that institutions built for children were not compatible with the idea that children needed a family environment, with two parents if possible, in which to learn and grow. This prevailing attitude about institutions and their costs encouraged counties, states, and private groups to try placements. Without standards or oversight, some placements were done in a way that put children into much worse situations than an institution.

Chapter 3 details the problems of abuse, neglect, and overwork that some children faced once they went into placement homes. These problems were not isolated to farm homes, but their presence in placement homes broke down the idyllic image of farmers as the best sort of people and caused reformers to call for vastly improved forms of supervision. Perhaps surprisingly, the most common issue facing placement children was not physical abuse but appears to have been the instability of the placements themselves. The accepted practice of allowing placement parents to return children to an institution at will created an exploitative system that fundamentally failed to give children the family home life placements were supposed to provide. This revolving door of placement homes no doubt caused anguish for some children and made it harder for parents to reclaim children or maintain any sort of communication. More difficult to find are the accounts of physical and sexual abuse suffered by placement children. These problems did occur, although with what regularity is challenging to document. Not all institutional managers kept good records of these problems, and an untold number were never reported at all. Newspapers sometimes carried the worst results such as the death of a child, but more often institutional records simply note "bad treatment" or "abuse reported," leaving little information about what was no doubt a more complicated story. The vulnerability of children placed into homes with strangers under no supervision left open terrifying possibilities. Both girls and boys faced the threats of sexual abuse, but no specific accounts exist involving boys.

Children did sometimes resist poor treatment in placement homes. The most popular choice was to run away or find a new placement family to take in a child. Older children did take these two options, but for younger children running away was not a real option. Some children did resort to violence or vandalism, with barn burning a recorded problem and a serious threat to farms. More common than the most outrageous cases of abuse or acting out are those of benign neglect, children who received no affection and simply lived and labored for a family until they came of age and tried to start out on their own. Even this reflected badly on the farm placement system because it failed to meet the goal of giving dependent children a substitute family to teach them faith, morals, and a work ethic and to provide a stable foundation for a productive life.

In Chapter 4 the efforts to remedy the problems with farm placements are examined. Child welfare advocates did not wait for Progressives to begin working on issues related to child dependency, but state boards of charity operating in the 1870s and 1880s had little power to enforce any recommendations, nor did they have any abilities to oversee private charities. These state boards tried to survey the child welfare practices in their states, and the Midwest formed more boards faster than other regions, but this powerless oversight did little to help individual children. Other efforts at supervising children began with county or local boards made up of volunteers who looked after children and helped institutions find new homes for others, but their efforts were local and therefore unevenly distributed.

Alongside county boards, institutions and eventually states hired visitors to staff supervisory departments for placed-out children. Like many Progressive Era reform efforts, this increased framework culminated in state-level departments charged with managing the work done locally in institutions and by placing groups but did not eliminate the use of private charity in the placing-out system. The two-pronged issue of mistreatment of children in placement homes and the resulting efforts to increase supervision ultimately forced placers and visitors to rethink their position on farm placements. Their suggestions included a return of direct aid, known as mother's aid or mother's pensions, as a way to preserve biological families, and more involvement by the courts. Judges gained more power over decisions regarding placement, institutionalization, and the awarding of direct aid. The results of these changes meant that superintendents of institutions sometimes had less control over their placement policies than in previous decades, ceding some of their control to state agencies, state visitors, and judges, and more children remained with their parents.

Chapter 5 explains how Progressive efforts at studying child welfare and farm life colluded to shed additional doubt on the wisdom of farm placements and free placements in general. The Country Life Commission and the Children's Bureau represent two forms of federal-level intervention that pointed out not only the issues facing farm families but also the things lacking from placement methods and supervision. While the Country Life Commission indicated that farm homes and rural schools needed updating, it undermined the notion that farm life was in any way healthier than life in urban or suburban areas. The Country Life Commission did little to directly affect children placed onto farms, nor did it develop any policies for placement children. In contrast, the Children's Bureau homed in on issues of child labor, and while it did not directly attack the practice of children working on family farms, the bureau did join the National Child Labor Committee in opposing the labor of children on contract farms. The bureau also supported mother's aid and criticized placement practices. The critiques from the bureau demonstrate a lack of support for child labor and its value for dependent children.[40]

The agency also sponsored research that provided additional evidence about the problems experienced at the local and state levels. In Wisconsin and other Midwestern states, the bureau lambasted the practice of farm placement as archaic and backward. These studies, published in the early 1920s, took stock of a declining practice that had been reduced because of social worker professionalization in towns and cities, direct aid for family preservation, and the lack of able-bodied children eligible for placements. Some institutions had already closed their doors, relying on agencies to find paid foster homes for children, and state institutions were making a transition to juvenile facilities treating troubled or disabled youth. Free placement homes on farms were no longer acceptable for most children.

The farm placement practices of the late 1800s had a profound influence on the changes that followed during the era of reform. The move toward paid foster homes, often categorized as the logical next step between institutional care and family care, was heavily influenced by the breakdown of the system that preceded it, the practice of placing out to farms. Institutional problems played a role in this transition, but in a less direct way because foster homes suggested a problem not only with removing children from institutions but also with finding enough qualified or appropriate homes for children. Farms, once used in this capacity, were failing, and an alternative was required. Thus, the transition to our current system of dependent child welfare is incomplete unless we take into account the step from farm home to foster home.

1. The Rural Ideal

Constructing a Myth

> "Say what you will about the general usefulness of boys, it is my impression that a farm without a boy would very soon come to grief. What the boy does is the life of the farm."
> —*Home Life for Childhood* (October 1923): 4, RJDL

Children gauged their experiences on placement farms in different ways. Some became giddy with the prospect of kittens and chickens, or interested when the oats, corn, and wheat were planted. Many wrote back to the institution with summaries of their new lives. A boy from the Michigan State Public School reported, "I have got a potato patch of my own to sell and buy me a Sunday suit . . . I had a patch of popcorn, but I planted it so deep it never came up. I don't go to school. I went a month and half last winter. I will commence as soon as the work is done and go all winter. I like farming real well . . . we have our harvesting all done now. The crops all look nice."[1] He helped the farm and the farm helped him.

A boy might represent the life of the farm, but during the second half of the nineteenth century the farm also meant a chance at a new life for the boy or girl. Children placed on farms were expected to learn the dignity of labor and skills to support themselves as adults. In addition to these skills, farm families could also provide children a "normal" family life consisting of parents, school, religious services, and healthy work. The dilemma of a failed row of popcorn contrasted sharply with imagery of children covered in industrial soot from a hard day of factory toil. Fretting about deeply planted seeds also contradicted the conditions of those living in the confines of a county poor farm, surrounded by sick and impoverished adults, or children crammed together in institutions. The farm was the foil to these negative scenarios. Conditions inside institutions prompted one reformer to refer to the poor farm as the "great nursery of pauperism and crime." The servile, dirty, and charity-dependent child would, it was assumed, grow up to be a drain on society, continuing the problem of dependency into further generations. For child welfare workers, the worry about systemic dependency and a belief in environmental determinism encouraged them to embrace the reputation of the farm as a place of normalcy to raise and educate children.[2] The commonly held idea that farm families represented the best of American life significantly influenced the development of placing out.

The notion that any farm was better for a child than an institution developed as a result of the American mythology that glorified agriculturalists. This myth influenced child welfare policy by encouraging farms as part of institutions, locating institutions in rural settings, and, most important, relying on farmers to provide homes for dependent children. Nowhere was this more apparent than in the Midwest, which was often lauded for its boring normalness. As historians of the region like Andrew Cayton have pointed out, the region, while sometimes the most challenging to label with regional identifiers, has long had a reputation for niceness. This nice, normal, rural background made it the most popular place to find farm placement homes for children.[3] Government officials and charity workers believed in the abilities of Midwestern rural residents to help care for dependent children because their assumed good moral natures allowed them to accept these children as part of their family and teach them positive values. There is no single child welfare policy that unifies the region; rather, its appeal as a location full of placement homes in waiting made it different from any other region in the nation. Solicitations seeking farm homes for children linked the positives of farm placement to the needs of dependent children:

> I have today about 120 boys and 54 girls that are almost entirely dependent on the farmers for homes, and I am happy to say we get the best results from those who go out to be farmers . . . All are anxious to get out into farm homes. If you ask for a boy to pick up stones, drop corn, or to do chores of any kind, the whole 120 want to go, and you can see how eager these little souls are to be busy. Why don't some of our intelligent farmers write to me . . . I want families that will make good, moral, and industrious men out of these boys.[4]

This reliance on a farm setting contrasted other types of child labor in its efforts to create what anthropologist Dorinda Welle refers to as "'industrious,' rather than 'industrial,'" children.[5] They supported the notion that "the well-regulated rural family, fits for life in a more complete sense than the ordinary institution does."[6] To give children these positive influences, hundreds of workers from institutions and associations fanned out across the Midwest undertaking the job of placement based on their understanding of a rural ideal.

The perpetuation of rural America as the foundation of democratic principles grew in popularity after the Civil War when urban growth, industrialization, and immigration all increased. The idolatry of American farmers was further reinforced as the federal government opened new land for Homesteaders to spread yeomanry to the plains and beyond; farmers would civilize the West. Other policies demonstrating a federal deference to farming included the Dawes Severalty Act of 1887 that expected farming by Native Americans, the Hatch Act also from 1887 that expanded the Department of Agriculture, and the Kinkaid Amendment of 1904 that expanded acreage of the Homestead Act. The focus on the farm as a provider of care for children reflected larger conceptualizations of the American rural myth. The agricultural lifestyle represented the ideal for many Americans, particularly during the late nineteenth century as more people moved away from land ownership; rural people embodied the self-sufficient egalitarian tradition held up as a foundational principle of American government. From the first decades of the country's founding, when Crevecoeur recalled seeing "wives and children . . . now fat and frolicsome, gladly help their father to clear those fields whence exuberant crops are to arise to feed and clothe them all," people associated the farm lifestyle with prosperity and vigor. Simply getting children into a rural setting, at a time when rural areas shared community and economy with agriculture, might help them achieve higher standing. Placement into farm homes was a way to indoctrinate dependent children into the American work ethos through productive labor and supported the stereotype that rural people embodied special virtues.[7]

Constructing the Rural Ideal

Thomas Jefferson became perhaps the most famous promoter of the small family farm and the notion that what farmers lacked in material possessions they made up for in morality. Jefferson linked agrarianism with citizenship by arguing that the ownership of a small farm helped families appreciate their liberties and continue to work as independent economic units. Additionally, he believed that farming served as a source of "human virtues and traits most congenial to popular self-government." He continued, "Cultivators of the earth are the most valuable citizens. They are the most vigorous, and they are tied to their country, and wedded to its liberty and interests by the most lasting bonds."[8] Those seeking to transform dependent children into productive citizens adopted his ideas joining farming and self-sufficiency. Antebellum agricultural reformers embraced not just Jefferson but George Washington as well, further strengthening the bond between farmers and the foundations of American self-governance. Historian Richard Hofstadter reinforces this notion when he links both the moral and the physical health of yeoman farmers to American civic virtue.[9] In this light, farm parents served as providers, protectors, and moral discipliners for a class of children who desperately needed such examples to block the influence of poverty and vice, whether it came from their own families or from the institutions where they lived.[10] Those who placed children on farms did not simply do so as a nostalgic recognition of American traditionalism; they saw farm training for dependent children as an affordable and useful avenue to self-sufficiency.

Historian David Danbom classifies two types of agrarian myths popular in the late nineteenth century: rational and romantic. The rational agrarian myth repeated stories about hard work and self-sufficiency, while romantic mythology sought to celebrate the morality and spiritual benefits of a rural environment.[11] Both types were used to support the placement of children onto farms. Dependent children were thought to need lessons to develop a work ethic as well as the steady, moral teachings of farm people to take the place of lessons not learned from their own parents. The farm could also help erase the stigma of pauperism. Rural residents—and farmers specifically—were selected to help dependent children because of long-standing beliefs about the good moral natures of farmers and their storied place in the formation of American democracy. According to Hofstadter, "The yeoman, who owned a small farm and worked it with the aid of his family, was the incarnation of the simple, honest, independent, healthy, happy human being. Because he lived in close communication with the beneficent nature, his life was believed to have a wholesomeness and integrity impossible for the depraved populations of cities."[12] Giving this wholesome environment to dependent children came in exchange for their labor on the farm.

Jeffersonian enthusiasts were not alone in their appreciation of farm life; popular culture also took up the practice of celebrating simple rural life. Fiction writers enjoyed success linking Midwestern rural images of fine farms, open spaces, and fresh air to the needs of children. Some of these accounts specifically discussed conditions for placement children.[13] Indiana native James Whitcomb Riley introduced his legendary orphan character, Annie—based on a dependent child who lived in his own childhood home during the Civil War: "Little orphan Annie's come to our house to stay, / an' wash the cups and saucers up an' brush the crumbs away, / An' shoo the chickens off the porch an' dust the hearth an' sweep, / An' make the fire an' bake the bread an' earn her board and keep."[14] During this time the Riley family owned both a farm and a home in town, and the real-life Annie, a girl named Mary

Alice, did tasks for the household as would be expected of most placed-out children. Riley held no illusions about why Annie lived with his family; she was there to work. Other popular tales of placed-out children happily working on placement farms include Kate Douglas Wiggins's *Rebecca of Sunnybrook Farm*, which featured an energetic orphan well-placed in the country, where her abundance of energy could be appreciated and directed properly, and *Anne of Green Gables* (although Canadian), the story of a girl accepted into her rural placement home despite the family's request for a boy who could provide labor.[15]

Other less well-known fictional placement children taught adults important lessons about piety. Abby Blake, the heroine of C. E. Bowen's *Bound Out at Farm Service*, arrived at her placement farm to find herself working for a couple who spoiled their biological child and regularly missed church services; they were not the archetype for the rural ideal. Even when the wife cuts off Abby's prized braids, the orphan reminds herself of the good fortune of her placement and how the lessons she learned at the orphanage helped her serve this family. In the end, Abby single-handedly taught the spoiled child to read the Bible and brought the entire family back into a faith-based lifestyle. This character embodied the belief that any farm placement provided children with an opportunity to better themselves and others.[16] Edmund Morris's *Farming for Boys* told the tale of one young orphan educated alongside a farmer's biological sons so that he might appreciate how hard work ensured success. This story epitomized one of the goals of rural placement: dependent children should learn to earn their keep because they always needed to work harder than others to succeed. None of them could count on family connections so their success would need to be earned.[17] Other authors such as Willa Cather celebrated farm life even as her characters struggled under the yoke of hard work and geographic isolation before finding salvation in the fresh air and constant labor.

This type of morality tale was repeated in farm journals and circulating publications. The *Ohio Farmer* published stories meant to inspire children to hard work and honesty, sometimes through poor-orphan-turned-successful-adult narratives. In one recounting, a boy living with a farmer is tested with a fifty-cent piece left on the floor, and after he dutifully returns it, an uncle appears to whisk him away to California and the farmer is left feeling justified in his testing of the young boy's integrity.[18] Author of *The Child*, Herbert Collingsworth, used his own experience as a placement parent as the basis for a successful book and syndicated columns. Having failed once at farming, Collingsworth tried again after he and his wife accepted a young man who arrived at their home having been rejected by a local farmer because of a bad arm, which rendered him unable to do enough work. After taking in this child, the Collingsworths took in six more children and moved onto a small farm where the children could participate in the garden produce business and reap small profits for their efforts. Thanks to the popularity of his books, Collingsworth weighed in on the importance of balancing work and affection in placements: "One farmer will take a boy or girl and work them until there is no vitality left. Another will heap kindness until the youngster grows up spoiled . . . Either case is a tragedy." The story of the Hope Farm and the Collingsworth family appeared to be an ideal pairing of dependent children and rural benefits.[19]

Other authors used imagery and metaphor to connect children to the land. By comparing children to agricultural products, botanist Luther Burbank gave additional reinforcement to children's advocates who wanted to place children in the countryside. Burbank compared children and plants in this way: "A child absorbs the environment. It is the most susceptible thing in the world to influence, and if that force be applied rightly and constantly when the child is in its most receptive condition, the effect will be pronounced, immediate, and permanent . . . Rightly cultivated these children may be made a blessing to the race, trained in the wrong way . . . they will become a curse to the State."[20] One Michigan woman took the metaphor further when she compared farm boys to a hardy stock of thoroughbred turkeys as she proffered advice on their proper raising, citing the importance of farm boys as "genuine American bred" and the "best American stock." The overwhelmingly positive portrayals of children and the benefits derived from rural life reinforced American mythology and encouraged the notion that farm placement served a greater good for all interested parties.[21]

In addition to the written word extolling the value of the farm experience, paintings and illustrations in publications such as *Harper's Weekly* lauded the pastoral imagery of quaint family-based production.[22] Religious leaders like Protestant theologian Arthur Holt spoke of his "vision of a just society . . . : only the small community could maintain the intimacy of primary relationships, direct communications, minor class distinctions, identification of self-interest with the public interest, and widespread community participation."[23] These impressions of rural life convinced people that the best way to prepare dependent children for a successful future was to place them in the middle of a "just society."

However, other authors demonstrated a familiarity with the more difficult aspects of farm life, particularly as it related to children. For example, in

Mark Twain's *The Adventures of Huckleberry Finn*, Huck claimed to be on the run from a bad placement with a cruel farmer. Other interpretations, such as those by Hamlin Garland, focused on the brutality of farm life. Garland gained a reputation for his expressions of rural misery and criticized other writers who "omit the mud and the dust and the grime, they forget the army worm, the flies, the heat, as well as the smells and drudgery of the barns . . . Milking the cows is spoken of in the traditional fashion as a lovely pastoral recreation, when as a matter of fact it is a tedious job . . . We hated it in the summer when the mosquitoes bit and the cows slashed with their tails, and we hated it still more in the winter time when they stood in crowded malodorous stalls."[24] In *Son of the Middle Border*, Garland described a return trip to the Midwest, where he rectified his softened memories with the harsh reality of conditions for farm families. As he described it, "All the gilding of farm life melted away . . . no splendor of cloud no grace of sunset could conceal the poverty of these people, on the contrary they brought out . . . the gracelessness of these homes and the sordid quality of the mechanical daily routine of these lives."[25]

Ironically, placers often used the farm to remove children from the "mechanical daily routine" of institutional life, with little consideration that farm work brought its own unique forms of drudgery. J. L. Irwin advised his readers to look closely at the farm boys in their midst, whom he described as "almost babies at the plow," and see how the drain of hard work slumped their shoulders and made them old before their time. He countered the popular notion that farm boys were the nation's healthiest, and he placed blame for such a plight on the farm parents: "While they should yet be attending school every day in the term, they are at home in the fields, doing a man's work."[26] Like Garland, his observances came after leaving the farm. Other, less polished writers struggled to balance their own memories of farm life with their desire to present it in a kind light. Liahna Babener has reviewed dozens of autobiographical farm writings that balanced bleak accounts of poverty, labor, and routine while trying not to taint the reputation of the farm. Many of the authors diminished the negative accounts with generalizations of happiness that contrast with their starkly detailed accounts of trouble.[27] Babener asserts that the difficulties provided clearer details than the general notions of happy times that emerge with distance and time away from an event. Many Americans believed in the idealism of farm life even after critics like Garland tried to dismantle it; the idea that farm labor did not necessarily equal citizen yeomanry went unrecognized in most child welfare circles.

Institutions and the Rural Ideal

Charles Loring Brace was among the first in the United States to act on the connection between the Jeffersonian ideology of agrarianism and the needs of dependent children.[28] He believed that moving children to farm settings, even across large distances, provided them with much needed positive influences. Brace often used agricultural metaphors in his writings and speeches to celebrate children growing up in a rural setting: "The hopeful field was evidently among the young. There, crime might possibly be checked in its very beginnings, and the seed of future good character, order, and virtue be widely sown."[29] Brace perpetuated the myth that crime, hunger, illness, and abuse miraculously diminished because of the rural setting.[30] He also relied heavily on the Midwest for his placement efforts, finding that "the best of all asylums for the outcast child [was] the farmer's home."[31] He based this conclusion on the labor needs of rural America and the arrangement where farmers would "train up children who shall aid in their work, and be associates of their own children."[32] In his perception of rural life, placement children would become a part of the farm family.

Brace spurred the acceptance of urban children in the countryside by emphasizing the farm labor that placement provided. He unapologetically used the potential for child labor to advance his plans for child emigration, noting, "There is an almost endless demand in the country for children's labor in families and on farms."[33] While the positive implications of farm life for children were well touted, the benefits for farmers also played a role in the longevity of rural placement. Tens of thousands of dependent children could not have found free homes if farmers in the post–Civil War era did not need affordable laborers. These children became practically free workers at a time when many farmers struggled to afford machinery and hired hands. During the same decades that farm placement was popular, the labor costs of hired farm workers and the need for seasonal instead of permanent workers increased. In turn, this move toward seasonal laborers probably contributed to the financial distress of families who relied on local institutions to care for children. This tumultuous labor market created an ideal circumstance to find farmers willing to accept children.[34]

To use the American rural ideal as a foil for urban poverty, the CASNY transported tens of thousands of children to the Midwest. In fact, Midwestern states took more children than any other region. When opponents challenged the methods of the CASNY and accused the organization of shoddy methods, they did not object to the idea of farm placement; instead, they protested the haphazard way the CASNY supervised and screened placement homes.

In 1880, facing criticism that his organization dumped children in remote locations, kidnapped them from parents, and brought vice to rural havens, Brace repeated his earlier ideas, arguing that supervision was not paramount because the homes were so often superior: "A child's place at the table of the farmer is always open . . . The chances, too, of ill treatment in a new country, where children are petted and favored, and every man's affairs are known to all his neighbors, are far less than in an old. The very constitution, too, of an agricultural and democratic community favors the probability of a poor child's succeeding." He continued: "when placed in a farmer's family, he grows up as one of their number, and shares in all the societal influences of the class."[35] Brace believed that people living on farms adopted the social tone of the farmer and his family, and that this cultivated essential character traits like diligence, thrift, and hard work. His methods attracted other followers, and child welfare experts who followed him, such as Homer Folks, agreed by seeking out "the ordinary, respectable, land-owning, country family" to take in dependent children.[36] Men like Meigs V. Crouse, who managed a children's institution in Cincinnati, compared the desire for farm homes to other choices this way: "of course, we will not give our children to people who belong to the class of laborers although laborers sometimes beg for our children, and might treat them kindly. Our aim is to place them with those who are neither rich nor poor, especially to put them with farmers."[37] In this telling, Crouse understood farmers to be situated in the middle of the economic hierarchy. Putting children with farmers would neither spoil them nor force them to live with day-laborers.

Other emigration groups reinforced Brace's lofty impressions of farm life and offered romantic updates of children's progress on farms. In 1879, *The Youth's Companion* printed updates of children sent to the West, with one placement parent promising devotion, two brothers visiting each other at Sunday school, and a former poor house resident exclaiming, "I am going to save money and buy a farm of my own." To tout the superiority of the country, one young man remarked, "I have everything I want. I wouldn't give up our farm for the whole of New York City." All the children, so the story told, took to the life of the farm quickly, with emigration groups maintaining that "in every case they have left want, and foul air, and vice behind them, and now are in a land of plenty, with the simple, innocent open air life of a farm to still their thoughts and in a church-going, religious community, the very atmosphere of which will protect them from crime."[38] In this depiction, life on the farm brought nothing but the best for the nation's most deserving dependents. Although the emigration programs came under attack by critics, writers continued to endorse the idea of sending city children west to farms, even noting that eastern farmers were less likely to accept children because "the cost of maintaining a boy in this section of the country is quite a consideration. Food, rent, and clothing are more expensive."[39] Not only was the Midwest ideal, it was a less expensive place to raise a child.

The affirmations of rural life not only affected the movement of children to the West but also influenced the design of institutions to include farms. Beginning with poor farms whose land and products helped offset the costs of shelter and food for indigent adults, children's institutions also used farms in a variety of ways, including for training and as punishment. In addition to institutional farm settings, city charities embraced a "back to the land" movement for children by sending them to farms during the summer. When the concept of children in the outdoors doing healthy activities became increasingly popular during the Progressive Era, cities constructed parks. These attempts to get children to healthier environments further reinforce how farm placement fit into a larger narrative of childhood necessitating access to nature and nonindustrial labor.

Often institutions used farms as a way to train children in agricultural labor and prepare them for placements on farms. This preemptive training developed both as a way to help children learn a skill and in response to placement parents who complained that children did not know how to perform basic farm work or housework. Indiana State Agent William Streeter reported, "The frequent criticism is made by foster parents that the children from the institutions do not know how to do things and must be taught the simplest tasks of farm and household duties."[40] Any refinement of manners, work skills, and schooling could improve a child's chances of finding a permanent placement. On the other hand, ill-behaved children might ruin an entire area for future placements.

The desire to outfit children with basic farm skills can be seen in institutions across the country. Outside New York, Cincinnati, Cleveland, and Chicago, institutions opened farms to prepare children unaccustomed to farming. Historian Leroy Ashby documents an increase in this type of institution after 1900, but even before then institutions connected farm training with successful farm placement. In 1872, the Children's Aid Society of Ohio, a charity group that helped place children onto farms, reported that almost half of the children living at its farm school went into homes having been trained to do various types of farm work.[41] If trained prior to placement, children might be more desirable to a "good farmer's family of easy, but not rich circumstances" while allowing dependent children to "work out in the open air and sunshine . . . as near nature as possible."[42] Farms used by city institutions for the training of urban children also hoped the experience would help alleviate some of the isolation experienced by those new to farm life. This was the case with the Brace Farm opened by the CASNY for older boys in 1894 in Valhalla and moved in 1929 to Bowdoin Farm in New Hamburg. According to the association, the goal of this facility was "to train boys in farm work and give them a taste of what to expect, before sending them to farms."[43] Providing children farm training, it was hoped, would make them more acclimated to farm work.

The Children's Home of Cincinnati opened its own farm home to teach boys how to do routine farm work such as orchard care, fence repair, stone crushing, and grinding wheat. It was managed by a farmer—not a specialist in child welfare—who kept the accounts and inventory for the facility. The orchard on the grounds became known for its varieties of pears.[44] The Michigan and Minnesota state schools maintained farms, as did the region's soldiers' orphans' homes. During 1899 and 1900, Minnesota's farm produced around $5,000 worth of goods to be used in the institution. The Illinois Soldiers' Orphans' Home operated a ninety-five-acre farm. The board of directors justified the added expense by noting, "The farm is thus made to serve a double purpose. It affords an excellent opportunity to the boys to acquire practical knowledge of tillage of the soil, and the growth of its various products, and, at the same time, it yields ample returns for all the labor bestowed, by the bounteous harvests of good fresh fruits and vegetables in their season."[45] Soldiers' orphans were not placed as often because their institutional care was seen as a service to their fathers, but the legislatures who funded the institutions connected the influence of farm work to a bright future.

Counties, many of which already linked dependency and farming together through county infirmaries, also used farms for their dependent children. During 1895 and 1896, the Lucas County, Ohio, children's home produced approximately $1,771 worth of produce, meat, milk, and grain. The children helped with the care of the livestock, which consisted of 65 chickens, 6 cows, 20 shoats, 3 horses, and 2 brood sows. Residents also assisted with the production of garments, including 183 pairs of pants, 81 dresses, and 50 towels. These efforts not only gave the children useful work to do, it provided them with healthy food and new clothing, luxuries that not all institutionalized children received. Six years later with 35 acres under cultivation, even more farm production was underway, and almost $3,000 of farm products came from the institution. The results were impressive; by 1914, the farm produced 4,000 heads of cabbage, 772 pounds of chicken, 3,500 pounds of grapes, and 225 bushels of tomatoes, among more than 4 dozen other crops. The older boys worked with the larger animals, and all the children over 9 years old received their own garden plots.[46]

Institutions with farms underscored the idea that "contact with the soil, both feet on the ground, has always been man's best insurance against most of his mental ills and physical failings."[47] Well into the twentieth century, institutions relocated to farms for the supposed benefits. In 1916, the Chicago Nursery and Half-Orphan's Asylum attempted to purchase property outside the city so children could enjoy the benefits of an agricultural setting.[48] The United Presbyterian Orphans' Home in Pittsburg moved to the country in 1929, and for three decades prior the institution sent children to the country for the summer. Parents of children living in this institution who paid board to ensure their children were not placed out on farms still consented to having their children removed to the countryside during the summer.[49] Nationwide, summer programs such as the one in Pittsburg demonstrated an allegiance to the rural ideal. Fresh air societies made arrangements to send children to farms on a temporary basis or created garden space in cities. In Cleveland, the "Hanging Garden" gave local immigrant girls the chance to grow produce on a rooftop under the supervision of a settlement house program. The entire concept of bringing farm life to children became so popular that groups moved children and adults to carefully selected farms whose owners received payment for housing and training the urban transplants.[50] Fresh air societies and institutional farms were joined by the School Gardening and Nature Study Movements of the 1890s, which sought to provide children with an education in growing food and working the land.[51] Political scientist Matthew Crenson suggests that the rise of groups such as the Girl Scouts and other "recreational enterprises" were a Progressive extension of order and regimentation outside of institutions, but these initiatives were also committed to bringing children into contact with nature, embracing the same ideas fueling the desire to find farm homes for dependent children. Likewise, Pamela Riney-Kehrberg concludes that reformers believed that the best combination for children involved not just fresh air but an appreciation for nature that encouraged curiosity. However, efforts to bring this appreciation to nonfarm children involved a "domesticated and gentle nature" as opposed to the often harsh conditions of a farm.[52]

Indian orphanages were among the wide variety of institutions to use farms as training tools as a way to help children provide for their own care while continuing the practice of assimilation. Although they used the labor of the children, some of these institutions supplemented child labor by relying on hired farm hands, cooks, and laundresses to ensure children were not overworked. They also hosted poultry classes, pig-butchering classes, as well as classes about agriculture and white society. Kate Bernard, commissioner of the Kansas State Board of Charities, encouraged the pairing of farms and institutions because, she said, "I believe farm life is healthier and better in every way for people who have not the prospects of financial help to put them in businesses in towns and cities."[53] To Bernard and others, farm work prepared children with life skills, not just trade-specific competence.

Institutional farm training was not a short-lived fad. In 1910, the Minnesota State Public School requested funding from the state to begin an "elementary school of agriculture" because "the state has the farm here, the boys are destined, and rightfully so, for farm homes, and so should learn how to succeed as farmers." This program did not receive the needed funding, but the state school continued to lobby for vocational training funds.[54] In 1912, when the Fraternal Order of Moose Lodges founded their own institution, known as Mooseheart, they purchased 1,014 acres in Illinois for the institution and farm. Board member Edward Henning justified the expenditure for the purchase when he related his opinion that public schools trained people for college but not for life; at Mooseheart, "agriculture will be taught in all its branches."[55] However, at Mooseheart and a number of other institutions, farm work was laced with mixed messages. Mooseheart staff sent misbehaving boys to Fez Hall, a farm dormitory where boys in need of punishment went to work off their demerits. Time spent at Fez Hall included long hours of work, isolation from other children, and a simple diet; boys could work their way to a clean record. Among the offenses that landed boys in Fez Hall were stealing popcorn, smoking, fighting, and disobedience. Girls could work off demerits in the main dormitories and did not face exile to the farm.[56]

Similar situations prevailed in juvenile detention institutions constructed for the reformation of youthful offenders. Institutions from prison-like facilities in Texas to the Ohio State Reform Farm featured agricultural work as a key part of inmate rehabilitation. The *Ohio Farmer* published an appeal to its readers about accepting boys and girls from the Reform Farm, even though they were normally not viewed as good candidates for farm placements because of their past behavior. The request suggested that the children there for minor offenses would benefit from a farm home: "Farmers need help in their busy times, and the housewife could make good use of willing hands and feet. The children could thus earn their board and keep, make friends with good honest work, and grow into right living."[57] Concerns about linking farming with punishment prompted agricultural groups to refuse an association with these institutions. As early as the 1850s, when plans for the Ohio Reform Farm were developed, the county agricultural societies and the Ohio State Board of Agriculture rejected proposals to become involved with the institution. Historian Robert Mennel attributes this to their desire to "protect the status of farming" and "portray their occupations in the best light."[58] Farmers did not want an association between their work and prison-like punishment, and these children were not likely to be made members of a new family.

Uniting an institution and a farm was a common way to bring the benefits of farm life to children, but ideally, dependent children would be moved from an institutional setting into a family sphere. In ways that an institution could not, the farm family was supposed to project their own value system onto the child, and their influences could wear away the pall of time spent living in an institution or surrounded by vice. Liberty Hyde Bailey, chairman of the Country Life Commission, referred to the city as "a parasite" in relation to the countryside.[59] Children living in the city were drained of life through industrial work, vice, and crippling poverty. With the temptations of the city inaccessible due to lack of transportation, farm children depended on each other—instead of street corners or back alleys—for recreation and socialization. The rural home offered the possibility of industriousness and strength of character. Though the isolation of being placed in a rural area caused occasional hardship, it nonetheless became a benefit of placing. As Brilla H. Cartwright of Madison County, Illinois, described, "The farm home is isolated, that is true—that is an old criticism—but therein lies its blessing. Rainy or inclimate weather forbids the going over a few miles to every concert, play, fancy fair, rink, ball and all the intoxicating and stimulating dissipations which spoil life's quiet nourishment." In this way, Cartwright surmised, "the nation's greatest boys and girls grow up to appreciate the little things in life."[60] Giving dependent children the same influences that produced the nation's greatest children would launch them on a new trajectory.

While farm institutions might train children for life on a farm, farmers who took in children received no training at all. The Children's Home of Cincinnati praised farmers who were willing to take children: "Our country friends have nobly done their part in obeying the Divine injunction to 'Deliver the poor and the fatherless and rid them out of the hand of the wicked;'" however, children needed to be deserving of the placement.[61] Farmers need not even be particularly successful at their jobs since "the homes most suitable to the welfare of the children are not always the wealthiest."[62] Finding homes to meet these specifications proved fairly successful; between 1904 and 1912, the Children's Home of Cincinnati placed roughly 45 percent of its children with farmers. During early decades the percentage was probably higher but harder to estimate given the lack of data. The remaining children found placements in the homes of families engaged in a variety of occupations, such as ministers, mechanics, doctors, and salesmen.[63] G. T. Green, who worked as the placing agent for this institution during the 1880s and

1890s, believed that as long as children were not exploited, the farmer who needed extra help or the farm wife burdened with chores offered the closest thing to an ideal home.

Associations like the CASNY, which also employed agents who worked in rural areas, learned that farmers were more likely to accept children before planting and harvesting season, and the CASNY sent more children to farms during these seasonal periods.[64] This seasonal demand continued to be viewed as an opportunity through at least 1899, when Edward T. Hall attested: "In the spring, a farmer's fancy . . . turns to thoughts of a good strong boy . . . who is not afraid to work."[65] Left unstated in Hall's summation was what happened when the farmer completed the spring harvest and was left with the child he took for the help. As explained further in chapter 3, administrators of children's facilities knew that the children they placed often returned after planting and harvesting seasons or during times of financial crisis.

The Midwest is Best

The reliance on the Midwest for placement homes began with the CASNY, which found early success in the Midwest, where established communities centered on family farms, local churches, and schools. By the time Brace started sending children to the area in the 1850s, the states of Ohio, Indiana, Michigan, and Illinois no longer suffered from the growing pains of pioneer life. These states combined agricultural maturity with profit and civilization, while the newer agricultural states to the West started farms from scratch. The CASNY and other groups had already sent thousands of children to the rural Midwest before institutions there began placing in earnest during the 1870s and 1880s. By the time legislatures in Ohio and Michigan required a surety bond for children imported from outside the state, the CASNY and others were already taking their trains farther west to take advantage of the labor needs of Homesteaders and western expansion.[66]

Farmers in the Midwest were some of the nation's most successful producers of foodstuffs. A Midwestern farmer worked for himself without having to break new land or live on the fringes of civilization to produce the raw materials destined for the homes of urban America.[67] Historian John Barnhart stresses the unpretentiousness of the region's residents, as fewer economic inequalities helped Midwestern society seem more equal.[68] States in the Midwest opened public school systems and founded public institutions of higher education, demonstrating a dedication not just to manual labor but also to the learned arts. Their small farming communities had churches, locally owned shops and stores, and a fairly well connected transportation system. By the 1860s, the region appeared to be balancing modernization with traditional values and work. Even the growth of cities did not disconnect it from rural life since major urban centers like Chicago and Kansas City developed as a direct result of the agriculture in surrounding areas. It did not take long to reach farmland after leaving the boundaries of Midwestern metropolises.[69]

The Midwest provided ample mythology to justify the confidence in the region's farmers. Stereotypes of the region relied "on an idealized vision of the Midwest as a place of 'white' family farms bereft of class conflict."[70] It was not just child placement workers who committed to this idea. The federal agencies trying to find workers for Michigan beet farmers during the early 1900s labeled Midwesterners obliging and patient. The perceived homogeny of the region actually embraced many groups of immigrants, including large numbers from Germany and Scandinavia and an increasing number of African Americans in urban areas. Historian James Madison refers to the region as one of the "most ethnically diverse regions on the face of the earth."[71] Kathleen Mapes shows that in 1910 Michigan had the fourth highest number of first- and second-generation immigrants living in rural areas. The native-born and foreign-born were almost evenly matched, with American-born residents numbering 745,000 and foreign-born numbering 720,000. In contrast, Indiana ranked as the least diverse state in the region.[72] Although their "whiteness" made them a part of the fabric of regional farm life, not all immigrants had the same notions about appropriate levels of farm work, and some German and Dutch farmers used family labor differently from their native-born neighbors, so that "the line dividing the work of men from that of women and children was even less clear in these families than in the native born farm families living in the same areas."[73] Status as an immigrant did not eliminate farmers for placement parenthood, nor did the existence of large numbers of immigrants dissuade placers. Regardless of their ethnicity, farmers in the Midwest desperately needed a ready workforce, particularly at peak times. Farmers of all types—immigrants; renters; owners; older couples; those with young children, older school-attending children, or no children at all—needed workers, and all were eligible for placement children.

The region itself has long suffered from its inability to compete historically with the other, more researched areas of the country. The East is the generator of commerce and American government, and its system of placing out paved the way for Midwestern emulation and eventual dominance; the South with its traditions of slavery and racial strife is the focal point of entire fields of study; the West, too, has its own origin stories and mythology that go well beyond the family farm. For these reasons and more, the Midwest has been left behind to gather regional dust, but in the study of child placement the region should be a focal point. As Andrew Cayton and Susan Gray note, "the Midwest became the place that best exemplified the United States. As it became the physical center of the country, so it also became the literal and spiritual metonymy of the nation."[74] The region shaped its own system based on the need to care for and place thousands of children, having already been the depository for children from the East. It adapted eastern methods, and western states emulated the Midwestern variety and desire for placement. The Midwestern methods, diverse as they were, were directly linked to child placement onto farms. As Cayton explains, regionality requires a connection with a sense of place, and while this is often a struggle in the Midwest, regionally, child placement onto farms resonated across the region.[75]

A Need for Labor

Farmers typically relied on family members to provide most of the needed labor on their land. Despite perceptions that technology lessened the labor requirements of farming, the amount of labor required did not necessarily decrease in the post–Civil War period, it just changed. Seasonal demands for harvest workers continued to make farmers vulnerable to labor shortages, and even during times of economic hardship, the need for affordable farm labor outpaced the availability.[76] In 1894, the *Ohio Farmer* printed a column requesting state intervention to connect out-of-work city residents with farmers in need of workers. According to one complainer, he went to Akron seeking a man for seasonal work, but "the ones I could get were ones I didn't want." Another woman said she tried unsuccessfully to get a homeless girl to come and work for her but was frustrated to hear many such girls lived in cities and griped, "The trouble with your city poor is that they prefer starvation in the city to coming to the country."[77] In 1907, Ohio's charity board recommended that vagrants be rounded up and moved to the State Reform Farm as a way to provide additional labor and deal with the perceived vagrancy problem all at once.[78]

For farmers, the need for efficiency to keep pace with commercial production highlighted problems with antiquated methods and a reliance on family labor. As the country industrialized, more and less-expensive food was needed for growing urban areas.[79] In adopting machinery for farm work, many farmers increased their acreage, not necessarily ridding themselves of the need for laborers. Farmers still needed help, especially seasonally, and this continuing need helped dependent children find homes, if only temporarily.

Historians Peter and Joanne Argersinger stress that technological improvement on Midwestern farms during the 1870s deskilled some of the labor needed from workers, which in turn might have made it more likely that a child could do the remaining work.[80] Tensions between farm labor and farm operators reached a fevered level in the 1870s as wealthier farmers invested in machinery to replace the daily work of hired hands, opening more lower-paid seasonal positions. This change in the labor market, which took place over many years, left farm workers in the unenviable position of unskilled and underemployed workers. In the same rural counties where farmers routinely took in placed-out children later in the century, the 1870s saw threats like the one to a binder-owning farmer in Knox County, Ohio, which read: "You better look out . . . we are watching you." Threats that turned to action through the destruction of equipment earned participants the designation of "Machine Breakers," and outbursts of this type were reported across the region. The destruction of equipment signaled a change in the relationships between farmers and hired hands during the post–Civil War period, but that did not mean that machinery replaced the need for work. As before, farmers relied on their own families to provide much of the year-round labor.[81]

Neighbor children offered an alternative to hired hands, but by the late 1800s even those positions garnered as much as $1 a day, roughly what the average hired adult made on the farm but without the room and board.[82] The high wages probably help explain why only 10 percent of the Minnesota farm wives surveyed reported having a hired girl. Twenty-three percent of their husbands claimed that finding good help was their biggest problem. Some farmers found it more profitable to hire tenants to work their land than to depend on the unreliable influx of hired men who demanded high wages or count on neighbor's children who left the farm as soon as possible for other opportunities.[83] Harvest work still attracted migrant laborers, but the help of children living in the household offered the best bargain. A reduction in the need for affordable workers is not one of the reasons farm placements eventually fell out of favor.

The federal government believed that the lack of willing adult farm hands quickened the move toward mechanization on many farms, and not the other way around. Farmers could increase the size and production of a farm with additional laborers or purchase equipment.[84] When posing solutions for the problems of farm life, experts and academics embraced the moral components of the rural ideal while simultaneously seeking ways to improve the physical and economic conditions of family farms.[85] These experts sought to manage farms in a more scientific way and increase efficiency through machinery, mimicking the transformation happening in other industries.

In southern Minnesota, U.S. Department of Agriculture (USDA) researchers learned that "machinery has influenced farm work greatly, but so also has the increase in livestock. This has made farm life more restraining and exacting."[86] Equipment purchased before 1920 was expensive; in 1870, prices for a McCormick reaper were around $200; a small threshing machine cost $160.[87]

Both farm tenants and owners who needed laborers could look to children's institutions to fulfill the need. Institutions wanted farmers of good character but were fairly unconcerned about the size of a farm. If the farm was large, it might be remarked on in the ledger or the child's file, but renting land did not prohibit farmers from being considered good candidates for a child. In 1900, Lyman Alden placed twelve-year-old Ed Adkins with the Wood family. They rented a farm, and Alden recorded that they were "rather poor but intelligent and kind and treat Ed well." Over the next few years Ed succeeded in this home; one visitor found him shocking wheat but struggling in school. When he turned eighteen the Woods paid Ed $50 and gave him a new suit of clothing. Although he could have left, he stayed with the Woods on and off until 1915, when Mr. Wood no longer had paying work for him. Ed was twenty-nine years old and had saved almost $1,000.[88] The record of twelve-year-old James Dwyer provides more evidence that a variety of farmers qualified for children. James first went to a "good farm" only to be returned because the farmer "did not need him." Next he went to a farm of eighty acres with a young couple who had a small child. One week later he came back, and next went to his uncle's farm of sixty acres. James stayed there for a couple of years before returning to the "good farm" where he had started. Using census records, the land status of farmers who claimed children in Miami County, Ohio, demonstrates that both owners and renters took placement children, but nothing can be concluded about whether the treatment of children changed based on the land status of their placement parents. Women, too, were able to get placement children, although they did so less regularly than men. Farm women claimed children, and so did those who lived in towns. Phoebe Young, a Miami County resident who cared for her paralyzed sister, took at least three different children from the county institution, presumably to help around the house.[89]

In the Midwest anyone desiring a child for their home or farm could fairly easily locate an institution from which to claim one, particularly after the institutional building boom of the 1880s and 1890s. Ohio and Indiana counties opened institutions, poor farms had children, state schools sent representatives to the country, and charity societies put advertisements in newspapers. Some farmers applied to a local children's home for a child, while others used institutions in nearby counties. It appears that neighbors often set an example for one another by using placed-out children, and people who were familiar with placed-out children also applied. Two neighbors in Sullivan County, Indiana, with hundreds of acres of land between them, took in Rose Orphan Home children, but one was returned because she was "saucy and couldn't work enough."[90] In 1880, Jacob Steinman worked on the Hancock County farm of his brother-in-law, Jacob Cramer, alongside a ten-year-old "bound boy." Cramer had a one-year-old daughter and a wife to provide for, and used the work of his brother-in-law and the placement boy to run the farm. Fifteen years later and now on his own farm, Steinman took Clifford Bennett from the Miami County Children's Home, but Bennett ran away in 1895.[91] Over time, some farmers took more than one child, as was the case for Lewis Frost, who went to a farm of seven hundred acres and a family who had already taken in another young man. Farmers who had previous experience with placement children often used that as a recommendation for another; Roy Hane went to a childless widower who owned 102 acres and at various times had taken in 3 other dependent children. Roy's mother eventually kept house for the farmer and married him.[92]

Farmers clearly used placement children to help supplement their existing family labor. In his investigation of agricultural labor, Tobias Higbee claims, "The earnings of farmers' sons and daughters helped sustain the home sphere at the same time that their families' reliance on wage labor tied them closer to farming-as-a-business . . . whether they were from a different ethnic group or simply ill-mannered, hired laborers represented the incursion of the outside world into the moral and economic structure of the farm household."[93] To avoid this issue—and the labor shortage faced by farmers who could not, or did not want to, hire wage laborers—dependent children served as an alternative, costing the same as other family members instead of the price of hired hands, and they were returnable. This could be particularly useful to farm families with children too young to work like Jacob Cramer's, childless couples, or those with grown children. Clarence Manning, a Miami County farmer, took in multiple placement children at different times to assist with the work while his own children were too young to be of help. Hal Rodney ran away from Manning's farm in 1914 after his first farm placement failed because he was "sassy and contrary." Manning must not have been discouraged because he then claimed Ray Gephart, an eleven-year-old who stayed on his farm from 1916 to at least 1920.[94]

Farmers like Manning had good reason to try another child if the first did not work out. During the 1870s, farmers who could not afford the going wages of $15 to $20 per month plus room and board hired "foreigners, [I] rarely keep one longer than a month or two, and they lose more than $6 per month from their ignorant stupidity, general incapability and from their quitting right in a time when needed most." This letter from Eugene M. H. Willoughby responded to claims by another writer that $16 per month should be plenty pay for labor. The real significance of this debate is that whether paying $16 or $20 per month, or more in some places as time went on, dependent children could be "hired" for a fraction of the cost.[95] Dependent children also fit Kathleen Mapes's description of hired hands who "expected agricultural labor to be part of an informal vocational education leading toward landownership." However, hired hands might be able to afford startup costs after years of working, whereas dependent children left with little more than work experience. Mapes explains the connection of hired hands to farm families this way: "[they] mirrored the families they worked for in terms of ethnic background, lived with the families for whom they toiled, and expected to be a part of the farm households economically, socially, and communally."[96] A dependent child could also fit this description but did not have to be paid. As Pamela Riney-Kehrberg establishes in her work on farm childhoods, most farm families could not afford hired help on a regular basis and needed their cash for purchases, which left family members carrying the labor burden of the entire farm.[97] Given the mobility of rural wage laborers and that "prices for that class [trustworthy men] have advanced very materially," the opportunity to use potentially stable and affordable dependent children gave farmers an advantage.[98]

The type and amount of work done by dependent children placed onto farms varied as widely as that done by farmers' own children. Daily chores might include milking, chopping wood, collecting eggs, or mending fences. Seasonally, farmers kept busy with planting, harvesting, livestock care, drainage, fence repair, and other tasks that varied in difficulty and length. Children reported they "cut and harvested wheat . . . I dragged in nearly all Mr. B's wheat," and "I like to go out in the country and work with the men and see the farm the pigs the cows the hens the chickens and the horses. All these things make me happy and glad."[99] While boys helped as physical laborers, farmers and their wives wanted girls who could assist with housework. Placed-out girls often performed jobs identical to those of the women of the house, who started their days by making breakfast before moving on to tasks such as laundry, ironing, mending, cooking, and farm chores such as milking, caring for chickens, gardening, or aiding in field work.

Despite the often heavy burden of work placed on farm children, placers believed these tasks provided positive work experiences for a child lucky enough to find himself or herself on a farm, so long as children were not doing all the work.¹⁰⁰ Placement parents who sent updates about children to institutions gave some positive indications that they intended to help the children in their care learn the ways of the farm and prepare for a productive life. Lyman Alden received this letter from one man who took in two boys: "The boys like their place, and I think we shall get along very well. They take an interest in the animals and like to fuss with them. There is a kind feeling all around . . . I shall try to make good men of them and give them a good start in the world."¹⁰¹ Children who became full participants on farms expressed the same frustrations with farm life as their placement parents. One young man finishing his indenture on an Indiana farm wrote, "I have got discouraged trying to farm. We have had two failures in crops straight ahead and have a poor prospect for this year. The farm is poor and we have had to rent ground and give one-third of the crop."¹⁰² Few early observers of placements believed that learning responsibility on a farm stole childhood or demonstrated placement parent greed; to the contrary, the hardships of the farm helped prepare dependent children for the real world.¹⁰³

Farm Trouble

The issue of affordable labor was just one problem that caused farmers grief during the late 1800s. Although they expressed pride that farms fed the nation and asserted that "the maintenance of a strong rural family and society was intimately related to the economic health of agriculture," groups such as the Grange worked often unsuccessfully to handle the problems of farming. The Grange attempted to harness the cooperative strength of farmers to gain better prices on items bought and sold, and gained popularity in the Great Lakes region of the Midwest.¹⁰⁴ Two decades after the start of the Grange, in the 1890s, the Populists attracted national attention to the problems associated with farm life by forming a political party and pointing out the discrepancies between their quality of life and the gains being made by workers in other types of industry. The group found an audience for their anti-monopoly, pro-regulation message but was never able to capitalize on a coalition with industrial workers to form a working-class party.¹⁰⁵ Although they were protesting the collusion of government and financial special interests, the Populist goals of the 1890s reinforced beliefs about the democratic impulses of rural people because of their message about the foundational principles of farming in the American state. Instead of this protest element in rural America dissuading child placers, the efforts of farm groups reinforced positive impressions of rural placement. Even though politically active farmers wanted to be recognized and respected for their contributions to American growth, which indicated that they did not feel their work was valued, their ideas tied directly back to the rural ideal. By demonstrating the "rhythms of family and community life in the countryside"; pursuing equal economic opportunities, assistance for small producers, regulation of large railroads and banks, and more power to voters; and pushing for prohibition, Populists espoused the conservative value system highlighted by those who supported farm placement for dependents.[106] The Grange's effort to support rural churches, social connections, and locally run cooperatives did the same. These expressions of farmer angst did not dissuade placers from continuing their efforts.

By increasing the demand for placement homes during the 1890s when Populists were nationally active, reformers selectively chose which ideas to accept and which to ignore: they underestimated the effect these farm problems had on conditions for placed-out children and rejected the conceptualization of dependent children as sacred, noncontributors to the household economy. Children who worked on a family farm fell between two polarized childhoods; they were neither idealized middle-class darlings nor pale-faced factory workers.[107] Increasing placements was a way to decrease the institutional population, and reformers were satisfied in their agreement that farm children worked hard and (presumably) played, attended some school, and contributed to the well-being of a family's enterprise—conditions suitable for dependent children. Issues for farmers, such as the growth of tenancy in the Midwest, which increased from 20 to 28 percent between 1880 and 1900, were of little practical concern for placers who did not preference renters over owners when selecting homes anyway. They were more likely to judge the fitness of the home and farm based on recommendations, as Lyman Alden did in 1902, when he placed a girl with a "first class renter" "highly endorsed by his neighbors."[108]

Even those who challenged the use of child labor did not fight the practice of rural placement. As Americans came to recognize childhood as a special and developmentally crucial period of life, farm children continued to work for the benefit of and alongside their families.[109] Farm children did not factor into national debates about child labor since they performed difficult but "healthy" work for their own family that built character and allowed them to enjoy the outdoors; on farms, children could still experience a childhood while learning all-American values. Like their colleagues who worked as institutional managers and charity agents, Progressive reformers argued that farm labor of the kind found on Midwestern family farms countered many of the wrongs of child labor in factories and as a result endorsed the farm placing system. Although they did not endorse all farm labor as positive, this inflated optimism failed to recognize that children laboring on farms often worked as hard as adults and that their outdoor environment could be dangerous.[110] This attitude demonstrates a failure to comprehend how farm skills trained children for little more than jobs as low-paid farm laborers; placers did not understand the financial challenges of starting a new farm or moving into the farm-owning class. In many respects, farm children suffered from the same plights as children working in industry; they attended school for a limited time, they could be injured, and they lacked the free play time of their middle-class peers. Unlike factory children, they failed to earn sympathetic recognition or pay. By separating the industrial work of children from the work of certain farm children, reformers failed to understand the point made by historian Jon Gjerde, who explains, "Whether or not free land made people free, it promoted a dependence and reliance within families that tended to trap certain members—such as children—in protracted subservient relationships."[111] The familial labor arrangement could benefit children who stood to inherit the farm, but for dependent children who had no stake in the property, placement meant that they worked for little long-term reward.

Placing advocates, with their objectivity clouded by the rhetoric of the rural ideal, often failed to see the potential danger of placing children on farms. These people had enormous confidence in the goodness of farm people, and many of them agreed with placement advocate Sophie Minton, who declared, "Rough conditions are nothing, if the [family] influence is good, morally and physically."[112] They consistently remarked that farm life offered values completely missing from industrial society; farm life centered on the family and advocated cooperation and self-sufficiency.[113] Charles Loring Brace sent New York children westward because he believed that putting children to work as farm laborers served as a middle ground between maintaining child-like innocence and participating in a family labor system. While biological children contributed to the family well-being through their labor, dependent children did not work alongside their own parents. Instead, they labored with and for temporary custodians, granting them uncompensated status somewhere between family member and hired hand.[114] As one of the few dissenting voices regarding rapid farm placements, Lyman Alden noted, "It takes more than a farm of 80 acres to make a good home."[115] Many of his colleagues might have agreed in principle but had little means to distinguish a good farm home from a bad one.

None of the advocates of rural placement feigned ignorance about the difficulties of rural life. To the contrary, childhood expert G. Stanley Hall joined Charles Loring Brace in believing that any hardships of rural life or hard farm work benefited children in the long run and provided them with opportunities other environments lacked.[116] Hall was not alone among Progressives when he maintained enthusiasm for farm life. Efforts like the Country Life Commission (1908) acknowledged the imperfections of rural life but linked those problems to a lack of services and modernizations on the farm.[117] Liberty Hyde Bailey, head of the commission, endorsed programs to improve the standard of living in rural America with the hope that young people would choose to stay on family farms rather than migrate to cities. If rural living standards could be improved, people would remain on the land—an important goal for those who believed agriculture still represented the foundation of American success. The commission did not launch an attack on a way of life that relied on child labor; instead they focused on changeable conditions. As further discussed in chapter 5, these reformers made recommendations about increased schooling for farm children and better services such as libraries but did not criticize the amount or type of work being done by children on Midwestern farms.[118]

In general, none of these protests or publicly acknowledged problems on American farms stopped child welfare workers from believing that farm life still represented the American ideal. It would take a combination of issues, not just those on farms, to dissuade people from the belief that placing dependent children on farms was a good choice. Many Americans thought that the countryside provided the quintessential values that children needed. No children required these influences more than those whose parents proved incapable of caring for them because of illness, death, poverty, crime, or vice. Despite evidence suggesting that farm life was more complex, writers, child welfare workers, magazines, politicians, and others regularly referenced the Midwestern farm as an ideal location for raising children. Those overseeing the care of dependent children appropriated these ideas when securing placements with farmers.

The quality of the rural experience varied widely, but the Midwest became the most popular setting not only for the myth of the ideal but as a depository for dependent children. The number of placements made throughout the Midwest—as well as the longevity of the practice—testifies to the significance of the region for placing dependent children. Reformers clearly believed that a home in the country yielded more positive results than a home in the city or in an institution. They relied on this belief when planning methods of care for dependent children and held on to these ideas, even when farmers themselves challenged the mythology of farm life. More farm homes would be needed for children as states, counties, and charities became responsible for an increasing number of dependent children during the last decades of the century, and conflict about the appropriateness of institutional care helped increase the importance of farm placements.

2. "Qualify them for the duties of life"

> "There is too much life and activity in this country for a boy or a girl long to remain in idleness. Qualify them for the duties of life, point the way, and they will walk therein, and be saved."
>
> —Albert S. White, superintendent, Franklin County, Ohio Children's Home, NCCC 1887

In 1857, directors of the Huron County, Ohio, infirmary indentured William Doyle, age two, to Comfort Lewis to "learn the trade of farming." This contract bound the two together for eighteen years. By 1870, the Lewises listed William as a member of their family by including him under their surname in the census enumeration. William's occupation was farm laborer. Apparently, William served out at least most of his indenture. A decade later William no longer lived on the Lewis farm, but two other young people—Elsie Mack, age seven, listed as "adopted daughter," and George Lavelly, age nineteen, listed as "farm laborer," lived in their home.[1] It appears that after William's time ended, the Lewises added at least one additional unrelated child to their home.

The number of institutions to serve the needs of dependent children in the Midwest increased in the decades after William's placement. By 1880, Elsie, if she was placed out, may have come from a children's home, whereas William came from the poor farm because almost no children's institutions existed in the state at that time. The growth in the number of institutions after 1880 came from a desire to give children a safer institutional environment, but the growth of institutions also fueled the desire to find more farm homes for dependent children. Between the 1870s and the 1890s, much of the discussion centered on the ongoing construction of new children's institutions and if those facilities properly served the needs of children. This was a timely debate because the number of institutions in the United States increased drastically. Nationwide, only 75 institutions for children existed in 1861, by 1877 that number had grown to 208, and at least 700 existed in 1890.[2] Concerns about children living in institutions provided the impetus for changes to child welfare in the Midwest. Beginning in the mid-1870s but increasing greatly during the 1880s and 1890s, poor farms were used less frequently for children, and counties, states, and charities built children's institutions. During most of William's childhood, county infirmaries served as the only form of public institution, and they placed children as they saw fit. The county officials and superintendents managing these institutions tried to locate farmers who agreed to train and provide care for dependent children. This basic idea stayed intact as the institutional landscape changed. States in the East like New York paid private charities to care for dependent children primarily in institutions, and Massachusetts centralized its care through a state institution. Midwestern states implemented a variety of methods, all having the option of farm placement. As states, counties, and charities worked to develop alternatives that removed children from negative adult influences, they considered the opportunities for placing out onto farms. By the 1890s, reformers believed that removing children from bad institutions would not be enough; families needed to be found for children, and the most desirable families were those living on farms.

The first part of the process in the Midwest removed children from county poor farms and put them in children's institutions, which marked an important step in efforts to increase farm placement. The overwhelming support for this idea did not necessarily provoke well-organized efforts. In the initial phase of reform between 1870 and 1890, many states ordered children out of poor farms, with the expectation that the new institutions built just for them would be a venue to help prepare them for family homes.[3] The new institutions were intended to serve as a means to move children into family units, not to become a substitute for family life. But placement did not necessarily go as planned, and many institutions filled with children. Starting in earnest during the 1880s, the entire idea of children living in institutions came under attack and fueled a nationwide reform effort to place as many children as possible with families. People recognized that farm placement did not just benefit the city child, it benefited all institutionalized children who lacked a proper family environment. Throughout the late 1800s, the notion that placement helped instill a good work ethic was omnipresent; but perhaps because of this, placers balanced two varying notions—children as viable components of a family workforce and children as requiring the protection and sanctity of a family home. In many instances, farm placement demonstrated that the two did not necessarily complement each other.

The County Infirmary

Indentures like William's were made between county infirmaries and local residents. In the Midwest prior to the Civil War, counties founded poor farms or infirmaries that housed people generally incapable of self-sustaining labor. Although the poor farm is often associated with working for room and board, counties that wanted a successful farming operation to help offset expenses hired local laborers to staff the farm and elected successful farmers to serve on the board of trustees. This had much to do with the fact that residents ranged from the insane, destitute, ill, elderly, abandoned, unwed, and illegitimate to the distressed and temporarily unemployed. Very few could be expected to provide full-time labor to a functioning farm.[4] Children sometimes lived in infirmaries with their parents, but when no other institutional options existed for their care, children also lived there alone. Children living in county infirmaries could be placed as the management or trustees saw fit, but typically children living there with a parent would not be placed out because this separated the family.[5]

Though many county poor farms did place children, it took extra effort on the part of the superintendent and the trustees. The thousands of children who lived in poor farms during the 1870s and 1880s raised the ire of reformers because of the conditions. Initially documented in the 1850s by Dorothea Dix, who toured a variety of institutions during her campaigns for the improvement of conditions for inmates, communities with neglected institutions faced a public shaming if visitors reported them to the local newspaper.[6] Precise information about the number of children who lived in poor farms and the condition of those institutions was not easy to obtain: Ohio's poor farms received sporadic visits from concerned citizens and state visitors beginning in the 1860s; Indiana did not conduct regular annual visits by state employees until 1889. Population reports outside the decennial censuses often went to the county supervisors and no further. When the conditions were recorded, the quality varied drastically between counties, and inspections were often performed by those responsible for the problems.[7] Reverend A. G. Byers, who headed Ohio's state charity board, which inspected public institutions, referred to the situation inside poor farms as "a spectacle of wretchedness and filth truly shocking."[8] In Van Wert County, an overflowing insane section prompted management to keep disturbed people in the main house despite fears they would set it on fire, and a children's room was set aside for the youngest residents of the institution. Along with these problems, the floor of the kitchen was reportedly decaying.[9] The conditions in infirmaries were aptly described after the 1888 Licking County, Ohio, infirmary fire as a "holocaust ... when the insane inmates, locked within their cells surrounded by stone walls and grated windows, were burned to death."[10] Because of the conditions and the associations made when children lived alongside insane residents, keeping children in these surroundings did not resonate with those who worried about the ramifications of environment for children. The Licking County fire prompted county officials to construct a state-of-the-art, $65,000 fireproof institution for children only. If city charities moved children away from vice and poverty, county officials needed to consider doing the same.

In response to the complaints that children should not be left in poor farms and other adult institutions, Midwestern states began mandating that children be removed from such places. However, they did not necessarily require public institutions be constructed for the care of children. The process of legalizing removal began in 1867 when Ohio authorized counties to build children's institutions, but it did not mandate such construction. To justify this change in policy, Byers used language recognizable for its rural metaphors: "Let those who appreciate ... childhood as the seed-time of life estimate, what it must be to have these impressions formed by association with the idiotic, the insane, and amid the loathsome moral corruption so common to our poor houses. Let them calculate the harvest not only to the future ... but to the State, which must be gathered sooner or later from such sowing."[11] Although the first efforts for removal began shortly after the Civil War, actually removing children from poor farms took decades. In 1894, Mrs. E. G. Kettering, a participant at the Indiana State Conference of Charities, claimed her experience visiting a county poor farm included "seeing a child ... who was seven years old, who was born in the county almshouse, and had never been off the farm. At a per diem of fifteen cents, that child had cost the county $400. Who can atone to this boy for a neglected childhood? Who can ever obliterate from his mind the memory of his early associations?"[12] The cost of maintaining this child irritated attendees of the conference, and so did the implication that the environment he lived in might cause life-long dependency. With little enforcement for removal laws, counties moved at their own pace and as their own treasuries allowed. Poor farms may have exposed children to vice and insanity, but new institutions cost money. In addition to environmental concerns about poor farms, placement was given as an additional motivator to putting children in their own institutions. Trying to find families to take children living in the poor farm proved more difficult because, according to one Indiana worker, "no one who wishes to take a child goes by preference to a poor asylum."[13] In other words, the condition and reputation of the institution itself made it difficult to place children with families.

The flaws associated with keeping children in adult institutions were some of the drivers of the institutional building boom that took place nationwide.[14] The largest amount of publicly funded institutional growth came because of the Midwest, where counties and states built their own children's institutions as an alternative to the poor farm. In Ohio alone, 46 counties had children's homes by 1890, and they had admitted more than 14,000 children. Almost 4,000 of those children had been placed out by the county homes.[15] Across the country, a variety of child-only care methods developed, but the Midwest focused on placing out, at least in theory if not in practice. Some states like New York saw a massive rise in institutionalized children because they paid for care in private institutions; Massachusetts paid for state institutions as well as placement options that included paid foster homes; states including Ohio, Indiana, Illinois, Kansas, and Iowa paid for soldiers' orphans' homes; Illinois allowed children to remain in poor farms while private charities took up the charge of finding them new families. Meanwhile, Michigan, Minnesota, Wisconsin, and Kansas all funded state institutions focused on placements, while Ohio and Indiana allowed counties to handle the details. No national consensus carried the day. The expanding institutional populations of children presented a new problem, as reformers determined that institutions were not necessarily appropriate for able-bodied children. By 1910, approximately 110,000 children lived in 1,151 orphanages across the country, and reformers raced to find family accommodations for as many as possible.[16]

Institutional Variety

Midwesterners authorized and supported a variety of methods for caring for dependent children, and almost all included living in some form of institution before a placement family could be found.[17] For example, Ohio counties began gradually opening their own children's homes or contracting with other institutions to care for dependent children as a way to remove them from poor farms. Although permitted to build a separate children's institution in 1867, most counties did not build until removal laws took effect. Miami County, Ohio, for example, opened its children's institution in 1880; the original residents were those children living inside the infirmary who legally needed to be removed. The infirmary, founded in 1840, held 116 residents but had no separate accommodations for the insane. Some children had a parent living there, while others arrived alone.[18] Once separated from parents through this new institutional segregation, children with living parents could be placed out unless a family member paid their board. These children were soon joined by others, and the superintendent sought out places on farms for the children. The Knoop Home, as locals called it, stayed in operation from 1880 to 1970 and housed approximately 1,500 of its 1,900 residents in its first 50 years.[19] The state of Indiana followed Ohio's pattern, with counties there opening their own institutions or partnering with other groups to provide care. In contrast, at the beginning of the 1870s, when Midwestern states were beginning to build public institutions, the state of Massachusetts began paying board for its dependent children who were too young to work. It took more than forty years for states elsewhere to adopt such a plan, in part because farm homes continued to need laborers and payments were seen as an unnecessary expense.

However, in the absence of a state mandate to remove children from poor farms, Illinois passed the Apprenticeship Act of 1874, which allowed local governments to bind out any child under sixteen caught begging or living as a ward of the county. In granting this permission the bill placed the emphasis on placement as opposed to institutional care. Children needed three months of school annually, a new Bible, two suits of clothing, and a minimum of $20. The state did not pass a poor farm removal law until 1895; thus, in Illinois dependent children often lived in poor farms well after neighboring states told counties to remove children from the damaging influences of an adult institution. By 1919, Illinois children could legally spend no more than thirty days in a county poor farm.[20]

In some locations, counties were relieved of the responsibility to build an institution by charity organizations that decided to take on the removal issue themselves. In Vigo County, Indiana, a plan for the county children's home was revised to reflect a generous endowment from the railroad magnate Chauncey Rose. When the facility opened in 1884, the Rose Orphan Home was a privately funded but public serving institution that removed children from the Vigo County Infirmary. While this arrangement seemed advantageous for the county financially, it denied local officials control over the institution, including control over which children were admitted. The Rose Orphan Home initially refused to take any illegitimate children or those with living parents.[21] Likewise, if the institution reached capacity, county officials had to make alternative arrangements for children. Almost twenty years after the opening of the Rose Orphan Home, Vigo County opened its own children's institution, the Glenn Home, because local officials wanted more control over the care of their dependent children.[22]

A more typical alternative to a county-operated children's home were privately managed institutions that relied on public funds. A women's group in Mishawaka, Indiana, took over the removal issue in their area, raising money for the care of children living in poor farms but relying most heavily on the per diem allowance received from area counties for the care of each child.[23] Vermilion County, Illinois, got its first children's home in 1894 in a similar way, when eleven "benevolent" women launched the project after reading accounts in the local paper about the children living at the county poor farm. Their purpose echoed that of other groups: "the ladies did not want them to go to the county home and have the associations of that place and people, they want these children to have the associations of home and of child life . . . many of these children come into this home from places where they would have been made criminals and pests."[24] This institution received money from the county board of supervisors (or trustees of the poor) to care for the children, a practice not uncommon in a region where privately operated institutions could be supported almost entirely by public funds.

Getting money from the county did not necessarily equal county management, and these private-public hybrids made their own decisions about a variety of things. The ladies board of directors in Vermilion County rarely accepted African American children, prompting a local woman named Laura Lee to step in and bring those children into her own home, where she too received small per diems from the county. The Rose Orphan Home very selectively placed children, but in Vermilion County the women received assistance finding homes for children from the all-male county board, particularly as overcrowding and costs increased. The Northern Indiana Orphans' Home also worked to find new homes for its children as a way to keep costs down.[25] Former Vermilion County resident Aggie Miller remembered that people were permitted to come to the children's home and select a child for domestic service jobs or for farm work. The 1889 newspaper expose that ignited Vermilion County's ladies to action noted that a large number of children lived in the poor house.[26] Since the state did not encourage counties to build institutions, Illinois relied heavily on privately managed facilities whereas counties in Indiana could choose whether to fund publicly or contract with private institutions. Illinois counties partnered exclusively with private agencies, such as the Children's Aid Society and the Children's Home Finding Society, for whose services counties paid a fee to help remove children from poor farms and place them in family homes.[27] In this way, Illinois became the Midwestern state most reliant on private placement agencies and charities.

The alternative to Illinois's lax government involvement was found in Michigan, which funded a state institution that counties used instead of constructing their own institutions. By making this decision in the early 1870s, Michigan's legislature made a unique commitment: no other state in the region had devoted as much money or effort to removing children from poor farms and only Massachusetts operated a similar institution. The Michigan State Public School in Coldwater used state funds to provide temporary care for children until they could be placed with a family. The entire goal of the institution was to prepare children for placement. Although the plan to place all eligible children from the state school met with mixed results, in part because the superintendent handled the operations of the institution as well as the placements until the mid-1880s, the Michigan State Public School set an example for effective poor farm removal and placement that the states of Wisconsin, Minnesota, and Kansas eventually followed.[28]

While states that centralized their dependent child welfare saw a drastic decline in the number of children living in infirmaries because counties avoided the burden of their expense by sending them to state schools, in Ohio and Indiana, the persistence of children living in poor farms can be attributed in part to the gradual construction of county children's homes. Although counties had state permission and were encouraged to open their own tax-supported children's homes, just twenty-eight of Ohio's eighty-eight counties built county children's homes before 1884, and those homes only placed out approximately 16 percent of their residents.[29] Most of the counties that opened institutions were rural or had small cities; the metropolitan centers relied on privately funded charities. Because of the low placement numbers, Ohio's county institutions came to be viewed by reformers as part of the problem with institutional growth; once children arrived, they never left. This did not halt the trend of construction, but the criticisms did help increase placement efforts. By 1904, fifty-five Ohio counties operated children's homes, with other counties contracting with one another for institutional space and at least two counties teaming up to operate one institution.[30] During 1900 and 1901, these homes had more than two thousand children in their care and placed more than one thousand children in family homes.[31] Despite this progress, counties still, if temporarily, kept children in poor farms, prompting criticism from reformers who claimed, "If the Legislature continues to ignore and permit this violation of the law by county commissioners and infirmary directors, it must be confessed that there is no remedy." When Judge J. T. Davis, of Newark, Ohio, proposed a bill for the mandatory building of children's homes for all counties, the legislature refused to respond to the suggestion.[32]

Despite the demands to remove children from poor farms, the admittance of families to the poor farm and a lack of other options in some places made it challenging for counties to completely comply. Ohio's state board of charity tried to assert that after 1880 no child had been "legally" committed to a poor farm, but the records indicate that committing and living there were two different issues.³³ Just 2 years later, approximately 2,200 children under the age of 16 cycled through Ohio's poor farms. They went there with family, or stayed there until other arrangements could be made.³⁴ Until 1900, Ohio allowed children to stay in poor farms with parents; children under the age of three were never legally denied admission if they came with a parent. Illinois simply refused to legislate for their removal, keeping children inside a poor farm but often together with family. As had been the case in earlier decades, removing children from poor farms often meant severing family ties. For example, Sangamon County, Illinois, maintained sixteen children in its poor farm during 1879, but only two of those children lived there without a parent.³⁵ With the laws written to allow temporary stays, counties without dedicated children's homes used their poor farm as a way station, keeping children until a placement or charity could take the child.³⁶ Between 1881 and 1885, the Martin County, Indiana, poor farm administrators placed thirty-three children in family homes. The poor farm manager handled the work after the county children's home disbanded due to lack of funds. Other children continued to live in poor farms because women used them as maternity facilities.³⁷

The number of children remaining in poor farms did, in the long run, decline. By 1892, 152 Ohio children remained in poor farms, down from 1,978 in 1880.³⁸ Of the counties disobeying the removal law in 1892, at least 4 housed more than 10 children in their poor farm, but it could have been worse. Until 1889, at least 10 counties in Indiana continued to lease out their poor to the lowest bidder.³⁹ Nationally, the trend moved even slower—Homer Folks documented that in 1890 almost 5,000 children between the ages of 2 and 16 remained in poor farms. Some states had no removal law, existing removal laws failed to provide for enforcement, and it remained more affordable for counties to keep children in pre-existing institutions. For states that did not want to invest in a children's institution, leaving these decisions to counties helped save state resources.⁴⁰

Like Ohio counties, Indiana counties increased the number of children's institutions as a removal strategy, and the number of counties contracting with privately funded institutions for children also grew. In 1890, Indiana possessed 38 county children's homes—eventually reaching a high of 47—but in 1894 almost 500 children under the age of 16 remained in county poor farms. The county institutions struggled to find family homes for children because they lacked staff and resources. With children remaining in various types of institutions, concerns grew about the lack of family influence. In the 1880s as the number of county children's homes steadily increased, the number of children placed out averaged less than twenty per year per facility.[41] Since initially these facilities were intended to place out children, the accumulation of children prompted calls for increased placement using whatever means necessary, including contracting with private groups and placing children into homes with little supervision.

Parents and Costs

The lack of placement happening at many institutions generated new concerns. Critics charged that institutions of any kind created a permanent class of dependents. Did a community encourage dependency because it was willing to help? Did more parents abandon their children because the county would pay for their care? Counties struggled with the reality that the construction of a local children's home resulted in that county caring for more dependent children than other counties without an institution. Clearly, these institutions were important stop-gap measures for parents in distress; they became "second homes" where parents temporarily placed children.[42] Although a need for this type of care existed, construction of local institutions was blamed for making child abandonment, even temporarily, more convenient for parents. The placement of children from the institution was viewed as a way in which counties might dissuade able-bodied parents from using the facilities for temporary care.

How parents used institutions is an important aspect of farm placement. Not only was placement used as a way to provide a family environment for children, it was also used to discourage parents from relying on institutions to provide care. This is significant considering that at least 75 percent of dependent children had at least one living parent. Parental reclamation of children removed as many, but in reality probably many more, children from institutions than placements. Through 1890, when almost 4,000 children had been placed from county institutions in Ohio, parents and family members had reclaimed 4,100.[43] Individual institutions shaped their own policies about ceding parental rights before placement, with some institutions requiring relinquishment, allowing board to be paid, or placing without the surrender of parental rights. As Jessie Ramey demonstrates in her book about parents using institutions in the Pittsburgh area, institutions served as a temporary measure for distressed families; however, unlike her urban institutions, where many parents paid board, few indicators show parents doing the same at public institutions in the Midwest.[44] Some limited examples show that parents did try to keep children out of placements by paying toward children's care. In 1902, Lucas County, Ohio, received almost $2,000 from parents, which covered approximately 15 percent of the expenses of the institution for the year.⁴⁵ Ramey identifies one Ohio father and farm laborer who removed his children from the Montgomery County Children's Home because officials wanted to place his three sons. Instead, he took them to Pittsburg and paid their board, which took almost all his monthly salary. In time he reclaimed the boys, and his costly decision to keep them out of a placement demonstrates the resistance and determination of some parents.⁴⁶ Paying board was often the only option for parents who did not want their children placed out. If payment stopped, children could be placed out, sent to another institution, or parents could lose contact. Reformers certainly believed that by placing out children, parents who might consider an institution a source of aid would be persuaded otherwise.

Those parents who could not pay board did not necessarily resign themselves to giving up their children. Often superintendents were forced to deal with the interference parents caused once children went into placement homes. In 1893, Lyman Alden placed Charles "Homer" Meissel in a home where he was described as "contented and happy." But a year later his father "coaxed" him away from this home. He stayed only a few weeks with his father before trying to return to his placement.⁴⁷ Other placement parents were bothered by the continued contact, as one placement parent complained, "She writes to her mother quite often and her mother still answers regularly. Her sister wrote a letter to try to induce her to come and live with her, but we did not permit her to answer it."⁴⁸ This family obviously wanted the girl back, but other children showed a willingness to choose where they wanted to stay, like one young man who reported, "My father came to take me away from my home. I don't intend to go with him, for I have a good home and I intend to stay."⁴⁹ Parents no doubt worried about the treatment their children received after placement. Addie Davis, an African American mother who left her daughter, Marree, at the Miami County Children's Home in 1899, wrote a letter to the superintendent in 1910: "Dear Sir. I would like to know if there is a colored girl in your home that Tayler Madison taken to raise I understand there have been some trouble if it is so would you please rite to me and tell me all about it as i am her mother her name is Marree(?) Vena When I put her in that home that was her name." In addition to knowing who had her daughter, Addie Davis also seemed to know that the Madisons had changed her name: she was listed as Viola in their household enumeration. Davis managed to reclaim one of her two daughters during the time Marree/Viola lived with the Madisons, but in 1920, with no account of the trouble Davis mentioned, Viola Madison was a lodger in Dayton, not far from where her mother wrote the letter in 1910.⁵⁰ Both fathers and mothers reclaimed children or contacted them in placements, although not necessarily with long-term success or in a timely fashion. They did so after children had gone into placements, sometimes claiming children directly from a placement home. Records indicate this process could take months or years and parents reclaimed one or two children but not others—leaving no indicators as to how they made that decision. Remarriage, employment, or recovery from an illness helped parents reconstitute their family. Superintendents and officials often let children remain with parents who went through such efforts to get them back, but placements of children to farms did make it more challenging for parents to contact children and upset parents who thought their children would remain in an institution.

Parents who made boarding payments or reclaimed children helped to offset the costs associated with operating an institution, which could be burdensome for governments and charities. Basic startup construction and property expenses for a county institution in the 1880s averaged near $10,000. During the 1890s, Ohio's county children's homes cared for almost 3,000 children at a cost of $204,505.[51] Michigan, which made a larger investment for bigger buildings and more property at its state school, spent approximately $150,000 to start the institution with annual expenditures around $35,000, which included the farm.[52] Using the Lucas County Children's Home expenses and receipts from 1902, the institution cared for approximately 100 children per day, costing the county $102.46 per child annually. In addition to the $2,000 from parents, the institution used another $2,000 of farm products, no insignificant portion of the $12,000 budget. Alongside the potential payments from family members, counties relied on farmland either to provide income or to offset the expenses of groceries. Counties that invested in farmland hoped to earn an income from the children's home's property.[53]

Whether or not to have a farm with a children's institution became a major dilemma. Not only did having an institutional farm promote a healthy lifestyle of work for children, but counties also maintained a farm to try and provide food for the residents and cut down on expenses, and the cost per child decreased an average of $12.00 annually with farm produce profit included. The sizes of these farms varied widely. In Ohio, the largest county children's home farm belonged to Fayette County, which owned a total of 210 acres, while Hancock County had a single acre of land. The average size of the farms was approximately 59 acres.[54] However, not all farms equated to cheaper operating costs; just like on a family-operated farm, variations in management, land quality, and the type of care given children in the institution all affected the outcome. In 1882, Miami County, which kept a farm, paid roughly $152 per child. Belmont County, Ohio, with half the land of Miami

County, spent just $77. The type of buildings, the salary of the management, and the level of care given to children probably affected these numbers more than the size of the farm. During this year, the Ohio County children's homes valued their total farm products at $6,781.33. Lawrence County, Ohio, on the other hand, located its home in the mining town of Ironton. With no property attached, the cost for caring for each child was $76. Lawrence County gained an additional benefit from locating the home in a town: the children attended local schools, reducing the cost of hiring a private teacher.[55] Over time the emphasis on having a farm declined, and Montgomery County, Ohio, trustee Charles Wuichet agreed with this concept. During the 1910s, directors of that county's children's home determined that they did not want a farm because they thought it isolated children and kept them out of public schools. Wuichet specifically cited the desire for children to blend into normal society as a reason to keep the institution closer to town.[56] Ridding an institution of the hassles of a farm and using a town institution might have been more convenient and also fit in with the coming trends to move all placement children closer to town, but the enticement of providing children with healthy air and exercise helped make most of these institutions rural.[57]

Those who argued that children's institutions needed a farm believed that children needed productive work to do outside of school—and they did help, but running a farm still required skilled management, which cost money. Children could not provide all the labor required on a farm any more than poor farm residents could. Still, the pull of the farm life was strong, and most public institutions tried to provide some type of attachment to the land. As one Indiana State Board of Charities member claimed, "Nothing could be better for such an institution than a farm with its varying kinds of labor. Boys who work on a farm feel that they are a part of the concern and that what is raised partially belongs to them." Like farm training programs at other institutions, these farms provided children with valuable work experience to prepare them for a farm placement.[58]

Contracts and Labels

Encouraged to place children with families by both the expectations of legislators who intended facilities to be temporary homes and by reformers who wanted children to have a family environment, but lacking any special skills or funds with which to supervise placements, children's home superintendents often followed the same techniques used by county infirmaries to secure children homes. Children regularly went into placements without a contract because they were "on trial." This meant that the children could be returned at any time for any reason; but in reality, they were returned at any time and for any reason even with an indenture contract. While the trial period usually lasted anywhere from a few weeks to a few months, children did spend a year or more "on trial" before formal indenture papers were drawn up. Each institution set its own terms, and those terms could be changed for a variety of reasons. As a baseline, the contract was between the institution and the adult taking the child. It typically noted that the child was to receive training and care, schooling, and a form of severance payment once the contract ended; girls' contracts often went until age eighteen, boys until age twenty-one.[59]

The trial period, coupled with the fluidity of indenture agreements, contradict notions about the permanence of indentures. Sociologist Bruce Bellingham effectively refutes the notion that the "adoptions" touted by the CASNY were somehow permanent or binding.[60] The CASNY had no more luck with permanence or encouraging better treatment than any other placing group or institution by refusing to use indenture documents. An example of how fluid placements were helps explain why indenture contracts were inconsistent and not always provided. Fourteen-year-old Nettie Lafevre went to her first placement in 1894. She stayed there from May until August, then was briefly back at the institution before heading to the Edwards's household. In February 1895, she was formally indentured to Mr. Edwards but was returned in September of the same year. Nettie's case is not unique; it demonstrates how time consuming contract writing could be with superintendents balancing trial periods, indentures, failed indentures, and re-placements. Superintendents expected the spirit of a contract to be followed even if the document itself was late in coming or altogether absent.[61]

Judging by a variety of examples, counties and participants modified contractual agreements to suit their needs. When a contract arrangement was drafted for a child, sometimes a preprinted form was used, like the one binding Frank Snow to the farmer Asa Borton in Fulton County, Ohio. Frank's indenture form was then altered because Borton did not agree to the standard payment of $50, so that amount was crossed out and $25 written in its place. This is perhaps a reflection of Frank being old enough that he would not provide many years of work, or of his ability to find wage work. Despite the existence of a formal document, he left before the 1901 termination of his contract and in 1900 lived with a different farmer where he worked as a hired hand.[62] Other situations relied on a simple handwritten note, similar to the one between infirmary directors in Williams County, Ohio, and Betsy Boyce, who took Bertha Bostater. The 1896 arrangement between Boyce and the trustees specifically noted that Boyce was bound to "board and clothe and care for her and not to abuse or neglect her." Bertha's mother granted written permission for her two daughters to be placed and promised not to interfere. By 1900, Bessie no longer lived in the Boyce household; instead, she lived with a different family and worked as a servant.[63] As an incentive for people to take in children, adjustments could be made to lessen the severance payment. In 1891, administrators of the Miami County, Ohio, children's home wrote indentures with no financial reward for children at the end of the contract as a way to encourage more placements.[64] This change in tactic may also reflect the competition for decent homes among the various institutions and agencies placing in the southwestern corner of the state. A typical contract from the Belmont County, Ohio, children's home asked that its children be given a Bible, two good suits, and three months of schooling per year. These were not necessarily generous terms since one of the home's indentures lasted twelve years.[65] Typically, most contracts specified a payment close to $100—a small sum for children placed at an early age, especially during a time when hired farm hands received approximately $16 per month.[66]

The standard contractual arrangement included a severance payment, the type of training to be given to the child, the age of the child, and the trade and address of the placement parent. The Greene County, Ohio, contract typified the terms used by other institutions, in which placement parents were expected to train the boys for "all kinds of farm work." The girls' contract specified that they be "furnished in accordance with her circumstances," and that they be treated in a manner similar to biological children.[67] Other agreements asked placement parents to bring a child into their home "on terms of social equality" and to "treat him kindly as his own child."[68] Some contracts expected that "the child be kindly treated, comfortably clothed, given medical attendance when necessary, and be protected from evil example and immoral influences."[69] These were fairly standard goals, indicating that children were not hired hands but in fact more akin to members of the family, but agreeing to them and keeping them were two separate matters.

What contracts failed to articulate were the actual relationships formed between children and families. Not all farm families took in children simply because they needed an extra set of hands. Childless couples, like Peter and Elizabeth Dewees, tried to complete their family by taking in ten-year-old Clara in 1885. Beginning in 1860 shortly after their marriage, census records do not show them having any children living in their household. It appears that the Deweeses, both in their forties, took Clara with the intention of raising her as a member of their family. In 1889, Peter was wrongfully convicted of arson and spent almost a year in prison before being pardoned. During the turmoil the couple returned Clara. The damage to his reputation had been done, and the Deweeses moved to Paulding County in northwest Ohio where they "took to raise" seven-year-old Martha. After Peter's death, Martha moved in with Elizabeth and in 1920 was in her household as a border. Farm couples with young children might have needed someone to assist them, but childless couples also used placement as a way to add children to their household for personal reasons.[70]

Census records can help explain how adults viewed their relationship to a child and indicate how varied the relationships between children and their new families could be. Placement children were defined in vastly different ways depending on whom they lived with and who counted the household. In 1880, the enumerator of Madison Township in Hancock County, Ohio, specifically labeled four placement children as "bound boy" and "bound girl." There were other terms used, including "foster son," "boarder," "lodger," "orphan," and "servant." There is little information to explain the changes in description or whether they came from the enumerator's evaluation of a situation or from the placement parents. The variety of terms in just this single township does little to clarify that these children were placement children.[71] Other examples suggest that relationships could change over time. Ben Ellis went to live with farmer Isaac Gruber where, in 1900, he was listed as a "lodger," occupation "at school." By 1910, Ben still lived with the Grubers, but after a decade in their home, he was listed as "foster son."[72] Similarly, seven-year-old Robert Faehl went to live with farmer John Gall and his family in 1914. In 1920, Robert was listed as "orphan," but in 1930 his entry with the Galls referred to him as "foster son." Robert farmed all his life, but despite his upgraded status as foster son, his death certificate listed his biological parents.[73] Robert's case in particular highlights the fluid notion of placement children in different families. He stayed with the Galls longer than required by his indenture, indicating a certain amount of satisfaction or loyalty, or both, but his name did not change, and neither did his identification with parents with whom he did not grow up.

African American Placements

While Robert gained a measure of familial status with the Galls, situations did exist in which giving the child a new family was not a goal of placement. Sometimes older children did not expect a new family because they were "to work for wages," and for indentures involving white families and African American children, any notion of being treated as a member of the family was not expected. These interracial arrangements were for labor, with girls such as Anna Belle Green living and working as a "servant" for the white

Seiberts, who operated a restaurant.[74] Eight-year-old Harriet Jefferson was placed with relatives in 1900, but they decided to return her, and in 1905 she "went to work" for a white female principal.[75] Unlike the forced apprenticeships documented by historian Karin Zipf, who describes southern families being stripped of parental rights so that their children could provide labor for powerful white farmers, these children entered labor relationships after a crisis altered their families' abilities to provide care.[76] Institutions serving African American children, such as the Home for Destitute Colored Children in Pennsylvania, also encouraged this type of arrangement, noting that residents would be "useful as domestics in families" and would be "bound to their employers, who become responsible for them until they are of age."[77] By embracing the already established notion of African Americans as household servants, the Miami County Children's Home and others followed practices that specifically stressed work instead of family and de-emphasized the farm in favor of any working opportunity.

African American children were the only group to have been placed out in two vastly different ways. If they were placed with an African American family, a chance at familial membership existed; but when placed in a white family, they were clearly there to work. Historically their indentures had categorized them as "others." For a period of time in Indiana when restrictions also existed on the civil liberties of black adults, indentured African American children did not have to be educated like their white peers.[78] Howard Brady experienced both types of placements. Born in 1883, surrendered by his parents in 1886, but reclaimed by them in 1890 only to be readmitted two months later, he then went to two different African American households between 1894 and 1896. In 1900, he was a servant in the household of William Kenny, a white shoe dealer who also had a white female servant living in his home. It is possible that the two African American families he lived with classified Howard as a "servant," but in their homes he had a chance of being treated as a member of the family.[79]

One of the other challenges surrounding African American placements was the relatively small number of African American farm families available to accept children. The rural Midwest did not have a large minority population during this time, owing to practices ranging from refusing to sell land to African Americans to neighborhoods of farmers refusing to hire black workers.[80] Facing such a shortage, institutions that usually preferred farm placements broke with this pattern and often placed children with African American families in towns or cities instead. Harriet's, Howard's, and Anna's placements are all examples of this. Miami County, where these children lived, had a larger than typical African American population thanks to an influx before the Civil War. The superintendent found homes for children in nearby Dayton, Piqua, and Troy despite strained race relations in the area. Miami County also sent a few children to Indianapolis, where a more substantial population of African American families could be found to house children and an institution operated by Quakers willingly took children for a fee. Sending these children to other facilities was not an isolated event; in the late 1880s, Lawrence County appears to have sent African American children to the state reform school as an alternative to keeping them in the institution or trying to find them a placement.[81]

In the absence of other options like an institution for African American children, parents and management used the resources nearby. In 1875, the Waters children of Defiance County ended up at the infirmary when their family fell on hard times. By 1880, their father, Harvey, classified as a mulatto farm laborer, managed to reunite his family, and the children did not go into a placement, probably because homes could not be located for children too young to be servants.[82] Defiance County trustees did successfully make arrangements for other African American children living at their infirmary, but smaller populations meant fewer chances for being included in the membership of a new family. In 1876, after the death of his father, Ben Butler was bound in apprenticeship to Gibbons Parry in neighboring Henry County. The Parrys were white and owned a large farm and raised stock. The Parry family had a steady stream of unrelated young men of both races working on their farm. In 1870, nineteen-year-old Edward Miller and eleven-year-old William Mason were both listed as farm laborers living with the doctor-farmer Gibbons Parry.[83] It is entirely possible these children were neighbor boys hired to work the large Parry farm, but it is unlikely that parents hired out an eleven-year-old. It is also probable that the Parrys took advantage of the local institutions for affordable labor.

Ben Butler was an exception to the typical institutional child in the rural Midwest because of his race; most placed-out children were white, and the majority were native born. A small minority population may have been made smaller after 1890 by the growing number of sundown towns and counties in the Midwest, making those areas hostile toward African Americans. As sociologist James Loewen documented, between 1890 and 1930 residents in rural counties of Indiana and Illinois participated in a racially motivated removal of the population, and by 1930 all-white counties existed. Rural residents in Ohio and Michigan also participated in these tactics, but to a lesser extent. African Americans left rural areas in the Midwest because they felt uncomfortable and because they were forcibly driven out, making it harder to find farm families to fill the need for dependent children.[84] Additionally,

Jessie Ramey notes a tendency for African Americans to keep their children out of institutions as much as possible and for kin or fictive kin to step in and recover children as an alternative to institutionalization.[85] In areas with an African American population, institutions specifically solicited for those families. An advertisement from the Lucas County Children's Home, located outside of Toledo, announced, "Colored Families Attention: Here are four fine mulatto children all homeless." This superintendent tried to provide a family instead of a labor arrangement.[86]

When families could not be found for African American children, they waited in institutions to come of age or for wage work to be found for them. Raymond, an African American seven-year-old whose mother had been in and out of the county infirmary, spent most of his childhood in the Miami County Children's Home until wage work was found for him and he left. His contact with the institution restarted in 1935 when he wrote requesting information: "Dear Sir, will you please look up my age when I was admitted to the Knoop home. I am trying to determine my correct age. Pap Jay, as I called him, was the Superintendent at that time. Please do this and oblige. Inclosed please find stamp for reply."[87] Having lived at the institution, Raymond seemed to have a fond connection to the superintendent, which might have been especially important since he had no parents and never went into a family. The residents of each institution reflected the makeup of the community that institution served. While a few institutions needed to manage the issue of race in placements, most had few if any African American children, and some, like Gibson County, Indiana, opened one for white children and another for black children.

Religious Interference

Matching children to a family of the right race could complicate placements, but religion and ethnicity factored in more often. Matthew Crenson and Linda Gordon establish the contentious nature religion played in the development of placement programs and institutional growth. Catholic, Protestant, and Jewish charities battled for the souls of dependent children, concerned that they were being undermined by other denominations. Opponents harangued Charles Loring Brace for both his lax methods of supervision and his habit of taking Catholic children and intentionally placing them in Protestant homes. In response, Catholic institutions started placement efforts to ensure their own dependent children stayed in the faith. Efforts to find Catholic families mirrored Brace's emigration attempts via long train rides, uninspected homes, and controversy. Linda Gordon explores the hazards of both religion and ethnicity in her work on the Arizona orphan abduction, when Mexican mining families offered to take in Catholic children from New York City but were undermined by white Protestant women who took the children. In that case, the desire for Catholic families was so pressing that the Catholic charity fought all the way to the Supreme Court to have the children returned so as to be re-placed with non-Hispanic Catholic parents. As Crenson and Gordon both note, concerns about maintaining the religious ties of dependent children caused groups to open their own institutions to protect children from conversion or identity loss, and some made concerted efforts to avoid placement at all cost in order to keep siblings together and control the religious education of children.[88] Crenson also documents that certain types of children were not necessarily welcomed into placements in the predominantly Protestant rural Midwest. Such was the struggle for the New York Juvenile Asylum's placing agent, who claimed, "Illinois farmers were 'as a rule prejudiced against Hebrew children.'" This type of problem heightened tensions related to placements in places like New York, but had less effect in placements closer to home.[89] Superintendents at nondenominational institutions who paid attention to the religious differences of their wards could, for a price, send them to institutions specifically matched to their denomination, such as the Cleveland Protestant Orphans' Home (CPOH), which employed its own visitors to find placement homes. Doing this lessened the burden of placement for county officials.[90] Putnam County trustees made arrangements for children by sending them to a variety of institutions like the CPOH across the state. When institution officials knew the religious background of the parents, they often attempted to place a child accordingly. Lawrence County officials made judgment calls, however, in some cases. Four-year-old Maud Dugan had a Catholic father and a Protestant mother; his habits were recorded as "not good and intemperate," while hers were "generally said to be good." They sent Maud to the CPOH for placement.[91]

The role of private institutions is apparent in the way public institutions utilized their services to make appropriate matches for the background of the child. At various times Putnam County contracted with the CPOH, the Sisters of Charity in Toledo, the Soldier's and Sailor's Orphan's Home in Xenia, and a Mennonite institution in West Liberty.[92] Wyandot County infirmary managers did the same, sending children to the CPOH and St. Vincent's for $1.50 per week. Efforts to make more accurate matches came as a result of overall better attention to detail. Like the requests for African American families, the Lucas County, Ohio, children's home also put out calls for "some specialties." Included in this flyer were "two Jewish children; brother and sister," as well as a list of "Negroes," one of whom was described as "quite white." There were plenty of options to choose from by the 1890s to specifically match children, and those options further expanded to include fraternal homes operated by groups such as the Odd Fellows and the Fraternal Order of Moose.[93]

Despite these attempts, plenty of superintendents spent little time worrying about a religious or ethnic match for children in need of a home. Lyman Alden said nothing about it in his overview about the purposes of the Michigan State Public School, and later when he worked in Indiana, Alden specifically noted that he placed James Dwyer with an uncle who was a Catholic, "as is James," only after trying two presumably non-Catholic homes first. Homer Folks blamed the desire to match children to families with the same faith as one of the causes for institutional population growth.[94] However, in 1905, Minnesota's juvenile courts and state school were legally obligated to try and place children with families of like faith, but trying and mandating it were two different things. Superintendent Galen Merrill noted his compliance with the law when he confirmed that race and ethnicity were recorded in the case files of the children: "we have to consider these questions in deference to the parties concerned."[95] Placement parents were expected to take children to church as part of their agreement, but presumably that would be the church of the placement family. If the child's background was not specified, mandatory church attendance could in effect change a child's religion.[96] Even when superintendents knew the religion or background of the child, like that of Roy Hane whose father was a German miner and whose mother was an American and a member of the United Brethren Church, there are few notes to indicate that an effort was made to match Roy with a family of similar characteristics. More common than seeking out specific types of families was the entirety of the Miami County ledger, covering more than 1,500 children, which featured not a single indicator of religious affiliation for anyone—not children, not parents, not placement families.[97]

Ethnicity also differed in importance depending on the institution. In some records, the ethnicity of the children's parents was never mentioned, and when birth locations were listed for children, most were inside the United States. More recently settled states such as Minnesota were exceptions, indicated by the number of immigrant children who lived at the state school, but even in nearby Wisconsin, most children were native born.[98] At these large institutions, intake records documented details of children coming from across the state. In smaller communities, particularly those with county children's homes, often the trustees and the manager knew the reputation of the child's parents and recorded that instead of ethnicity or religion. If they did note ethnicity, they did not necessarily make an effort to find a family of similar background. Notes such as "in jail," "no good," "veteran," "in state hospital," "abuse reported," "illegitimate," or "in workhouse" indicate that often the county officials knew something of the families from which the children came but prioritized parental behavior over background. They noted when parents were separated, divorced, or dead.[99] Catering to specific religious and ethnic backgrounds happened, but not with any regularity. While this can be seen as a purposeful omission designed to ignore certain faiths, it is equally possible that the absence of information is evidence of administrators lacking the time to handle such specific issues. In Lucas County, where the possibilities of finding both Jewish and African American families for children existed because of the proximity of both Toledo and Detroit, specific advertisements served as a way to increase the chances those children would be placed with families. Overall, the dearth of placers willing to prioritize ethnicity or religious preference invigorated the building of population-specific institutions where children could be cared for by their own group.[100] Nondenominational institutions showed some interest in appropriate matches between children and placement parents, but did not let the lack of a match prevent a placement from happening.

The Superintendent

Finding a suitable family to accept a child regularly fell to the most overworked individual in institutional care, the institutional manager. Referred to as a superintendent or matron, this person served on the front lines of placing. Superintendents managed the upkeep of the institution, found homes for children, readmitted and then re-placed children multiple times, dealt with biological parents, and sometimes oversaw an institutional farm. At county institutions trustees of the poor or county infirmary directors helped the superintendent with placements. In unique cases like that of county official Asa Borton and Frank Snow, the dependent child he took in, the trustee became the indenter. At larger institutions a staff assisted the superintendent. To enable placements, these men, and some women, sought out homes, signed the indentures, and at some institutions, supervised the children after a placement.

Early placements done by trustees were essentially all managed by men because the positions were elected, but women became placers when they were appointed to county boards by judges, when they worked as professional placers for agencies, and when they accepted jobs as children's institution matrons. In 1891, Ohio took specific account of the people managing institutions, and there were almost forty male superintendents of children's homes compared to three women.[101] Women were more likely to independently manage private facilities, and women like Laura Lee from Vermilion County, Illinois, took the initiative to open their own facilities to care for children and spent their own money to do so, which is also how the first county children's home in Ohio was founded. Women were more regularly employed as visitors whose job it was to check in on children already placed, and states and charities hired them for this work beginning in the 1890s. Women whose husbands worked as superintendents for children's institutions also played a significant role as matrons of the institutions.[102]

When children's institutions replaced county infirmaries, the task of handling placements could be turned over from county officials to superintendents, but often the superintendents lacked the time or motivation to complete such work. In fact, in institutions where costs were paid by the county on a daily rate per child, superintendents had no motivation to lessen the institutional population lest they lose out on needed funds. In other circumstances, such as at the Michigan state school, placement was an expected role of the institution and thus a mandatory part of the job. When Lyman Alden took over in 1874, he relied on a less than dependable network of county volunteers to help him find new homes for children and to supervise placements. He also increased the amount of time children stayed in the institution, worrying that immediate placements only created more work because they were more likely to fail. The Children's Home of Cincinnati hired a full-time visitor to handle its placement needs, which in turn made it appealing to counties that wanted to subcontract care of their own children. Institutions with a visitor separated the tasks of superintendent from placements, leaving the superintendent to manage the institution and the visitor to deal with children outside the institution.[103]

Most institutions could not regularly afford the luxury of keeping a visitor on the payroll. This omission would have been fiscally sound had these institutions had resources to keep children for the long term, but many overfilled because no placing was done. When recommending the construction of county children's homes as an alternative to poor farm care, the Ohio State Board of Charities never intended the facilities to become permanent residences for children. Instead, it hoped that children could be kept safe until a placement family could be found. In 1882, Ohio Governor Charles Foster suggested that agents be hired to find homes for children as a way to support the mission of children's homes, but counties hesitated to make this financial sacrifice in addition to the costs associated with the institution itself. At most, some contracted with facilities like the one in Cincinnati to provide professional placement services.[104]

Without a plan for placements, county institutions lagged behind their state counterparts in placement numbers, in part due to the overwork of superintendents and the need for per diems of the residents. In Ohio, around a dozen private institutions cared for and placed roughly twice the number of children as the county institutions.[105] Institutions with better funding and organization developed systems for good placement practices before the intervention of the state and trained social workers. Both Lyman Alden and G. T. Green, the man hired by the Cincinnati children's home, demonstrated the potential for placers who performed their jobs conscientiously. Most of Alden's adult life was spent working at a children's institution. In Michigan, hundreds of children needed supervised placements each year and dozens more waited to be placed. To attempt this feat he corresponded through letters with the children, their placement parents, and occasionally their biological parents. He also took tours around the state to visit some of the children personally, and they invited him for visits in many of their letters back to the state school.[106]

Green did not have the extra task of managing an institution while performing his work, but his supervisory job required an enormous amount of travel due to the preference of the Cincinnati institution for rural farm homes for children outside the city. Prior to his hiring, the institution relied on a network of local committees in rural Ohio, Indiana, and Kentucky to find families for children. These committees sought out placement homes and shared the responsibility of supervising the placed-out children living in their community to prevent abuse or other problems. Many of the communities were Quaker settlements, and they took in children even though most, if not all, were not Quakers originally.[107] When administrators hired Green, they hoped that a full-time placement agent would increase the number of children placed. Between 1864 and 1875, the local committees found "country homes" for 719 of the 1,906 children who lived in the institution.[108] Hired in 1877, Green placed advertisements in newspapers, lectured at community events, wrote letters, and met with local interest groups to try and encourage rural people to accept children from his facility.[109] He traveled almost 25,000 miles a year to stop what institution superintendent Meigs V. Crouse believed was a great problem for the institution. Crouse explained, "If we waited for people to come after the children, we might place the larger boys and girls for help, and the pretty little girls for pets, and we have so many applications every day for such children that we pay little attention to them."[110] It was hoped that Green could eventually find homes for all the children inside the institution, not just those wanted for work, but that goal never materialized;

still, he did find homes for approximately 125 children annually and visited hundreds more.[111]

Efforts to place children shaped working relationships between public and private institutions in the region. While Green worked in Cincinnati placing children from as far away as Marietta County, which hired him because officials there believed him to be the best placer in the state, other private institutions in Ohio also took public wards for placement.[112] One of the other private institutions often used by counties, the Cleveland Protestant Orphan Home, reported that in 1882 it received almost 1,200 applications for children but only placed 103 children with families. The management prided itself on selectivity.[113] Cincinnati solicited business by sending letters to county institutional management for additional children who could be placed for a fee. The trustees of Fulton County saved this advertisement, which discussed the practices of the Cincinnati home and offered to keep children at either the main institution or their farm branch in Hamilton County. For $30 per child, the Cincinnati institution would place and supervise all fit children, diminishing that burden for counties.[114]

One of the benefits of subcontracting placement services involved supervision. Green and Alden both agreed that visiting or at least hearing from a child once a year should be a priority, at least until the visitor could be sure that the family was upstanding and the child felt safe and at home. Both men independently made this recommendation a decade or more before state agencies set the same goal.[115] In comparison, emigration groups like the CASNY struggled to locate their children via letter. The notion that a letter to check up on a child would be a suitable form of supervision seemed foolhardy, as critics pointed out as early as the 1870s, but it continued to be the method used by many institutions because it was cost effective. Otherwise, for a flat fee, children living in public institutions became the responsibility of the private agency, and the placement and supervision of those children was their burden. Only when children proved unplaceable or unfit to remain in a home would they be returned to the original institution. The concept of regular visitation helped protect children from mistreatment, but it did not guarantee good matches. Green spent most of his year on the road and rail visiting children, and over a 16-year period he visited at least 2,500 children, earning him the nickname for his initials G. T., "I Get There." Green and Alden, who worked hard to place children in good homes, re-placed almost as many children as they placed for the first time, indicating that finding the right fit between child and home was a constant challenge.[116]

As a result of his experience in Michigan, where supervision did not meet his standards, Alden criticized the emphasis on finding farm homes for children and the notion that any home was better than an institution. He noted that sometimes homes that seemed satisfactory would not, in fact, be good for a child. In 1885, having left the state school for the Rose Orphan Home, Alden presented his concerns about placement in a widely circulated paper entitled "The Shady Side of Placing Out." In it, he made strong recommendations for better supervision and longer periods of institutionalization as ways to ensure the safety and happiness of children. In spite of the caustic title, he did not out rightly reject the notion of placements; rather, he cautioned that the optimism of his peers regarding the idealism of farm homes was misplaced. While he did not stop placing, the Rose Orphan Home never placed children for other institutions, and he believed that children needed to stay inside institutions until they had a solid foundation of education and training. Alden placed children with whom he had regular experience and still made mistakes. In 1899, he "placed Frederick Adkins with Thomas Stevenson who owns 300 acres. He is a brother of the man who took John Ruessler and did so well by him." This man's land holdings plus his well-behaved relations qualified him for a child. Later, neighbors reported that Mrs. Stevenson did not treat Frederick well. Based on this report, Alden moved him to a second placement, where he stayed for five years. As he neared the age of eighteen, the second family did not want to pay him the $50 owed him. They may have been decent enough for Frederick to stay for five years, but balking at such a low payment speaks ill of their true nature.[117]

By presenting his objections to the type of farm placements being done and his suggestions for improvements, Alden collided with a growing majority inside the national child welfare movement who believed that institutions, despite their increasing number, were not good places for children to live. An extension of the thinking about infirmaries and poor farms, this argument posited that institutional life scarred children, making them lifelong dependents, unthinking cogs, and adults who lacked life skills. Optimistically, they believed most children would find permanent placement, keeping the costs of operating a facility low. As the notable New York charity advocate William P. Letchworth noted, "In the placing out of children, two objects are to be considered. One is to save the county the expense of maintaining them, and the other is to save the children."[118] In reality, children stayed in county institutions an average of four to five years, and the costs associated with keeping children increased the longer children lived in institutional care.[119] Alden's successor in Michigan tried to reverse the practice of keeping children in the institution, bragging that he shortened the stay of children in the institution from approximately twelve months to around eight.[120]

The Trouble with Institutions

Keeping children too long in an institution was an oft-heard complaint and touted as a reason to place children out. Inexperienced employees, poor locations, and bad conditions in the facilities all contributed to the problems of institutional life. Officials from Stark and Columbiana Counties received low marks from visitors for the health care at their children's home, the Fairmount Children's Home, because there was no way to separate sick children from the healthy. Residents suffered from damp and "unfit" conditions blamed for a recent outbreak of diphtheria.[121] As in other counties, this institution housed a number of "imbecile and idiotic" children who needed to be moved to state-operated facilities. Combining fit children with disabled or sick children reminded visitors of conditions inside poor farms.

Problems with the physical condition of institutions were also reported. Counties purchased single-family farm homes and attempted to convert the space for the use of dozens of children as a cost-saving measure. These homes did not always have a good water supply or modern safety upgrades like fire escapes. Lack of maintenance and overcrowding quickly took a toll on structures, but despite the problems, Indiana visitors believed that children's homes received better maintenance than poor farms, an indication that county officials treated children as more deserving of decent facilities than dependent adults.[122] On Union County's sixty-one-acre farm property, the farm provided income and good food for the institution, but needed supplemental labor because the able-bodied children were the first to be placed out due to the local need for unskilled labor.[123] Facing a similar demand for labor in his community, the superintendent of the Harrison County, Ohio, children's home reported that almost no children came to the institution and expressed a fear that the reason for the low admissions involved the practice of township trustees secretly leasing out children privately—keeping the admissions to the county children's home low—in order to save money. If true, that meant that children went out to local families with no accountability and no method of supervision. This institution could hold sixty children, but only twenty-five lived there when the report was filed; the county paid a per diem for the care of each child. Indiana counties faced the same dilemma. Those that supported a handful of children at the poor farm refused to undertake the expense of building an entire institution for such a small number of children. Counties with few children to care for found it more fiscally responsible to contract with another institution or continued to house children at the poor farm until other accommodations could be found.[124] A daily rate for each resident, whether it came from parents or the county coffers, was important revenue for children's institutions. Although an institution needed this money to operate, the pressure to place children increased during the Progressive Era when reformers vilified institutionalization. All the aforementioned problems made the children's institution look less helpful and more like a place that encouraged life-long dependency. It also made Lyman Alden's assertions that properly run institutions could give good influences for children seem like an unattainable goal.

Placing more children with families was touted as a solution to the institutional problem. However, the way in which an institution undertook the task of placing a child in a home proved entirely up to the discretion of management. Urged to explain her placement techniques, the matron of the Johnson County, Indiana, children's home said she most often arranged for the placement of younger children in the hopes that they were too young to be used for drudge work on farms, but trained the older ones for labor. This training certainly included farm chores and housework. Through these efforts she decreased the number of children living in the home from fifty-two to thirteen and was lauded for her efforts.[125] Interestingly, she did not say how this decrease in population affected the income of her institution or how she supervised the placed-out children. The ability to work made older children more appealing to farmers, with children older than eleven or twelve years of age most sought after. Older children required less care and upkeep than younger children and better withstood the rigors of farm life. Unfortunately, older children also needed to be re-placed more often because they acted out, were overworked, or became dissatisfied.

Long-Distance Placements

By the 1890s, more institutions were trying to place children in response to national outcry about institutionalization and financial pressures due to an increasing institutional population. Public and private institutions alike tried to locate decent farm homes for their able-bodied children, but all these efforts competed with agencies still bringing children into the region from outside the Midwest. Orphan train children filled places in farm homes, making them unavailable to local dependents. Between 1857 and 1893, Ohio accepted more than four thousand placements from the CASNY alone. Indiana received thousands of children from the CASNY and the New England Home for Little Wanderers.[126] One attendee of the Indiana Board of State Charities meeting summarized his frustration with the importation of children: "[these children are placed] right in the neighborhood of county homes that are almost unable to find places except as they get old enough to work out, when they are in demand, not for their own sake, but because they are cheap help."[127] Ironically, the same states that placed legal barriers to importation allowed their own children to be moved out of state. In particular, institutions near state lines did not allow boundaries to stop placements.

Institutions had good reason to competitively seek out homes for their children. As the CASNY moved farther to the west in response to partial restrictions by Ohio and Michigan, the New York Juvenile Asylum advertised "mostly boys" in an 1888 Illinois broadside. E. Wright, the agent for these children, posted that "homes are wanted for these children with farmers . . . [they] have received instruction and training preparatory to a term of apprenticeship." For terms, boys were to receive $150 dollars, girls $50, after their indenture ended—but all children "will be placed on trial and indentured free of charge." Interested parties could meet these children at the Hotel Holland and take one home.[128] H. D. Clarke, a placing agent for the CASNY, made frequent trips to the Midwest. He placed advertisements about children needing homes in local papers and distributed flyers. The information given to potential placement parents about the children encouraged farm families to respond: "Here is Sarah, she is German . . . Her father is living but does not provide for her, her mother died recently. She has an older brother or sister somewhere. She would like to be on a farm. If you will give her a few chicks to care for and raise and let her have a portion of the egg money, it will make Sarah a very happy and obedient girl."[129] There was just enough information about Sarah to elicit sympathy but not too much to damage her chances of being selected. Additionally, her skills and aptitude recommended her to farmers. Clarke stopped in towns along rail lines serving rural areas where he typically sought Protestant farm families for the children. Clergy references on behalf of prospective parents helped the process.

With competition from multiple eastern groups as well as institutions located inside the region, placers followed similar advertising practices in the hope of finding farm homes for children. Lucas County published pamphlets containing photos and brief descriptions of children needing homes. In one edition, Benjamin, nine years old, "A German boy, big, healthy, and well mannered," was paired with Henry, twelve, "A boy with a natural inclination to work." While the children's home superintendent often tugged on the heartstrings of possible placement parents by calling them to the "missionary" work of needy children, these images and their captions were intended to attract those who needed a worker and played on the stereotype of German Americans as sturdy, hardworking people.[130] The Fairmount Children's Home in Alliance, Ohio, placed its request in the *Ohio Farmer*, a sure way to target the right audience. Singing the praises of farmers, Superintendent M. M. Southworth advertised almost 170 children ready for farm homes in April 1895. He reminded readers that his children were "eager . . . to be busy" and that farmers with references would be able to get children "out of my flock." Southworth had good luck using the *Ohio Farmer*; he mentioned that after a reader recommended farmers take children from his institution in the publication previously, he received more than one hundred letters and placed eleven children in Hardin County alone.[131] Southworth highlighted the benefits of taking a child and contributing to the greater good by trying to appeal to people's better natures, and seemed unconcerned that Hardin County was located across the state from the Fairmount Children's Home.

The tactics used to try and find homes for children, including ads touting their strengths, training them for placements, and putting them in distant counties, all indicate that finding enough good homes to take in children was a difficult task. Despite their almost unanimous dislike for the CASNY and other groups bringing children to the region, Midwestern superintendents placed children using newspaper ads as far away as Kansas and Nebraska, where homesteading farmers needed hands to clear land and start a farm.[132] This happened as states took legal steps to prevent the importation of children into their own states by imposing bonds paid by the placing agencies. Illinois placers, almost all working for private agencies accepting public funds for their work, routinely sent children elsewhere while Illinois farmers simultaneously accepted children from out-of-state institutions. In 1912, well after the period when states determined that accepting children from other states did not benefit their own dependent children, approximately one hundred Illinois children went to twenty-eight different states—some as far away as Washington.[133] The Woodford County Poor Farm in Illinois sent children to Iowa, Missouri, Ohio, and Indiana. A majority of the Illinois children placed out of state went to neighboring states.[134] In turn, institutions from nearby states sent children into Illinois. While sending children out of state, Illinois' State Board of Administrators complained that Missouri should be stopped from "dumping" children across state lines from St. Louis.[135] The practice of moving children across state lines lasted decades, but did slow down in the 1910s because it made supervision difficult if not impossible. Even when institutions used other facilities inside the state, children still ended up far from home. Fulton County, a rural area in the west-central part of Illinois, sent children to the St. Charles Home for Boys outside of Chicago. The St. Charles Home for Boys, in turn, placed out more than one hundred children each year to states as far away as Oregon.[136]

Illinois was not alone in this long-distance quest for rural placement homes; the superintendent of the Belmont County, Ohio, children's home took two trips to Kansas, taking children from the home each time to place them in that state. One of the children from Belmont County who went on the western trip already had ample experience in placement homes. In 1886, at the age of eleven, she had spent a summer and harvest season living with a family before being returned to the children's home. The following year she went into a placement home for two months, but the family returned her because she was too young. In December 1888, she made the trip to Kansas, but this placement did not work either, and a new home in Kansas was found for her six months later, probably through letters to the children's home. Between the ages of eleven and thirteen, this child lived in four homes in two different states in addition to time spent in the county children's home.[137] In 1871, the training given at the farm operated by the Children's Home of Cincinnati was credited for seventy-seven requests for children from farmers in Ohio, Indiana, Kentucky, and as far away as Kansas.[138] Two decades later, in 1892, Ohio institutions reported that 480 children were placed in their home county, 250 in a different county, and 150 children out of state during the year.[139] Lawrence County, located on the Ohio River, used families in West Virginia and Kentucky regularly, but they also looked farther to find homes, including Texas, where at least one child was sent at the recommendation of a local doctor. In 1893, the local paper printed up the story of an institutional resident bound for North Dakota to live with "our former townsman." The boy went alone to Chicago, where he was to meet one of his new family members, but he arrived late, having spent a day at the World's Fair.[140] With many institutions and organizations moving children for the purposes of placement, children were often subjected to the luck of the draw when removed from their home county.

Moving children away from negative influences—such as family members—was often given as the prime motivation for transporting them away from home. But management also worried about local people knowing too much about a child's background. S. J. Hathaway, a vice president of the Ohio Board of State Charities, worried about local placed children: "their very names had evil associations and their pedigree was well known . . . people who were given to genealogical studies would trace out its [the child's] pedigree to prove that nearly all the criminals and vagabonds in the country were connected or related to the child."[141] His concerns about the treatment of children once their "pedigree" became known speaks to a larger issue about whether or not farmers, or anyone for that matter, could bring a child into their home knowing about their tumultuous family history or the reason for their dependency. Taking a child to a different county or state did not just sever the ties with family members, it also gave a child a chance at a fresh start.

There were questions about how far institutions should go to alter a child's environment. In 1892, representatives from Ohio children's homes disagreed about the proper geographic location for placing children. Removing children from their home county might provide needed distance, but it complicated the system of supervision after placement. Hathaway noted an increasing need to move children outside the county so that placement parents would not be distracted by the "fateful" history of children. He suspected placement parents might be more inclined to include children in their family if they knew nothing of their past. The institutions that placed away from their own county managed to place more children, leading the Ohio Board of State Charities to conclude that this system was more successful.[142] To make placement easier, institutional managers like Meigs V. Crouse of Cincinnati said, "We will not be overparticular and captious in our requirements. A fair share of the work and of the buffeting of life will not hurt the boys but bring out their best qualities." If no one determined what a fair share of work and the buffeting of life meant, children could be left to languish far from their placing institution. The need for laborers on farms far outpaced the ability of institutions to track and supervise children sent into other Midwestern states for the purposes of placement.[143]

Getting a Child

Whether nearby or in a distant state, people requesting children often divulged their motivations and information about the type of home they could provide. Some institutions advertised their children, but when the requests came in, not all were approved. Minnesota Agent Hannah Swindlehurst printed excerpts of some of her most notorious requests, including a farmer with no hired help who wanted a sixteen-year-old boy as "company for my wife," and a couple who included a lock of dark hair expecting a child with hair no lighter than the sample.[144] The Lucas County Children's Home denied almost half the applications because people wanted workers. A request to an Indiana placer explained, "My wife is not very strong, I am away from home a good deal, we live in the country, and want a little girl about thirteen to help for a little while."[145] Such a blatant and temporary labor arrangement did not receive approval, but at a different institution that letter may have merited a child.

In some locations people actually came to a children's home with the intention of taking a child. That they did so gives credence to the concern that a poor farm was not the sort of place people wanted to come for a child. At the Washington County, Ohio, children's home, the state's first county home, the administrators did not initially intend for people to select children directly from the home, but between 1868 and 1889, local residents showed up and took children after providing the superintendent with a "certificate of good moral character." S. J. Hathaway, speaking for this institution, worried, "The evil of the present system of waiting for people to come and select children, is that, as a rule, people leave the dull ones in the homes who, most of all, need foster fathers and mothers, and again, those who seek children at the homes are too often not seeking children for their sakes, but for some ulterior purpose."[146] While applicants agreed to treat the children properly, send them to school, and give them a payment when they came of age, such assurances did not eliminate the risk of "ulterior" purposes; people who approached children's homes to select a child did not necessarily do so because of a dedication to the child. People produced false references and lied about their willingness to make the child a member of their family. Mary Dykeman, who worked at the Cass County, Indiana, children's home, claimed that anyone could and did get a decent reference letter in order to take a child.[147] Dykeman might have discounted the reference letter, but other counties relied exclusively on its merits. Lucas County, Ohio, told perspective placement parents that "these children will be given away to people of good reputation who apply for them." The goodness of their reputation needed to be backed up by references.[148]

Once a home had been found, superintendents often relied on correspondence to keep up with the children. After placement parents got a child, the Washington County Children's Home asked them to write once a year about his or her condition, but most people did not fulfill this request; children were not instructed to write. Other options for supervision, like the township trustees, did not do much to help. Even though this home placed most of its children locally, the county trustees proved too busy with their own affairs to check in on children. In hindsight the administrators realized that if parents took pride in the child and treated him or her well, they would correspond about the child. These problems supported the worries of Lyman Alden and G. T. Green that more placements without improvements for supervision created a dangerous combination. Without good methods for measuring their results, the administration from Washington County estimated that half of their placed children "got along alright and grew up to be good men and women." They made no guess about the other half. In 1892, Hathaway told the Ohio Board of State Charities that the home had changed its policy in order to better track the children.[149]

With plenty of examples of haphazard placement techniques, conscientious county officials tried to improve. Lewis Miller of Akron, Ohio, told the Ohio State Board of Charities that his county declined to place children until their institution superintendent could personally visit the potential placement family. Miller claimed, "We think the personal observations are worth more than all the recommendations we can get from the neighbors."[150] Local officials did sometimes take their assignments seriously; Perry County township trustees joined other county officials and helped their children's home administrators supervise and find homes for children.[151] This work served the best interests of the counties; fewer children inside the institution meant less money from the county coffers for their support.

County infirmaries were among the first institutions inside the Midwest to take up the task of rural placement. Despite often being located on a farm, these facilities did not meet the standards of providing children with a positive environment because children shared space with destitute adults. Although implemented unevenly, state-mandated removal of children from poor farms launched an institutional building boom that included both public and private children's institutions. After the transition from poor farm care to children's institutional care began, more institutions placed children on farms, but their efforts had almost no cohesive strategy for effectiveness. As a result of the inconsistencies, heated debates took place between child welfare workers regarding the problems with institutional life and the benefits of placement. These disagreements did not produce homogenous results, and leading into the Progressive Era, the child welfare system in the Midwest featured a vast array of options, with institutions placing carefully, others placing hastily, and some not placing at all.

The issues relating to religious matches between children and placements that dominated much of the urban child welfare work played a less significant role in the Midwest. Some institutions tried to move children to religiously affiliated homes and institutions, while others appear to have neglected such details not necessarily out of a concerted effort to convert children but more likely due to the rigors of institutional management and placement. African American children faced different challenges, and stood no chance of being treated like a family member when they went into the homes of whites.

Farmers accepted dependent children from their own counties and from other locations, enticed by advertisements and the affordability of placement children as workers. Children placed out in the Midwest faced challenging circumstances—not the least of which was the lack of supervision. Unfortunately for some children, the lack of oversight forced them to live in situations that proved unsuitable or hazardous. By the 1890s, with the transition from poor farm, to children's institution, to placement farm home well underway, Lyman Alden's ideas about the benefits of institution life seemed passé. Institutional workers and government officials appeared to be supportive of farm placement, the farm lifestyle, the needs of dependent children, and how those things complemented each other. Their efforts at increased placement revealed evidence that not all farm families lived up to the rural ideal.

3. "The hideous consequences"

> "I found the wrongs which dependent children suffered from being placed in unsuitable homes . . . to be very great."
> —W. P. Letchworth, "Dependent Children and Family Homes," NCCC

During the first months of 1870, ten-year-old Phoebe Ann Moses left the Darke County, Ohio, poor farm, destined for a farm placement home in a neighboring county. Anne, as she was called, represented a fairly typical placed-out child—her widowed mother could not provide for all of her children and so sent two of her daughters to the local institution. When a man came to the institution looking for a child to help his wife around the house, the Darke County Poor Farm superintendent sent Anne home with him, believing she would be a useful helper to a farm household with younger children. In July, census enumerators recorded Anne in the household of the Bosses, an older couple with a large farm who lived with their four-year-old, their married daughter, her husband, their baby, and another placed-out child, thirteen-year-old Solomon, the son of a widowed woman from Darke County.[1]

For two years after the enumeration no records exist for Anne, but during 1872, she returned to the poor farm a beaten, battered, and terrorized runaway. When the superintendent's wife, Nancy, saw the child's green-hued skin and learned that she had been unable to sleep on her back for weeks, she reported the problem to her husband. They assigned Anne tasks around the poor farm, ensuring she would not be placed again.

Years after her ordeal ended, the world came to know this battered child by the name Annie Oakley. Her shooting skills developed because of the need to earn her keep in the home of her still-struggling mother. Before she became one of the nineteenth century's most famous women, Annie labored in a placement with an abusive farm family. Later in her life, when Oakley recounted her experience, she referred to the couple who abused her as the

"Wolves." Annie said little about these dark years, but described one encounter this way: "Suddenly the 'She-Wolf' struck me across the ears, threw me out into the deep snow and locked the door. I had no shoes on. I was slowly freezing to death. So I got down on my knees, looked toward God's clear sky, and tried to pray. But my lips were frozen stiff and there was no sound." Her biographer Shirl Kasper believes that Annie's experience with the "Wolves" left a deep impression on her and filled her with shame—enough shame to shape the rest of her life.[2]

At the time of Annie's placement, states across the country were determining how to define treatment of children "within the bounds of reason and humanity." Each state defined child cruelty and prosecuted cases as local officials saw fit.[3] Although too late to prosecute the "Wolves," Ohio passed legislation in 1884 that clearly defined penalties for torturing or neglecting children and articulated that torture, torment, cruel punishment, and the deprivation of food, shelter, and clothing could result in jail time and a fine. This law and others like it acknowledged a problem and demonstrated a willingness to interfere in households, not just for placed-out children, but for all children. This time period is more often characterized by a rise in interest by private societies seeking to protect women and children, but placed-out children also drew concern from those connected to their cases. By the early 1900s, abuse that might hamper a child's ability to function as a self-sufficient member of society was deemed particularly hazardous.[4]

We know that concern about the treatment of dependent children increased because the calls for better supervision often focused not just on physical abuse but also on what would be considered neglect. Claims of abuse and neglect became an important way into placement families' homes, but the measure of mistreatment remained subjective. As Minnesota's state visitor noted in 1900, "There have been no cases of shameful abuse or neglect. Some have been reported, but on investigation little or no real abuse was found."[5] Little abuse to one visitor might be grounds for removal from the home for another. His co-worker recounted one abusive situation: "A boy, whom a former guardian could not control without using such severe means that I intervened and removed to another home, has only been punished twice in nine months [in his new home]."[6] For this visitor, some punishment was permissible, but he drew an undefined line for severe correction. As these two visitors demonstrate, determining what counted as abusive treatment was in the eye of the beholder.

While scholarship like that of Linda Gordon focuses more attention on the better-documented abuse cases of the twentieth century, the threat of abuse for children in placements was obvious well before the era of state visitors, social workers, and friendly visiting. This prior knowledge did little to slow the pace of placements, and often nothing happened to those found mistreating children. Significantly, as placement became more firmly entrenched in the policy of institutions and charities, placers recognized they had a responsibility to monitor the well-being of the children they placed out; as they increased supervision, more cases of abuse and neglect were therefore recorded. This does not mean that more cases were prosecuted; since the abusers and neglecters were not the parents of these children, the easiest solution was to remove the child from the home. That required little paperwork or court involvement because the arrangement existed between an institution or agency and the placement parents. The "Wolves" were never charged for their mistreatment of Annie, although the superintendent and his wife knew about the abuse. There would have been little with which to charge them without definitive and life-threatening injuries.[7] In the era prior to regular supervision, children like Annie stood little chance of anyone standing up for them; she was readmitted to the poor farm where she established herself as an able, if overused worker, taking charge of the institution's twelve-cow dairy. For children in her position, being re-placed was a possibility. Anne avoided that fate by making herself an indispensable helper.

Abuse, neglect, and overwork all emerged as serious and problematic issues facing advocates of free placement homes because they refuted the notions on which rural placement was based. The assumptions that the farm was healthy and farmers inherently good paved the way for abuse and neglect because many institutions saw little reason to invest money into supervising farmers. Placers relied on farmers for their supposed morality; they believed farm work to be healthy work; but this confidence could be misplaced. With increasing oversight came more awareness that children did not receive proper treatment. Historian Patricia Rooke identifies the distance of children from their families as one reason placed-out children were vulnerable to abuse.[8] Ironically, distance from relatives was one of the reasons farm placement became so popular in the first place; however, removing children from institutional settings sometimes put them in situations where they could be unnoticeably exploited. Distance contributed to their isolation, as did the fact that these children did not attend school regularly or live in a public, urban space where they could be seen regularly by others.

The social welfare networks constructed in cities during the late 1800s coincide with rural placement, but no similar associations formed in rural areas. Instead of moving children into urban families where they might be monitored by such groups as the Society for the Prevention of Cruelty to

Children (SPCC), placers focused on the positives of rural isolation and relied on the reputation of farm families. Gordon's work on the abuse of children in cities relies on reports from the visitors and volunteers of the SPCC, who found children, a few of them placed out, in homes where they were victims of incest and abuse.[9] Those children's location and the existence of the SPCC helped facilitate their removal from bad situations. As Elizabeth Pleck, Ann Vandepol, and Gordon all note, the nativism that drove groups into working-class homes did not extend to rural areas. When SPCC workers visited urban homes, many of them belonging to immigrants, they "discovered" dreadful problems, including intemperance, malnutrition, contagion, and a host of other ills. These plights reinforced the notion that the countryside provided a better life for children. With little friendly visiting happening in rural households, they maintained an elevated status.[10]

Family violence, overwork, and child neglect were not problems new to the late 1800s, but in previous generations, propriety limited intervention into immediate families, and apprenticed relationships between children and unrelated adults could be policed by the child's parents. As Pleck and Gordon both explain, the Progressive Era brought outside intervention into the family sphere as well as different ways of thinking about the power of parents over children. No longer would parents be permitted to treat children as property, and the working-class home became a venue for interference. What placers and child welfare workers came to see was that suffering for placed-out children happened not only as a result of abuse. Whether through isolation and dependence on the farm family or overwork and seasonal placements, the farm contributed to the hazards facing placed-out children. It is clear that most children placed on farms did not experience the cruelty that Anne did, but the incidents discussed in this chapter are not unique because they are so rare; instead, they are unique because evidence for them exists through newspaper reports, institutional records, or accounts from the victims and witnesses. Propriety drew a veil over recording explicit details involving bodily harm, which is particularly true for sexual abuse.

Problems with the treatment of children placed on farms led to a transformation in placement policies. As the number of rural placements increased during the Progressive Era, calls for improved supervision that resembled visiting done in cities were met by states and charity groups. The emphasis placed on visits and inspections eventually became standard practice but began because a problem already existed. State agencies were ultimately deemed the most effective way to monitor, remove, or re-place children living in placement homes, but the institutionalization of that support system did not begin until the 1890s and did not gain substantial funding until after

1900.[11] Supervision did not stop the problems; a number of the best accounts of abuse, neglect, and child resistance come from these visitors. The examples here draw attention to the types of problems that undercut the rural ideal, as well as demonstrate the limited documentation of these issues. Each child welfare worker determined how serious the problems with children were, with W. T. Gardner cataloguing crimes against children as "obtaining cheap labor . . . obtain girls for prostitution . . . treat children with the greatest indifference and even with severity amounting to cruelty."[12] But Gardner's list was limited: the seemingly benign habit of moving children in and out of placements seasonally, the crueler and telling physical abuse cases, and the examples of sexual abuse indicate that placed-out children faced a myriad of troubling circumstances. Children responded by running away, by contacting family members, or by fighting back through physical means. Although they were often voiceless, children's resistance can be seen through their behavior, pleas to relatives, letters to an institution, or leaving the placement. By far the largest difficulty for placements was the number of times children went into and out of homes. The sheer number of children placed multiple times indicates how challenging making good matches could be and suggests that farm families were not as accepting of needy children as placers believed. Multiple placements cost institutions extra money and effort and no doubt caused children heartache and confusion.

Multiple Placements, Overwork, and Neglect

In July 1911, Mary B. Favorite went into an indenture with Charles Cadmus. In October of the same year she was returned because the Cadmuses were "going away for the winter." Three years later, still in the institution, Mary was surrendered to the Children's Home of Cincinnati because they had a home available for a girl her age, but no girl available at their own institution. The institution thought this family was so good they sought out a child to fulfill the request. Three months later she returned because the Cincinnati staff "saw fit to remove her from the home." No further information was provided regarding the unfitness of the home. Mary's record specifies no physical abuse, but instability and a lack of affection cause different forms of suffering for children. Gardner catalogued it as "treating children with the greatest indifference." Certainly returning a child because of winter travel plans counted as indifference.[13]

According to advocates of the farm placement system, by putting children into farm homes, those families would provide dependent children with a stable, morally sound place to call home. They would be treated "as one of the family." This specifically supported the effort to remove children from institutions and place them in farm homes. In spite of this, records indicate an overwhelming number of children who went through multiple placements. In Cincinnati, where G. T. Green worked to find homes and re-place children, the placement data confirm the semi-permanent nature of placement relationships. Out of 787 children, 263 were placed twice, 102 a third time, 39 a fourth, 5 a fifth, 4 a sixth, 3 a seventh, 3 an eighth, and 2 children were placed 9 and 10 times. One-third of the group was moved at least once after initial placement.[14] These numbers bolster other data like that from Miami County. Between 1880 and 1930, roughly 40 percent of the children studied were returned to the institution at least once; approximately 80 percent of those children went to at least one additional placement home. Likewise, in the decade between 1887 and 1897, the Minnesota state school re-placed 67 percent of children from their first home. In the following ten years, less than 20 percent of children ages eleven and sixteen reported being happy in their placements. During both 1899 and 1900, the Minnesota state school re-placed almost as many children as it placed the first time, but the school's officials pointed out that a majority of the re-placements came for children out on trial, and not those officially indentured.[15] Time did not necessarily improve success; Cincinnati continued to re-place at least 40 percent of its children over six years old, noting that three homes on average needed to be found for each re-placed child.[16]

Cycling through one or two homes until a good fit was found happened regularly, but it often took more than two placements to make a match. The case history of a five-year old girl from Champaign County, Ohio, suggests the hardships faced by children who went through multiple placements. This child moved between the county children's home and the same placement family three times in a single year, once from August to February, again from March to June, and then for the last time in August. No explanation was given, but it is possible that the farm family who took in this child needed the small amount of extra assistance she could provide or perhaps could not decide whether or not to keep her permanently. For a five-year-old, the constant movement between county children's home and a family must have been confusing. Indeed, the records for children as young as five indicate a willingness on the part of placement parents to exchange children often. Edith, also five years old when she arrived at the Miami County Children's Home in 1888, went out on trial seven times and was formally indentured twice between 1889 and 1898. All nine trips out of the children's home were to different people in different locations across Ohio. She spent her entire childhood bouncing between families and the institution.[17] Even finding stability in a good placement home could be ruined by unforeseen circumstances. Benjamin Vickroy was six years old when he went to live with the Kearns family. Eight years later, in the fall of 1912, Mrs. Kearns died. Eventually, Benjamin, who spent most of his childhood with this family, was returned and in 1918 transferred to the Ohio Board of State Charities for a new placement.[18] Dorothy Abel was adopted in 1903 by the Langfords, who owned a small farm in Indiana. She was almost fifteen at the time, fairly old for an adoption. Two years later Mr. Langford "says he is sorry he adopted her." Apparently her contact with her biological mother had created hostile relations and severed the ties between herself and the Langfords. In 1911, a now-married Dorothy wrote to the Rose Orphan Home claiming that Mr. Langford nullified her adoption. If true, she wanted the back wages of $1.50 a week she should have received for the time she remained with him after turning eighteen.[19] When a home did not work out, regardless of the reason, children often moved out of one family, into another household, or back into an institution before being placed into another new home or making their own way.

Moving children in and out of homes did not physically harm children, but it did help dispel the notion that farm families wanted children for the right reasons. Children seen as disposable had not been included in the fabric of a family. The trial periods, informal adoptions, and breakable indentures allowed placement parents to return children, often with no notice, to the institution. Even the long-time advocate of placement Homer Folks admitted that farm placement parents did not volunteer evenly throughout the year, an indication that they wanted children when the need for workers peaked. He further claimed that volunteers wanted the most attractive or able-bodied children and returned "the weaker ones and those not quite old enough to work [and those who] seem[ed] especially liable to be morally perverse." Folks resigned himself to the fact that without a payment attached to their care, placement children "are poorly supplied with clothing . . . they are not in any sense made members of the family. They see of the house only the kitchen and their sleeping room, which is shared by the hired man; they are shut off from the refining influences of the family, and work without pay. Thus many come to regard the days spent at the institution as their best."[20] In Minnesota, the superintendent of the state school noted that the only difference between a trial period and an indenture was that after an indenture was signed, the parent needed to gain the permission of the institution before returning a child. Yet, he noted, "permission is invariably granted," and the statistics from that institution indicate that more children were returned during the trial period than from indentures. Farmers often agreed to a trial period during peak times of work, only to return a child once the work ended without ever having to enter into a written agreement.[21]

Many cases demonstrate that the chasm between what people thought about how children would be received into placement homes and how children were really treated once there was fairly wide. The idea that any family home was better than the best institution was challenged by cases such as Myrtle's. Myrtle, who entered the Rose Orphan Home as a ten-year-old in 1897, was noted as a "good girl," but her record demonstrates how the instability of placements could negatively affect even the best children. Myrtle's first placement family returned her because their business failed. Her next placement father died, having helped her through teasing at school, which forced her to stay home for extended periods of time. At fifteen, her third placement family, who operated a farm of 234 acres, returned her because she was "saucy and couldn't work enough." Family number four also faced economic hardship. After six months living with an older farm couple, Myrtle was again returned because her placement parents "were afraid she might have consumption." Apparently she simply had a cold. By the age of seventeen and in home number six, problems became apparent. The Malones, who raised another placement child from the Rose Orphan Home, returned Myrtle because she was "immoral and slovenly." She admitted to having sex with their hired hand. Family seven claimed she was "too old to learn the ways" of their farm, landing her in home eight, which she aged out of a year later. Ernest Alden recorded that Myrtle was "doing as well as could be expected."[22] Myrtle's case may not shock those familiar with the twenty-first-century foster care system, but this constant movement contradicted why farm homes had been recommended in the first place.

Myrtle's case showed how economic distress, death, and dissatisfaction led to the return of placed-out children, but other cases illustrate that farmers purposefully took children with the intention of returning them after a season of work. Initially, seasonal placements were embraced by groups like the CASNY, which exploited farmers' seasonal need for workers. Not everyone agreed that seasonal placements led to good long-term solutions, but they did meet the needs of farmers, who after the Civil War increasingly specialized production and needed "the accumulation of labor at certain seasons, the cessation at others."[23] Minnesota Agent Herbert Lewis warned that "mercenary" requests for children "made it possible to keep a few more cows, and to get the corn husked and the potatoes dug a few days earlier in the fall." Indiana State Agent William Streeter stated, "It has not been at all uncommon for parties to take children out of the orphans' home in the spring, work them all summer, and bring them back in the fall, ragged and dirty on some trumped up excuse to the effect that they 'didn't suit.'"[24] The seasonal trend can be seen in the timing of placements. During 1893 and 1894, officials in Brown County, Ohio, placed more children during March and April and September and October than any other months; the Michigan state school had similar seasonal patterns, with 45 percent of all placements happening between March and June.[25] As the 1893 record for one Clinton County eight-year-old noted, it was "not the fault of the boy, ['C'] managed to get a summers work and then returned him."[26] This type of exploitation remained possible as long as placements were viewed as flexible arrangements.

Short-term placements make it difficult to accept the labor exchange between child and farmer as healthy. Several farmers took children for days or weeks at a time before returning them for unspecified reasons. John Brookman's first placement came at the age of ten when he went to Charles Pond for one week. Charles himself appears to have been bound out as a child to a local couple. In 1891, John went to the Andersons for one month, waited six months in the institution, then started the spring of 1892 with a new family. The same day he returned to the institution in August 1893, he went back out into a new placement, which he ran away from nine months later. Given John's age during this series of events it is likely he was viewed as a promising worker on these farms. Irvin Layer went to a home for four days before they returned him, but one year later was re-indentured to the same family. The short-term work he performed apparently met the needs of the family and recommended him for another trial period the following year.[27]

Farmers preferred children like John and Irvin who were over the age of ten because they could perform a full day's work. Those between the ages of five and ten were more likely to stay in institutions until they became old enough to place, or, in other words, old enough to work.[28] Seeing people claim children because they were old enough to work drew the ire of those working to assist dependents. In Ohio, F. M. LePage used a rural metaphor to advocate for short-term job training inside an institution as an alternative to placements: "if the child is taken as a farm is rented, for the most that can be got out of it for the time being, at least cost, it is a cruel and wicked thing."[29] Mrs. W. B. Campbell from the Orphans' Home Association of Anderson, Indiana, perhaps overstated her point, but it contained at least a bit of truth when she told the audience that families took girls "for what they can get out of them, and nine times out of ten the girls are imposed on."[30] Even though they knew placements made children vulnerable to this type of neglect, placers struggled to differentiate between good and bad families because there were few resources with which to investigate the homes.

Officials who admitted that children received poor treatment is only part of the evidence showing that children placed on farms were not given the type of care expected. A letter from one placement mother described her delight with the diligent and unsupervised work of the girl she took in: "I have just returned from an unexpected absence of three days, and found all the housework attended to just as if I had been here to see to it." The visitor H. J. Jaeger noted that this girl, who had previously destroyed things in her old placement home, now was credited as a "faithful and willing worker."[31] One Ohio visitor found a girl wearing rags, who did nothing but fetch coal and work in the kitchen for her placement family. The visitor removed her from the home although the family indicated they wanted to formally adopt her. G. T. Green, noting that appearances could be deceiving, found a boy living in a seemingly satisfactory home eating alone after the family finished their meal.[32] Placers came to understand that taking time to select a good family would reduce the number of available households but also discourage the "families who want an unpaid servant to talk of adopting a child . . . the relation thus formed is a relation of servitude and dependence."[33] Treating children like servants violated indenture contracts in which placement parents agreed that they would treat children as members of the family, but the only recourse institutions possessed was to remove children from homes. Many superintendents hesitated to do this unless the child faced truly abusive treatment.

Across the country, experts struggled to balance between advantaging the labor of placement children and potential abuses. The NCCC committee for child saving complained that the appearance of benevolence masked other intentions: "Very often the requisition reads this way, 'I want a boy not less than fourteen years of age, of good size, strong, and not afraid of work.' Hold the requisition before the light, and a farmer may be seen . . . he may give the lad a good home, suitable food and clothing . . . but he has driven a hard bargain for the bone and muscle, and placed in question the wisdom of the guardianship."[34] In this way, placers came to understand that exploitation of children was not isolated to orphan train children, but was a problem based on the placement parent and not the origins of the placement child. This made their task of supervision all the more important. One respondent to a Charles Loring Brace presentation claimed that "men who take children out West are apt to look at a boy or a girl just to see how much they can get out of them, just as they would look at a cow, or a calf, or a colt, to see how much they can get out of *them* [emphasis mine]." He continued, "There are very many homes in the west unfit for children to live in."[35] Minnesota State Agent Herbert Lewis found two CASNY children and two state school wards suffering from aggravated cruelty. He removed his own wards but could only report the other cases of "gross abuse" to the CASNY, which took "decisive" action on at least one count.[36]

Farmers demonstrated their expectations for labor when they returned children because they were "too young" for the purposes of farm work or offered to exchange them for another who better suited the needs of the farm.[37] This happened on farms varying in size and quality, with renters and owners. Nine-year-old Clara Lawson went to a childless farmer described as owning "160 acres of rich prairie land," but she was returned because she was "too small."[38] Fred Moore went to a thirty-acre farm in Indiana at the age of thirteen. He was returned after a year of work "because he was not large and strong enough for farm work."[39] Twelve-year-old Willie was returned after the placement mother worried that "some of the relatives think they ask him to do too much and she fears it may cause unpleasant relations." Willie apparently agreed with the relatives and said he was happy to be back at the institution, "on account of being so dissatisfied. Had to do so much housework."[40] For children like Willie, being back at the institution was often a preferable option to the rigors of placement life. The hardships of being a placed-out child, whether physical or emotional, are indicated in the commentary by children themselves and the memories they left behind. In 1882, one of the earliest children to be placed from the Michigan state school wrote Lyman Alden the following lines:

Dear Friend,

I thought I would write a few lines to you. I am very anxious to know where my sister is. I have written to her, but received no answer. I feel interested in hearing from the school. Are all the girls gone that were there when I was? Do you know if my mother is living? I am happy and have a good home, and am trying to do the best I can. It seems lonesome sometimes to think that I have no relatives but strangers. But I am going to try and make a good and useful woman. I wish you would write and tell me where she is, so that I could write her a letter and be sure that she will get it . . . Give my love to all.[41]

This young girl found more companionship and family in the institution than she did in her farm placement, and with a mother and sister of her own somewhere, she longed for a deeper connection and reassurance. Homer Folks was right when he said that the institution gained the loyalties of children over itinerant placement homes.

Some applicants for children showed their true colors by asking for an ablebodied child for work, but others waited until they had a child to complain about their abilities. In 1877, a man wrote requesting a boy for his sick father, "to see to the chores or to work without hiring." He went on to insist on the urgency of his parents' need, "as soon as you can send him, and would like one that is large enough to plow."[42] Other comments from placement parents show that they had lofty expectations of the children placed in their care. A man complaining about the child he took to help on his farm phrased his request to exchange the boy this way: "If I raise a boy I want one that has got some life in him. I have tried the bud on him three times, twice quite severely, and it done no good . . . I would like to exchange him for one who does not eat so much. It makes him stupid and it's a hard matter to stint a child when victuals taste so good." Another woman who took a young girl with a bed-wetting problem wanted to make a deal with the superintendent: "if you have one that you can recommend, about her age, I would be glad to exchange; if not, send those papers and drop the fifty dollars and we will try her a while longer." Both of these placement parents obviously expected more than they got with a child and wanted a more advantageous situation for themselves.[43]

Aside from taking a child in as cheap labor, plenty of evidence shows that placement parents understood the arrangement to be contingent on convenience. A change in the occupation or residency of placement parents provided a motivation for returning children. As families stopped farming and moved on to other opportunities, they returned children, with one man commenting that he "did not need Harry and wanted to return him."[44] Among the other reasons given for the return of a child were "she didn't suit," "had no further use for him," and simply, "don't want child."[45] These returns explain much about the relationship of children to the placement families and about persistence rates on farms. A farm family leaving Illinois for California left their teenage placement son behind, so he worked part-time in a coal factory before heading west to work as a migratory harvester.[46] The Children's Aid Society went so far as to commend farmers who agreed to keep children when they were not working on the farm. One of their placement parents wrote trying to strike a deal: "He does not want to leave us, though we do not need his services during the summer, as we have rented our farm this year . . . we accept your proposition [to keep him] provided you pay his tuition at the graded school."[47] This arrangement, as understood by the farm family, needed to be adjusted because the child no longer provided them with enough value; in the absence of his farm labor, they expected someone else to pay for his schooling.

While problems stemmed from the misunderstandings that placement parents had about their responsibilities, placement methods also lent a casual air to the process. Institutions advertised the availability of their children as a way to find them homes. Ads like the one entitled "Homes for the Homeless," published in the *Marietta Daily Leader* in 1897, specifically promoted "the advantages of placing out children at some distance from their native place and especially away from their connection." Mary Workman, who visited and placed children for the Belmont County Children's Home, had these advertised children waiting for new homes at a local hotel where people could select a child knowing that he or she possessed no contacts in the county. Coming to the hotel to select a child probably represented the sum total of the screening process.[48] Dispensing children from a hotel room helps explain why some placement parents might not have seen the relationship as permanent.

Other tactics, such as allowing an adult to come to an institution to select a child, left little doubt as to the amount of supervision children could expect. That is how Anne Moses and countless other children found new homes. General S. J. Jones, Superintendent of the Soldiers' and Sailors' Orphans' Home in Xenia, Ohio, related to his colleagues that a well-recommended and childless man came to that institution requesting two girls, ages seven and nine. Having brought the appropriate paperwork from references, he left with two children. He later charged the Soldiers' and Sailors' Orphans' Home with fraud, claiming that the children were not "good hands to fork onions." While the fraud charges never amounted to anything, the institution did nothing to suggest that this would be an inappropriate use of the girls. Jones wanted other Ohio institutions to do a more cautious job when screening for potential placement homes.[49] Stanley Griffin, agent for the Michigan state school, recalled that during the financial crisis of the 1890s, other institutions in the state ceased operations because of financial difficulty. As a result, those institutions rapidly dispensed more than one hundred children into homes and then closed—providing no supervision and no contact person for the children or placement parents.[50] This type of institutional neglect did little to discourage the worst tendencies of some placement parents.

Superintendents managed the comings and goings of children and the return requests of placement parents. These parents did not necessarily mince words in their complaints. One woman vented, "She is so saucy, and lazy, and ugly, and quarrelsome, and causes me so much trouble."[51] Nine-year-old Anna Lewis was returned because the wife of the family was jealous of her husband's affection for the child.[52] In other situations, when placement parents asked to return a child but did not get a timely response from the institution, they took it on themselves to find a new home for a child.[53] A Michigan State Public School placement parent requested permission to return the boy he took in because the young boy would not mind the man's elderly parents, with whom he shared a home. He blamed the child's temper, describing it as "one of the worst I ever saw." This man wanted so badly to be rid of the child he offered to find a different local family to take in the boy if the institution could not take him back.[54]

Children helped find themselves new arrangements when they felt overworked or mistreated. Alice Chapman from Lawrence County, Ohio, went to six different placement homes—one returned her in 1883 without "notice or reasons given." In another home, Alice removed herself because "she wanted to go to school and disliked being treated as a servant."[55] Thirteen-year-old and full orphan Minnie Asher was returned from a farm home because she "was not satisfied."[56] Other children vowed to make the best of whatever situation they found themselves in; one young man wrote to his cottage matron at the Michigan State Public School: "You have been more than a mother to me, and now that my own mother is dead and gone I am left without a friend in the world but you." The child closed with assurances to make the best of his placement home.[57]

Not all children promised to be obliging and well behaved since their behavior was one of their only forms of control and power. David Knight's placement parents returned him for being "a thief and liar"; twelve-year-old Charles Reeder's placement father claimed he had "immoral practices"; James Lee "could not control" Norris Hackett, who was returned from multiple homes because he was "not right," "wouldn't mind," and "wouldn't talk." Fifteen-year-old Gertrude's fourth placement with the Malones on their large farm seemed to be going well, but Mrs. Malone reported she had run away suddenly at the urging of her biological mother. Ernest Alden wrote the mother for an explanation and learned that Gertrude "is getting wild . . . runs out with the boys." Alden next wrote directly to Gertrude, who denied such behavior. His last report came from the police matron of Bloomington, Illinois, and by 1910 Gertrude was living at the Girls Industrial Home from which she ran away.[58] One of Lyman Alden's charges claimed that his placement dad was never satisfied with his efforts and after a month and a half of hard labor "he did not pay me one cent or buy me any thing so I have hired out." Like other placement children, earning $10 a month was preferable to staying in an unhappy arrangement.[59]

Physical Abuse

No comprehensive record keeping or method for dealing with abusive treatment existed. Superintendents did not have to report abuse cases, record them in a ledger, or contact law enforcement. Knowing how many children suffered from abuse in placements or institutions (or in their own homes) is impossible, but enough accounts exist to explain why the treatment of children in farm placements was one of the reasons farm placement declined in popularity.[60] In 1885, a twelve-year-old girl went missing after living at the Illinois Soldier's Orphan's Home for seven years. The superintendent had no record of who took her. After an abusive eight months, she returned to the institution, having run away from her placement home, only to be given away by one of the institution's trustees to a family heading to Florida.[61] The superintendent of the home did not arrange her first, abusive placement, nor did she know how to locate the girl once she headed to Florida. Record keeping gradually improved, but not enough to assess any patterns among institutions or placement parents. When abusive conditions were found and children were removed, superintendents recorded few details. Miami County superintendents recorded incidents in these clipped notations: "Brought back because abuse reported," "not being treated as we thought right, being kept out of school and required too much work," "abuse reported, investigation proved true," and "returned because of abuse."[62]

The accounts of both physical and sexual abuse hint at the vulnerability of children once they went into a home and the potential for further problems since many went to different homes after being removed from abuse. Most did not, like Anne Moses, remain in the institution after returning. In 1895, Clara, a six-year-old from the Perry County, Ohio, children's home, was removed from her placement after suffering three months of physical abuse. After six months in the children's home she left again for another placement, staying six months before returning again. Clara went back out to a different home in April 1898, only to return to the children's home in September; one month later she went out again. In March 1900, she returned for a fifth stay at the institution, but stayed just a week before another placement family was located. Between the ages of six and eleven Clara lived with five placement families—two of which she was removed from because of mistreatment.[63] The fact that her first placement home resulted in abuse serious enough to cause a removal from the home may have affected this young girl and the way she viewed other placement parents—but it did not stop the institution from trying to find a family to accept Clara.

This appears to have been standard practice. Nellie, who prior to her tenth birthday had already lived in three different homes, also suffered through physical abuse. The matron of the Lawrence County Children's Home learned that Nellie was missing school while out on trial. The information probably came from a neighbor or a teacher. On investigation the matron "found the child with a bruised and swollen face so [she] brought her home despite the entreaties of the man and his sister. The cause was not that hard to find, for upon an examination of her body, after the return to the home, she found her full of bruises and black marks." Although the sheriff swore out a warrant, the ledger book indicates nothing came of attempts to locate Nellie's abuser. After a stay of indeterminate length at the children's home, Nellie was placed again.[64]

Nellie's and Clara's cases have several things in common; both girls went through multiple placement homes, both benefited from supervision, and both lived close enough to the institution to receive prompt help. In Nellie's case, a conscientious matron pursued her abuser. This could only be accomplished when placers knew where the children lived—visitors in Indiana found more than a few instances of false names and addresses being given by placement parents; specifically, the fake references of one man resulted in his taking a thirteen-year-old girl whose location could not be determined after her departure.[65] Complaints about abuse came from a variety of people, including institution employees, neighbors, teachers, casual acquaintances, and newspaper reports. This piecemeal network of informants could be effective if the adults knew who or which institution claimed ultimate responsibility for a child. Reports of abuse had to be followed up once received. With good supervision, like that provided by the Minnesota State Public School, accusations of abuse could be taken up fairly quickly. State Agent Albert Harpman responded to a concern about a ten-year-old boy, whom he found "shamefully beaten." Harpman filed charges against the placement parent, resulting in a guilty plea to cruel and inhumane treatment and a $20 fine, which Harpman believed was "none too large for such treatment."[66] Rarely, newspapers picked up the story of an abused placement child. In Minnesota, a local paper criticized a county judge when he dismissed the abuse case of Lulu Connor, who had been whipped by her placement mother.[67]

Getting direct reports of abuse was more challenging the farther away agencies and institutions placed children from their point of origin. As early as 1869, the Ohio State Board of Charities published concerns about abuse that resulted from placing children away from their home county. The recommendation of the board to place children in their home county came as a result of an incident in Greene County, shortly before Anne Moses went to her placement home nearby. A seven-year-old girl went to a family in a "remote" part of the county, but no record of who took her existed at the county poor farm. The abused child was returned to the poor farm where a visitor recorded her impressions of the child's condition: "God only knows what she had endured during these two years. At the time of her return her flesh was livid with terrible beating. From her shoulders to her heels, body, and limbs, there was scarcely an unbruised spot, and around her neck, the well-defined bruised line and abraded surface, made by a rope with which she had been hung." The adults responsible for her abuse were arrested and tried, and at least one was fined as a result.[68]

When placed closer to the institution, children benefited from local informants reporting their condition. This was true for seven-year-old Henry, one of the Miami County children: "May 18, 1904—Indentured to John . . . Reported that they had abused the boy on investigating found was true. October 1, 1906—Indentured to James . . . Left James in January 1909 went to uncle at Covington." The ledger makes it sound like a routine issue: the abuse accusation made by a neighbor or concerned citizen triggered a visit to the child, the abuse charges appeared true, and so trustees removed Henry from that home until another could be found. Henry eventually ran away from a subsequent placement in order to locate biological family members.[69]

Helpful volunteers who reported abuse rescued an untold number of children, but accusations of abuse also appear to have been a way for angry neighbors to cause trouble. In 1906, Frank, a former resident of the Cincinnati General Protestant Orphan Home, was living in Miami County with a farm placement family. Concerned neighbors reported abuse, neglect, and truancy to county officials from the Miami County Children's Home. These officials did not know if the child was in their jurisdiction since they did not place him. A month passed before Miami County officials launched an investigation with the help of local law enforcement. The farmer and his wife admitted to the truancy but defended themselves by explaining that Frank was there on a six-month trial period and his school books were too expensive to purchase, and they asked if he might not stay with them for a longer period of time; they denied all charges of abuse and neglect. As the investigation continued, officials discovered that the person who initially filed the report of abuse was a neighbor who locals believed to have "quite a feeling against orphan children and has frequently made the statement that he did wish there was none of them in his neighborhood." In this case, a report of abuse provoked investigation and the possibility for removal, but in the end, Frank wrote to Cincinnati and asked to remain in his placement family.[70] While the record for Frank is complete with reports and correspondence, often the reason for removing a child from a placement home was veiled under vague remarks in a ledger. Notations included comments such as "family unfit" or removal for "ill treatment." These vagaries leave open a broad spectrum of possibilities.[71] It is particularly troubling when the language suggests something worse, as was the case when a teenage girl was removed from a Warren County, Ohio, farm for "ill treatment" by the farmer.[72]

"Ill treatment" could refer to any number of problems, but it was often used as a synonym for sexual abuse. Although the risk of sexual abuse existed for both boys and girls, reports about girls make up the entirety of the documentation. In Children's Bureau publications, workers fretted about the potential threats to girls in placement homes with male hired hands or boarders, indicating that bureau workers were more concerned about outsiders than members of the family.[73] Inspections of potential placement homes completed by agents from the Wisconsin state school reveal their wariness of all men in the home. Working on an 1890 application from a widower, the inspecting visitor noted that the applicant was "requesting girl, 12–14. He is a widower, and I do not think it best to place a girl there." Another case in 1903 determined that "three worthless boys" lived in the house under investigation, and as a result the visitor did not want to place a girl in the home.[74] In Lawrence County, Ohio, the matron and trustees decided to remove two sisters from their uncle's house where they had been placed because "we did not like what we heard of the sons and deemed it best to remove the children." They believed that something about two young girls living in this home with their cousins was not right.[75]

The cases of Amy and Emma clarify what happened to girls who suffered from sexual abuse in placements. Amelia (Amy), nine years old in 1889 when admitted to the Rose Orphan Home, faced a difficult childhood. One year into her second placement she was returned "at the request of the superintendent because he thought the home was not a good one." Nothing else suggests what Lyman Alden thought what was wrong with this home. In quick succession Amy went through six placements. By the time she was eighteen an informant wrote that Amy's placement father "has been too intimate with her." Two years later Lyman Alden recorded that Amy was living in a convent "for immorality."[76] Emma, eight years old when she went to live with a Wisconsin farm family, had this notation in her file by the time she was twelve: "Emma had a disagreeable experience with Mr. C and was in the Woman's Christian Home at St. Paul for one year. C was arrested and sentenced to Waupon for the term of fifteen years . . . Emma was then returned to the school." Despite the trauma of being raped as a preteen and having given birth as a result of the abuse, after she returned from the unwed mothers' home, Emma was re-indentured by the state school.[77] Other pregnant girls faced similar circumstances. In 1901, the dissolution of a coal mining family in Perry County, Ohio, sent at least two of the children to the children's home. Twelve-year-old Cornelia went to a local farm family where both parents were in their sixties and their twenty-year-old son lived at home. Roughly three years after her placement Cornelia returned to the institution pregnant. When the children's home sent her to a maternity home, her placement father paid the bill. After the birth, the infant disappears from the record, but Cornelia went to the industrial school for girls. For girls like Cornelia and Emma, whose presence among "good" children at their old institution might be unwelcome, the reform school system was their destination even if they had been victims of assault.[78] Minnesota's records contain additional examples of pregnancies as a result of sex between placement fathers, placement brothers, and placed-out girls.[79]

Although exceptionally rare, events that resulted in the death of a placement child did occur, and some were the result of abuse while others appear to be accidental. Minnesota summarized the cause of deaths for children living specifically in placement homes in one annual report. The review indicated that in fourteen years of operation, the state school lost one child from a kick by a horse, two because of accidental gun shots, one because of freezing, another due to drowning, one having been run over by a car, and another child poisoned by opium.[80] The few incidents that specifically relate to adult-on-child violence come from across the country, but those that made headlines show the very worst of adult behavior toward placement children. Some resulted in prosecutions, but due to the isolation of many placement children and the prevalence of childhood death in the nineteenth century, cases certainly went unreported.

A few of the deaths of placed-out children were followed by additional savagery through lynchings, which helps explain the publicity surrounding their deaths. Three publicized cases exist in which a placed-out child was killed, and then the accused assailant was lynched by angry locals. In 1870, a Kansas lynch mob murdered a man who had abused and whipped to death a young child classified as an apprentice. The child's body was found at the bottom of a well in a "mutilated" condition, but the placement father insisted he ran away from the household.[81] Another lynching related to the death of a dependent child occurred in Missouri in 1892. Twenty-two-year-old Dick Cullen of Marshfield, Missouri, was accused of dumping a four-year-old down a well because he did not want the young child to share in his inheritance.[82]

In 1884, one of the most notorious lynchings in U.S. history took place in Colorado. A placed-out child named Mary Matthew died at the ranch of her placement parents, Michael and Mary Cuddington. Her placement had been arranged through a Catholic placing agency. Because locals suspected foul play, the child was disinterred and an autopsy performed, leading to the conclusion that marks and scars on her body were the result of abusive treatment. Mary Matthew's death generated enough angst that a lynch mob killed Michael Cuddington and his pregnant wife, Margaret. In response to the outcry of the death of Mary and the lynch scene that followed, Father Robert Servant publicly claimed that he saw no signs of abuse when he visited Mary at the Cuddingtons, although apparently two claims of abuse had been reported. Servant, who placed the child with the Cuddingtons six months prior to her death, claimed that he specifically asked the child if she was being mistreated. In his letter to the *Denver Daily News*, Servant explained that he was being wrongly implicated in the tragic death of this little girl; he did not believe that the Cuddingtons abused or killed the child. He may have also feared for his own life in a climate that was considered to be highly anti-Catholic.[83]

Other child death cases resulted in prosecution. In 1902, a Washington Courthouse, Ohio, grand jury indicted African American Henry Cross for the first-degree murder of nine-year-old Ralph Thompson, who was found beaten, burned, and frozen. Six weeks earlier, Ralph had gone to live with Cross and his wife, Nancy, who took him from the Fayette County Children's Home on trial. In 1900, Henry Cross was living in the local jail, so why a child was given to this couple is unclear, but there may have been a limited number of local African American families to take him in. After Ralph's death, a coroner confirmed that the child showed signs of having been tortured. Both the Crosses were arrested, but Nancy Cross was released from custody after telling jailers she was afraid of her husband and that he beat Ralph in the head with a club. After the threat of a lynching passed, Mrs. Cross visited her husband in his cell, where he stabbed her twenty-five times with a homemade shiv and then tried to cut his own wrists. Nancy Cross managed to survive this attack, and her husband stood trial for Ralph Thompson's death.[84]

During the 1890s, newspapers picked up additional stories of violence against placement children. Walter Fidore lived in the Rockwell, Iowa, farm home of Peter McMahon. At the time of his death, he showed signs of having worn a harness, being stabbed with a pitchfork, and suffering kicks and blows to the body, and had frozen feet.[85] Questions remained about the case of Charley Henderson, whose placement father claimed he had gone out to tend stock near Vandalia, Illinois, and never returned. Charley was found dead in the creek; his clothes were on the bank, his face was bruised, and he had swollen lips and a gash on the head.[86] Ten-year-old Frances Will told investigators in the Nebraska hospital shortly before she died that her placement parents abused her. As the reporter noted, the attorney general did not believe that there was enough evidence to charge the parents, but the doctor treating the girl had a stenographer take an official statement anyway. Having been brought to the hospital for illness, nurses soon saw black bruises and wounds on her body. Frances claimed that she was not strong enough to do the work expected of her and "told a story of blood curdling cruelty and abuse almost beyond belief and enough to make a man's hair stand on end."[87] In Iowa, John Ewing and his wife were accused of beating and burning their placement child, whom they got from the foundling home in Springfield, Illinois.[88]

Other deaths were suspicious but not classified as abuse. Preston Green was returned from a placement and died one day later. He was not alone. Abraham Bradley died shortly after returning to the institution from his placement as well. These two boys, both African American, may have gotten ill or may have been mistreated. No cause of death was provided.[89] In 1885, fourteen-year-old Gertrude left the Montgomery County, Ohio, children's home for a placement home near Celina, a farming community about seventy-five miles to the northwest. Gertrude stayed in her placement home approximately two months before apparently killing herself. She had been there such a short time that no one at the children's home had been in contact with her, nor did they know why she committed suicide.[90]

The fact that children in placement homes often suffered abuse and neglect and those children left unsupervised might not even have their plights reported struck a chord with reformers. In 1899, Edward Hall, a member of the subcommittee for dependent and neglected children at the NCCC, summarized his general concerns about mistreatment when he claimed that placement parents treated children "with much less consideration than humane people bestow upon dumb animals." Not even the use of "Christian" homes in remote country districts necessarily protected children who were "provided with poor clothing, received no wages, and were worked hard from early morning until late at night; and, when they were old enough to understand and appreciate their position, they ran away."[91] As adults tried to remedy some of the problems with placement, including the isolation of children, the mistreatment, and the lack of supervision, some children took matters into their own hands.

Resistance

Children were not always passively resigned to their placement. Some like Anne Moses simply ran away, others wrote to a family member or talked to a visitor about their problems. Leaving without permission was the easiest way for children to escape placements, but it could be dangerous. In 1889,

May of Mexico, Missouri, was assaulted by a strange man after running away from her placement home. The local paper described her as "in quest of a home." William Hooten, the assailant, was convicted of assault and sentenced to a $50 fine and thirty days in jail.[92] Irene Francis, a sixteen-year-old from Minnesota, eloped to escape abusive placement parents.[93] Bertha from Vernon County, Wisconsin, ran away with the hired man working at her placement parent's farm. Her brother had similar ideas and ran away from his placement too. Children also requested permission to leave, like one young woman who asked Lyman Alden's permission to marry before the end of her placement:

> Mr. F. [placement father] has been trying to coax me to stay until I am 18 years old. He has always treated me very good in every way. But this is not my home. It does not seem like home to me, and I would rather have a home of my own. I know how to cook. I do most of the cooking all the time for five, and am sure I could cook for two and I know we could agree all right. Probably if I should wait till I was 18 no telling where I would be. I am quite sure Mr. F. will consent if you will. So please don't interfere. I will wait until you answer this letter. I would much rather have your consent than to be disgraced by running away.[94]

Requesting a change of placement also occurred when children did not enjoy life on a farm. One boy placed at Berea College in Kentucky requested a move to the brick factory because he disliked working on the college farm. The college shared his disillusionment, complaining that he left his work to attend baseball games.[95] Other children thought it best to hire on with another farmer or move back to the institution until they reached majority age.

It is reasonable to assume that personality conflicts played an important role, perhaps more so than abuse, in children's decisions to leave a placement or request a removal. The dissatisfaction of placement families and children led to repeated changing of homes, as evidenced by the multiple placements. Finding the right fit between a child and a home took massive amounts of time and energy. Spending a long time with a family did not necessarily obligate a child to stay. In 1893, a nine-year-old boy went from the Montgomery County, Ohio, children's home to a farm in Kearney, Nebraska. Ten years later he refused to stay any longer. By breaking the contract that bound him to the farmer, he left with no guarantee of a severance payment for his ten years of work.[96]

As placed-out children got older, the likelihood that they would run away increased. Like the young man in Kearney and the eloping teenager in Minnesota, older children understood that their work had marketable value.

Edwin Kellogg left his 1890 farm placement "thinking that he could earn a good deal of money among farmers." He was thirteen. After a day or two of roaming, Edwin decided to return to his placement farm, but that arrangement was temporary, and he continued to float around the county for almost a year. In 1891, he returned to the door of the institution "in a very dirty and dilapidated condition ... acknowledging he had made a great mistake in leaving." Edwin finally settled into a farm placement and was still doing farm work in 1901 when he was seen in Terre Haute selling a load of hay.[97] In the challenging labor market of the 1890s, a young teenager trying to make a living might have struggled; in a different economic environment he might have found success like the young man who, in 1881, told Lyman Alden he was getting $30 and board for his labor.[98] One twenty-one-year-old man who stayed through his entire indenture told his visiting agent, "I am not such a fool as to leave before I get my money."[99] He was right to think so; leaving before the end of the agreement often meant placed-out children cancelled a chance of receiving their remittance from their placement family, but abandoning a placement home gave children the opportunity to control their own labor or possibly reconstitute their own family. In 1917, the Indiana state visiting agent reported that over a 10-year period, 300 children out of 3,700 in placements ran away.[100]

Instead of running away, children could express their displeasure by acting out or disobeying placement parents and institution managers. Delia, a ward of the Rose Orphan Home, spent many of her teen years creating trouble for the superintendents. In 1898, Delia was a ten-year-old with a dead mother and a divorced father. She left her first placement after two years because she was not happy or "well liked." Next she lived with a former Rose Orphan Home employee, but was returned because "she was so fond of the boys and had gone to a student's room for half an hour and Mrs. N was afraid that something would happen." Delia was around twelve years old. Over the next three years Delia was returned again for her behavior with boys and eventually worked for the institution earning a wage. But, this did not last either, and she was taken before the local judge because of theft, placed on probation, and in 1905 sent to a convent. After she escaped the convent, the Rose Orphan Home continued to track Delia—in 1912, she visited with her son and was described as "a very pretty, stylish woman."[101]

Other children resisted the work expected of them on a farm. A Michigan parent described his placement child as "very pleasant if I don't call on him to work." He did not like to work, did not go to school or church, and did not tell the truth. One of his state school classmates was described by her placement family as "not such a girl as we want to bring up our children with."[102] Little reasoning needed to be given for the rejection of a child. Roy Hane was returned from a farm home as an eight-year-old for being "unreliable." After his mother and stepfather reclaimed him, they continued to contact the institution with updates. Roy went to reform school for theft, found work, and married. But an update to his file in 1927 noted that Ernest Alden visited Roy in jail where he was being held for the rape of a fifteen-year-old girl. Three years later the courts sent Roy's two daughters to the Rose Orphan Home; he was apparently out of jail and working, but his wife was prostituting herself in town and the children had been removed from the home.[103]

How many of these incidents were because children disliked their placements and how many reflected legitimate behavior problems is impossible to know. It is likely that children who did not want to leave the institution used their behavior as a way to be returned.[104] Children sometimes liked the institutional environment while others left siblings behind when they went out to a placement. One child noted, "I don't like my place very well . . . I wrote to my mother and she did not like it because I went out to a home. She said she wrote you not to let Henry and I go out of the school, and I want to go back again."[105] This child's placement parent said he could return, but bad behavior was another way to be sent back. Betty Jane Morton would not mind her placement parents, and they claimed she was "mean to small children" of which they had three.[106] Charles Bell, who rejected a "good home" and bounced between family members, remained in the record books because he was caught stealing a gold watch and two revolvers. The Rose Orphan Home tracked him as a young man and recorded his arrest for a horse theft. Yet after this difficult childhood, Charles became a seemingly responsible man. In 1942, he contacted the superintendent for his birth certificate in order to claim a pension. He had worked on a survey crew for almost thirty years.[107] In 1900, the Neclys took in thirteen-year-old Ralph Achors to live at their 160-acre farm in Illinois. A year later, Mrs. Necly wrote that "Ralph is so disobedient, untruthful, and deceptive that she cannot and will not keep him longer." Ralph returned briefly to his own father before causing additional trouble, stealing toys from children, running away, and in time landing himself in the Illinois Reform School. By age sixteen, Ralph was making headlines that were clipped and added to his file: he sprained his knee jumping off a train, was wanted for robbing a man at a boarding house, and ended up at the county poor farm because he became ill while in jail. In 1908, Ralph became the second resident at the poor farm to die from typhoid.[108]

Aside from behavior that placement parents found intolerable, which litters institutional records, the accounts of violent behavior are few. One way to protest farm placement was to destroy the farm; fires on farms always provoked fear because of the potential damage to stored crops, equipment, animals, and buildings. Raymond Wagner's mother tried to reclaim him once but was forced to return him to the institution. Farmer John Kilngfelter returned him after he set straw stacks on fire.[109] In 1891, twelve-year-old Louis lived on a Grant County, Wisconsin, farm, where he, too, "set fire to hay stack and was very mischievous and unruly." Even though Louis posed a threat to farm property, he was re-indentured before running away in the spring of 1893.[110] Another young man set his placement family's home on fire and ran away, having given them no other indication of his unhappiness.[111] Guernsey County, Ohio, officials refused to pay for the property damages incurred because of one of their placements; instead, they instructed the placement parent to have the young man arrested.[112] Fires set by children on farms, were not, of course, confined to placed-out children. The problem became so serious in Ohio that the state fire marshall published a special dispatch in papers, quantifying the loss of property by fire-starting children at $200,000 annually. He claimed that children would be turned over to juvenile authorities and institutionalized if caught.[113]

Children were arrested for wrongdoing while living in a placement. In 1886, teenager Isaac Lucas went to the Boy's Industrial School (formerly the State Reform School) for assaulting the five-year-old daughter of his placement parents. He had lived with them for four years. The family moved to the Dakotas after the assault, but they accepted another placement child into their home before moving. William Church was charged with killing his placement parents, Henry and Nettie Yeater, in Warrenton, Missouri.[114] Although newspaper reports claimed that William had lived on the Yeaters' farm since age seven, in 1900 he appears to have been living at the Missouri Reform School for Boys in Boonville. Of the killings, William said, "for more than a year before I had thought about murdering the old couple. I had nothing against them, only we quarreled once in a while." Six months after the crime, William was arrested in Philadelphia, having joined the marines. He was executed in January 1907, unsuccessfully petitioning for a new trial and an insanity plea.[115] Often the punishment for serious acting out in placements was a trip to the state reform school, which usually meant more farm work. In 1887, while working on the institutional farm an inmate of the Boy's Industrial School almost killed a shop overseer using a wheat cradle scythe. His choice of weapon may have been an apropos protest about the work expected of him—especially since he seems to have known how to wield it effectively.[116]

Revealing the Problems

One of the ways to protect children from mistreatment was to supervise placements more carefully. In recommending this solution one worker claimed, "Children have been beaten, starved, and worst of all, defamed."[117] To combat this trouble, states involved themselves in the process, and the idea that a professional class of visitors should supervise rural placements gained popular appeal. As the following chapter details, developing networks of workers to supervise dependent children created a government framework that continued the pattern of mixing public and private resources for dependent children.

The isolation and work relationship on the farm exacerbated the problems found there, but problems existed elsewhere as well. Abuse and neglect did not happen only to placement children on farms; during the Progressive Era, reformers focused on working-class and immigrant parents who mistreated children. In fact, increasing efforts to save children from neglectful or abusive parents resulted in an increasing number of children being removed from their own homes and, in turn, increased the number of children in need of rural placement. Undoubtedly the short-lived enthusiasm for removing children from biological parents put some children in additional danger by putting them in the homes of strangers.

As rural placement became more prevalent in the decades after the Civil War, the lack of supervision and record keeping made placed-out children exceptionally vulnerable. The implementation of organized supervision during the Progressive Era provided more examples of problems, even if they failed to specifically detail the abuse or neglect. In extreme cases this abuse resulted in the death of a child at the hands of a placement parent. More often, cases of physical and emotional abuse sent children running for other homes or back to institutions. The isolation from family and friends caused a few placed-out children to act out, resulting in property damage or violence. The threat of sexual assault created additional hazards for young girls, and certainly boys. Over time, the dangers of the farm—always present for children working with animals and machinery—began to look to reformers more like industrial working conditions, and they objected to children performing such work.

While maintaining a spirit of idealism about the farm environment, calls for better supervision and regular visits put a serious strain on resources. Calls for change were made by reformers who claimed "the practice of giving children away without legal procedure of any kind, as though they were valueless chattels, cannot be too strongly condemned. It is the outgrowth of carelessness and ignorance."[118] References to cruel neglect, hasty placements, unsuitable homes, and brutal treatment all color reports from institutions and visitors. Finding good people to accept children made the work of placement challenging, leading one placer to remark that "some seem to act as if they thought the mere act of their being tax payers entitled them to a child if they desired it."[119] Part of the problem might have been the behavior of children and the lax treatment of institutions, but much of the burden for trouble landed on the placement parents. By examining the problems plaguing farm placements, it is possible to better understand the increased intervention of supervisory agencies during the early 1900s. Eventually, improvements in supervision designed to protect placed-out children overhauled the entire rural placement system.

Although it is challenging to form a definitive idea about how placements affected children historically, some studies of the modern foster care system suggest that the problems of abuse and neglect in placements correlate to recent research. In 1991, researchers claimed that anecdotal and clinical evidence supported the idea that children living with one or more nongenetic parents were more likely to suffer abuse, or in the words of one study, had "an elevated risk of lapses of parental solicitude."[120] If living with unrelated adults heightens the risk for abuse, then placed-out children would have fit into this category. Other studies indicate that harsh punishments and an "insecure attachment" to foster parents creates more external behavioral problems, or acting out, while internalized behavior problems such as depression, anxiety, and withdrawal come from overall poor treatment by foster parents. These modern child studies suggest the array of issues placement children might have also faced.[121] In the early decades of the twenty-first century, child welfare experts agree that the breakdown of a family can have tragic effects for a child, and the influences and socialization of children during and after this event help shape behavior and long-term perspective. These data support efforts to try and keep children safe, secure, and well adjusted in foster care, but it also highlights the significance of events in the nineteenth century as children moved from their family environment, to an institution, and then into placements. The problems stemming from the methods employed for placements generated calls for improvements and increased oversight.

Map of Ohio Counties with Children's Homes. Erin Greb Cartography

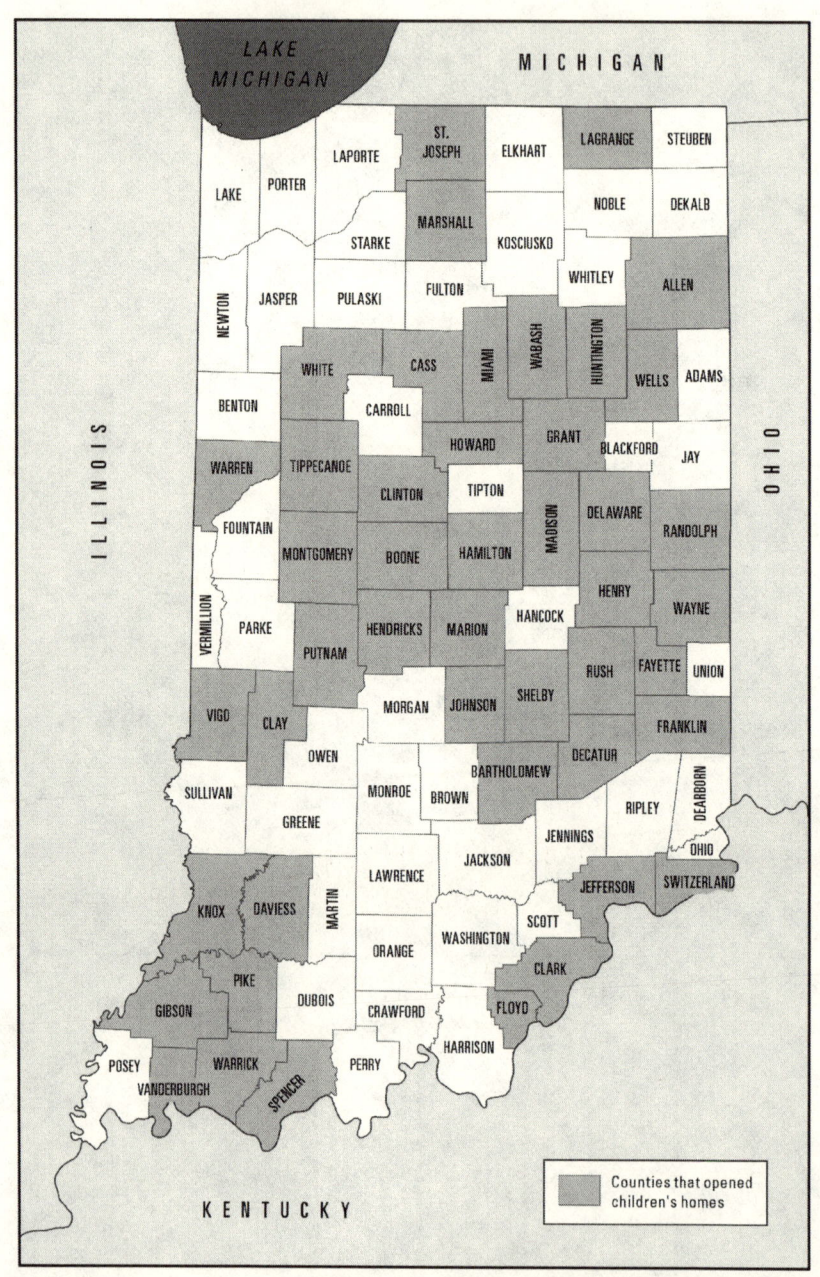

Map of Indiana Counties with Children's Homes. Erin Greb Cartography

Logan County Children's Home building. The original Logan County Children's Home opened in 1885 with a sixty-eight-acre farm. A fire destroyed the main building in 1907, prompting the county to rebuild the institution, which reopened in 1909. Collection of the author

Darke County Children's Home in background, children in pasture in foreground. Darke County spent close to $40,000 for approximately 50 acres of land and the building of and improvements to their children's home. The first thirty-eight children moved in during 1889. Trustees wanted a modern building that would accommodate the future needs of the county. Out buildings, including an ice house and an annex, were added later. Collection of the author

Child surrounded by pumpkins. The Lucas County Children's Home received at least a few photos from placement parents, showing children happily enjoying life on the farm. This child may have been responsible for the pumpkin patch or is simply enjoying the bumper crop. Courtesy of Center for Archival Collections, Bowling Green State University

Girl standing with chickens. Sending photos of a child in a placement was thought to demonstrate caring and competency on the part of placement parents. This girl, while perhaps not used to farm life before her placement, is doing a typical farm child chore of working with the chickens. Courtesy of Center for Archival Collections, Bowling Green State University

Two children smiling in front of home. This brother and sister were lucky enough to be placed together and are posing in front of their placement home in everyday farm clothes. In the early 1900s, Lucas County made efforts to place siblings together by advertising them as pairs. Courtesy of Center for Archival Collections, Bowling Green State University

Children picking apples. While awaiting a placement, children at the Minnesota State Public School learned farm skills by helping on the institution's farms. These children are picking apples for use in the institution's kitchen. In 1900, 53 bushels of apples were harvested, worth an estimated $45. Courtesy of the Minnesota Historical Society

Children working in field of produce. These boys are working on one of the many types of produce grown at the Minnesota state school. Among the crops destined for the kitchen were cabbage, kohlrabi, lettuce, cauliflower, celery, and beets. Courtesy of the Minnesota Historical Society

Boys working in field of wheat. Minnesota children also helped to harvest hay and straw, which the institution used for its own stock raising but also for sale. Sixty loads of straw and one hundred tons of hay were harvested in 1900, a slight decrease from the year before but still valuable to the financial success of the institution. The pasturage and fodder grown on the farm contributed to the valuable dairy herd, whose milk was valued between $2,500 and $3,000 in 1899 and 1900. Courtesy of the Minnesota Historical Society

4. "The right of the state to interfere is unquestioned"

> "We put a little, defenseless child into a home, and in that home it may be abused worse than any slave in the Southern states. This whole system is under very serious ban by some people. It is denounced as the new child slavery."
> —*Indiana Quarterly Bulletin of Charities and Corrections*, December 1896

In 1893, the Indiana Board of Charities received newspaper reports about a placed-out child who had been raped. The victim, a twelve-year-old ward of a county children's home, left the institution with a strange man by order of a township trustee. The man then assaulted the child and left her for dead. This terrifying attack occurred in part because the trustee made a decision on his own, apparently without the input of the institution's superintendent or other trustees. Because supervision by institutions varied widely in quality and children suffered as a result, states built frameworks to oversee children in placements and determine the direction of child welfare policy that included the work of private charity groups. This Progressive Era response not only began to centralize child welfare work with the state, it also acknowledged a problem with rural placement. That the state board was even notified of this case indicates a changing relationship between local operations and the state, but that they got a newspaper clipping and not a report from the institution demonstrates one of the challenges of moving supervisory power from the institutional to the state level. The board received information but had no power to prevent the situation or reprimand the trustee. Before improvements to placement practices could begin, states needed to convince citizens and child welfare workers that their right was, in fact, unquestioned.[1]

The first oversight of institutions began at the county level with elected trustees. At the state level, a board to collect information about public institutions served as the first stage of state oversight, but these boards possessed little to no regulatory power, and until the 1890s, counties were not required to report to the state about their public institutions. State inspections of institutions were permitted but limited by staffing and funding. Counties also formed voluntary oversight boards and committees to inspect institutions and assist with the distribution of aid, and state boards hoped county officials and boards would report to them. During the Progressive Era, state boards gained more power from legislatures to oversee not just institutions but also placements as a way to introduce better policy and rationality to divergent practices. Using this power, they authorized state visitors to supervise dependent children and encouraged better use of the court system in child welfare cases. By centralizing supervision through one department, states and institutions would, according to the Child Saving Committee at the NCCC, "lessen the waste and failure incident to the multiplying forms of unsupervised and misdirected effort."[2] In regard to dependent children, the state boards wanted more children placed out and fewer living in institutions. Successfully lobbying legislatures to hire state visiting agents, the state boards gained more oversight of dependent children and used the evidence gathered to help shape additional legislation about supervision and care. Visiting agents who supervised children in placement homes joined the professionalizing class of workers trying to improve case records and institutional care. Social workers joined these ranks, as did specialized courts; together they helped reverse the trend away from direct aid and focused on keeping families intact.[3]

During the construction of this larger, state-driven framework, rural placement was still the most popular care option for children. With the intention of standardizing placement methods and screening homes more effectively, reformers hoped to remove the stigma of the "new child slavery." The boards, visitors, and courts are all examples of methods used to improve placing out. Refining placement methods so that children would not be "very friendless, isolated, and subjected to abuse and neglect" was one of the goals of the new system of oversight, as was finding more homes for the children still living in institutions.[4] However, as boards, visitors, and judges gained a better understanding of the realities of farm placement, they shaped new opinions about its desirability, gradually leading to a rise in paid foster care, which made supervision easier because it could be done in town, and encouraged formal adoptions of the youngest children.

The use of Progressive notions about organization, professional expertise, record keeping, and intervention can be clearly seen in the development of state supervision for placed-out children. Those who supported improvements had high hopes. At the 1899 NCCC meeting, Canadian Children's

Aid Society leader J. J. Kelso struck an optimistic tone when he claimed, "We are gradually learning to do this work, and in time to come this will be the great system."⁵ Midwestern states set an example by contributing to the "great system" by attempting to build politically neutral state and county boards to supervise child welfare and increasing the number of children placed out from institutions. Additionally, during the 1890s the region advanced quickly as states hired paid visiting agents, involved the courts in placements, and were among the first in the country to award mother's aid during the 1910s. These efforts demonstrate not only the popularity of Progressivism in the Midwest among policy makers but also the significance of placing out in the region. Having led the nation in the number of farm placements, Midwestern states would now try to lead the nation in supervision of those placements.

In order to effect the type of state-level involvement desired by reformers, institutional workers and those staffing private charity agencies needed to release some control over their own placement decisions. Professionals who had experience in the field led the way, and men such as Alexander Johnson, the first secretary of the Indiana Board of State Charities who delivered the "new slavery" line, encouraged more state involvement as a solution to overwork and abuse and to increase the number of children living in placement homes. These efforts took the state into institutions as well as family homes all in the effort to bring consistency to the methods of child welfare. All too often visitors came across institutional managers like one in Illinois, who bragged that he could operate an even less expensive orphanage if he had "a few more children and a bunch of cattle."⁶ Supervising placements was one aspect of the challenge; changing the mindset of institutional workers who wanted to run their own fiefdom was another. Reform came gradually; the inconsistencies of institutional care and placement practices meant that some children were well supervised while others had been failed miserably because their institution had no order to their methods, failed to keep records, or refused to place children at all.⁷

The challenges in the transition from local to state control of dependent child welfare support the idea that the supervision of dependent children was contested space. The impetus for state involvement came from outside the institutions where reformers advanced their agenda, sometimes over the objections of institutional workers accustomed to shaping their own plans and making their own way as a loosely affiliated community. To counter claims of malfeasance, matrons and superintendents like J. J. Kelso who defended the positive aspects of placement claimed: "It is not right to let the impression go abroad that these children are wanted simply for their work . . . thousands of these children are doing remarkably well."⁸ Those doing their own placement work did not necessarily want to turn their jobs over to the state, while others saw state intervention as an opportunity for improvement. Institutional managers not interested in placing were typically uninterested in state intervention, creating tension as the consolidation of power took place and initially causing a hybridized system of state, local, and private involvement.[9]

State Boards of Charity

The state board of charities, also called the state board of control (which often specifically handled state funded institutions) or the board of state charities and corrections, and referred to here generally as state boards, were the groups charged with studying the conditions of public institutions. The Midwest followed the early lead of eastern states such as Massachusetts in forming boards, with Michigan, Ohio, and Wisconsin among the earliest to do so in the 1860s and 1870s. Founded to exchange information about all types of public institutions, including jails, poor farms, and children's homes, state boards attempted to ensure the humane institutional treatment of residents. Board members included prominent men and women with experience in institutional care, medicine, and religious and public charity who were appointed by the governor. Bridging the partisan divide surrounding state institutions and supervising institutions in the state represented two of the primary functions of these boards, but they could not necessarily rise above the political fray. Legislatures gave and took away the boards' power as they saw fit, and the initial operating budgets did not allow members to be paid. Nevertheless, members tried to work on the real and perceived problems of welfare in their states. Institutions in bad condition, too many children living in institutions, too much local outdoor relief awarded, and children placed from outside the state were several of the issues worked on by state boards.[10]

During the 1880s, the number of state boards grew even though their powers did not. As the *St. Paul Globe* bragged in 1890, "An unbroken chain of state boards of public charity now stretches its length from Massachusetts to Kansas."[11] By the 1890s, Midwestern states almost all had boards at a time when only twenty-five existed nationwide. The boards reported to the legislators and governors with data about the issues of charity and correction in their state. The state meetings and board publications became one of the ways institutional employees communicated about trends and dispersed data. Well-known reformers of the region, including future Children's Bureau head Julia Lathrop and social gospel leader Reverend Oscar McCullough, served on state boards.

Although they were not particularly powerful in the 1870s and 1880s, one of the earliest influences of the state boards can be seen in the efforts to remove children from poor farms. In addition to lobbying for separate children's institutions, board members influenced legislation encouraging specialized institutional care for the sick, the insane, and the delinquent while advocating for better placement practices. In general the state boards often focused their attention on the shortcomings of public institutional care as opposed to private because they possessed influence in that area, but including the state in local decisions did not come easily. During the 1860s and 1870s, the Ohio board could not even depend on all counties to file a report about institutional care—the most basic way to share information; in 1868, seventeen of the eighty-eight counties in the state failed to provide any information about their public institutions to the board, and this pattern continued through the 1880s.[12] With so little power granted to the board, there was no penalty for not participating in reporting, nor were there penalties for noncompliance with the laws it helped pass. In 1885, the Ohio board commiserated that counties were not following the removal law for children living in poor farms: "The same indifference to the law seems to prevail in these counties as has heretofore characterized the treatment of dependent children." To remind county officials of their obligation, the board helpfully reprinted a copy of the state law in its annual report.[13]

With no enforcement power, when problems like children living in poor farms came to the attention of state boards, little could be done except to shame the county or legislature into making improvements. In 1903, the state board of Nebraska discovered that an institution manager was embroiled in controversy, having refused to return custody of a child to its mother. Based on this case, the board hoped to convince the legislature to grant it supervisory powers over all children's institutions in the state.[14] Instead, the board continued to have the power to visit public institutions until the 1910s, when the board at least gained access to the records and facilities of both public and private charities handling the cases of children.[15] Noble County, Ohio, received bad publicity when the board printed the following report: "The Children's Home of the county [is] a part and parcel of an infirmary which has been for years absolutely disgraceful . . . these instances are cited with sincere regret." The state board could not force Noble County to build an institution "in harmony with the magnitude and importance of the public interest."[16] They could, however, make it known that Noble County did not keep the same standards of care as other counties in the state.

Sociologist Theda Skocpol refers to the habit of pitting government entities against each other to encourage reform as competitive emulation.[17] Although she references state-level reforms, the shaming of counties by comparison to one another by the state encouraged the laggards to improve their care methods. Until the state boards gained strength of oversight and enforcement, nurturing competition was often the best they could do. Counties did take notice when the board complemented or critiqued their institution. The local paper for Logan County, Ohio, published an update from state board Secretary A. G. Byers that "reports that the infirmary is in first-class condition, and compared favorably with the best conducted institutions of the country."[18] Making these reports was initially the limit of Byers's power; the Ohio board was so ineffective that for a few years during the 1870s, it was inactive until re-forming in the 1880s, when neighboring states such as Indiana also formed their own state board.

Hoping to build a comprehensive picture of welfare work in their states, boards tried to make comparisons by gathering information, sending forms and questionnaires out to institutions. Because their large centralized children's institutions depended on state funding, the boards in Michigan, Wisconsin, and Minnesota had more success gathering detailed information about dependent children, institutional expenditures, farm products, and placement histories. However, in states such as Ohio, Indiana, and Illinois, where the state board had no control over funding, boards struggled to compile information about dependent children, including the number of children placed out or the expenses of the institutions. Counties that paid for their own institutions owed nothing to state oversight boards. Even though the particular power dynamics did not reflect strong centralized organization during the early tenure of the state boards, Ohio Secretary R. Brinkerhoff optimistically declared, "Now that the people of Ohio have been convinced of the value of the board, they don't see how they ever got along without it." Residents might have preferred life with a state board, but politicians did not necessarily feel the same.[19]

Like the efforts to remove children from poor farms, state boards took up the issue of patronage jobs in children's institutions because the practice of appointing political friends negatively affected care and placement. In the 1895 report of the Indiana Board of State Charities, members blamed politics for keeping poor farms inefficient and indebted while claiming that placement systems "range from having very poor to none whatever in the different counties." In a number of institutional scandals, political appointees earned the ire of charity experts for abuse, overspending, and mismanagement.[20] The history of the Illinois Soldiers' Orphans' Home provided a variety of examples to justify removing politics from institutional care and was notorious for bad conditions. In 1880, two hundred children in the home contracted the measles at the same time because money to build a sick ward had been tied up in state political haggling; sixty children contracted spinal meningitis, resulting in two deaths; in 1897, more than one hundred girls suffered from an outbreak of gonorrhea because one girl transmitted the disease through common bathwater and shared towels.[21] The Illinois state board pressed for the superintendency to be awarded to someone trained for the job, as had been done in Michigan and Minnesota, instead of to a political associate, but changes were slow to come. The Ohio state board also complained that county trustees often became the leading abusers of the patronage system, making trained institutional managers or matrons "figureheads" while they controlled the budget and the supply contracts.

As long as control of local institutions stayed local, and elected state officials controlled state institutional appointments, these state boards gained little traction in the fight against patronage or in favor of placements. In 1891, the Ohio board proposed a law to prevent county residents from managing institutions inside their own county, reducing the potential for superintendents to give contracts to friends or neighbors or for trustees to appoint cronies. This law failed to pass the legislature.[22] Battles about patronage jobs illustrated how little actual power the state boards possessed to deal with the pressing problems of dependent child care and how tenuous their early positions were; in 1907, Nebraska's legislature abolished its board after a controversy about paying the travel expenses of the members.[23] Despite trying to be a-political in nature with charters stating that the board should be split along party lines, board members were appointed by governors and political factions disrupted the administrative services of boards. In 1901, Julia Lathrop was one of two board members who resigned from the Illinois board after the new governor appointed friends instead of charity experts to fill vacancies. Critics of Governor Richard Yates Jr. claimed that by appointing his friends to the board "he is trying to degrade this otherwise useful body to the purposes of spoils politics." Board members led by a secretary, who was paid a salary, wrestled with the need for political connections to get advised legislation passed while maintaining political neutrality.[24] In some cases the expenditures required to make changes dissuaded legislatures, as happened in the decades' long effort by the Indiana board to get the legislature to fund a state school like the one operating in Michigan. Ernest Bicknell, who reported on behalf of Indiana's state board to the National Conference of Charities and Corrections, tried to be positive when he noted that while the legislature refused to fund a state institution for able-bodied dependent children, improvements to record keeping and supervision "hoped thus to secure many advantages of the Michigan system."[25] Improvements and the funds needed for them were limited by the generosity of the taxpayers and elected officials.

As the notion of relying on experts to steer policy became more palatable, the balance of power shifted between local and state officials, but conflict developed as a result. Initially only public institutions had to report to the state boards, but even that limit caused controversy. Commissioners of Stark County, Ohio, ignored a ruling from the Ohio board and its secretary, J. P. Byers, when the state tried to interfere with the construction of new children's institution buildings. Commissioners went to Columbus to meet with the board and present their plans, but they only saw Byers. When their proposal failed to pass a subsequent vote of the board, commissioners publicly announced that they believed Byers never submitted their proposal to the whole board, and that he made the decision on his own. Claiming "we know what the county wants better than he does," the Stark County officials moved forward with their building plans. Byers responded that there was no penalty for breaking the law requiring state board approval of institutional plans.[26] Even though the board demanded approval of plans, they had no legal standing to prevent construction of a building to which they objected. Stark County went on to use this facility for its own children and leased out space to a neighboring county. Stark County officials won this contest, but state boards gained more power during the Progressive Era, which they used to influence the direction of legislation providing more state funding for oversight.[27]

The mandatory inspection of public institutions was one of the first changes to take place in the supervisory power for dependent children. Experts-turned-reformers, like Amos Butler in Indiana, wanted states to supervise children both inside and outside the institution, which provoked tension because it fully conflicted with institutional management. Beginning in the 1890s, state officials went into children's institutions and were not pleased with what they found. The placement practices, or lack thereof, did not comply with the growing national push to place all able-bodied children in homes. The Indiana board publicized its policy to urge placement in private homes as opposed to maintenance in institutions because "it is not desirable that children grow up in such institutions without adequate knowledge of the conditions under which they are to live when they start out in life for themselves."[28] Recommendations for increasing placements began as soon as institutions opened their doors, but in reality institutions placed slowly, if at all, and many provided no supervision. Board Secretary Butler and other Indiana reformers pushed for state supervision and formal county visiting boards because they believed the system to be inefficient and local elected officials to be untrained; these people allowed parents to use institutions at their leisure and institutions to hoard children. The board blamed institution superintendents for being backward, inefficient, and unwilling to place because they needed the funds provided for the children's care. Butler believed that the existence of local children's homes encouraged parents to rely on the charity of local government. As a remedy he suggested sending children away with a state agent to unknown parts of the state as a way to encourage parents to maintain their children at home, but such a plan cut out local institutional management from placement and criticized their abilities to run their facility.[29]

County children's home superintendents in Indiana fought against their state board's recommendation to place out children because without the per diem paid by the counties institutions would close, leaving those same employees charged with filing the reports and doing the placing jobless. The board claimed that paying for children using a per diem system "places the matron's personal interests directly in antagonism to the interests of the children."[30] In 1897, the state passed a law on the board's recommendation, requiring institutions to try and place eligible children, and county children's homes capitulated, using either a soon-to-be-funded state visitor or closing the doors to the institution and hiring out care elsewhere. When it was announced that parents had to release claims on their children to ready them for immediate placement, an "unexpected event" of parents reclaiming their children rather than having them placed with another family took place. While Secretary Butler thought this ample evidence that parents took advantage of institutional care, it also indicated an acknowledgment that the terms of county care were changing and an unwillingness to have one's children laboring for strangers without supervision or the possibility of revenue.[31]

Laws encouraging placement also required increased reporting about institutional populations as a way to make counties accountable to the state board. In 1900, the privately managed but publicly funded Jefferson County, Indiana, children's home lost its contract with the county after a report indicated that the association operating the institution hired out children to local people on a weekly basis. The income the children earned went directly into the association's treasury. To maintain this arrangement, the home's management kept a larger number of children at the institution than would otherwise be expected. Under new management, the number of children at the Jefferson County home declined from forty-four to twenty-one.[32] This institution came back into favor when county officials demanded increased placements and met the standards expected by the state.

County Oversight

At many local institutions across the region, county personnel handled most of the child welfare work. From poor farms, county trustees took charge of indentures, sometimes finding homes and checking on the children from time to time. These officials occasionally aided the county children's home as well. Legislatures made increasing demands on county officials in an attempt to standardize and improve local care, but not necessarily place firm rules about the care of dependent children. States did, however, want better accountability for direct aid and as such, required trustees to report to county commissioners on their spending for relief. States also permitted the formation of local volunteer boards to assist specifically with institutional inspections and the supervision and placement of dependent children. Not all counties formed boards, but some boards had active members, like Judge S. B. Davis of Indiana, who summarized his experiences of having seen "children beaten, starved, and, worst of all, defamed," noting that "eternal vigilance is the price of successful 'placing out.'"[33]

Typically, county children's homes in Ohio and Indiana initially relied on trustees to help superintendents with the supervision of placed-out children, and in at least one instance a trustee took in a dependent child and certified his own indenture.[34] As mentioned in chapter 2, Frank Snow was indentured to trustee Asa Borton. It appeared that the two knew each other because the young man spent just one night at the poor farm before being retrieved by Borton, and while this was probably a favor to a neighborhood child in distress, it was also a conflict of interest. Most county officials did not take in children, but they still had business and personal relationships with the people in their townships and thus may not have provided the most objective supervision for children. Reformers saw this type of arrangement as lax and wanted to ensure that children like Frank had proper supervision and that homes like Borton's were appropriate places for a child. Although counties implemented volunteer boards differently, the precedent in Ohio formally began after an Ohio statute of 1891 required township trustees to annually visit any child in their township who had been placed out and registered with the county or township clerk.[35] This reliance on the trustees to supervise children depended on the willingness of institutional managers to register the children with the proper authorities and of those authorities to then go and see the children and make a record of their contact.[36] It extended the work of trustees, who were also charged with overseeing institutional care and direct aid. As an alternative, county trustees could share the responsibility with a volunteer board, and a number of counties chose this option. In 1901, Washington County was applauded by the state of Ohio for its unique division of board business by committee. The board appointed two members each to the following standing committees: children's home and placed-out children, commitments to and discharges from boys and girls industrial schools, county jail and lockup and recently released inmates, county infirmary and city charities, outdoor relief, and soldiers' relief. This breakdown of assignments puts into perspective the amount of work that fell to trustees and explains why a volunteer board helped offset the work.[37]

Washington County earned high marks for organization, but other counties did not emulate this style of leadership, leaving county oversight somewhat ineffective. In Ohio shortly after the passage of the 1891 law, county board appointments went unfilled because the attitude of "everybody's business is nobody's" prevailed.[38] Appointing a board did not necessarily mean that board would or could do the work to which it was assigned. Boards received little financial support and possessed little power to change the methods of placement, and if members were not elected officials, they needed to work with, not against, elected officials in charge of poor relief and institutional management. All county officials and boards were encouraged to report their findings to the state in an attempt to connect work done at the county level with supervision by the state. In places where volunteer boards did work, children received more supervision and more homes were found for those living in institutions.

Volunteerism was a popular way to supplement supervision of children. In the 1870s and early 1880s, Michigan, because of its state school, used county volunteers to supervise and place children from the school. Superintendent Lyman Alden worked with individuals he described as "county agents" to find homes for children and to check on their progress. But he came to the conclusion that such work needed paid agents instead of volunteers. Forced to rely on the volunteers during his tenure at the institution, he indicated to his colleagues, "I am strongly impressed that no children should be put out in counties where they cannot have the care and protection of the county agent . . . I should be very loth to send out children to such counties without the strongest assurance that the guardian was all right, and I should want it from undoubted authority."[39] Alden discovered that local people did not necessarily make the best choices, as they sometimes shirked their duties, did not want to travel without pay, and gave children out based on reputations or to those who needed workers. In 1885, having used the county volunteer method and finding it lacking, Michigan agreed to hire a professional visitor to supplement the work.

The Indiana legislature formalized volunteer county boards when it authorized the counties with the largest populations to appoint citizens to a board dedicated to child welfare. The idea was patterned after the formation of such a board in Indianapolis at the behest of the Charity Organization Society (COS).[40] The COS gained nationwide recognition by systematizing aid in the city and keeping case files across charities and is one of the most recognized elements of social gospel charity work in the United States during the Progressive Era. In 1889, Marion (Indianapolis), Vigo (Terre Haute), and Vanderburgh (Evansville) Counties formed what became known as the County Boards of Children's Guardians (CBOCG) to investigate cases of child neglect. The requirements of a county board included judge-appointed membership for three men and three women. These urban boards dealt less with placed-out children and more with inspecting suspect homes. This casework marked an important transition to better organization and oversight, and they eventually expanded their work to visit dependent children, but prioritized children whom they suspected might soon become dependent. In Indiana, the CBOCG possessed the authorization to remove children from their parents' homes and place them in temporary care. The boards then relied on both public and private institutions to care for the children after removal. The primary task of the CBOCG was to investigate reports of mistreatment, child labor, and abuse and to work with the courts to enact change.

The boards became a new type of intervention, visiting family homes and inspecting them for appropriate care methods. Like similar charity visiting societies such as the SPCC, these publicly supported boards targeted immigrant and working-class parents suspected of being immoral or intemperate. Between 1889 and 1891, the Marion CBOCG supervised 105 children; 49 went into institutions, 30 went into placement homes for a trial period, 12 were placed for adoption, 10 were indentured, and 4 died.[41] Around 1900, a few county boards in the largest Indiana counties began opening and overseeing their own children's institutions. The Glenn Home in Vigo County was an example of this effort; it opened as a rival of the privately endowed Rose Orphan Home and accepted children with fewer restrictions. The CBOCG facilities were intended to serve as receiving homes, temporary places to keep children until they could be placed or returned to their families and in this way the CBOCG became directly involved in placements. The relationship between this type of institution and privately operated ones was sometimes strained. The case of Mary Adams demonstrates how the decision making at the Rose Orphan Home and Glenn Home differed. Mary came to the Rose Orphan Home in 1900 as a "very peculiar" six-year-old described as "high tempered and vicious" and who bit and hit other children while calling her house manager an "old devil." But she could also be affectionate. The Rose Orphan Home management believed she needed to be sent to the state's feeble-minded school. However, the Glenn Home received her instead and placed her, but she was returned quickly and described by the placement mother as "no good whatever." The Glenn Home through its partnership with the CBOCG placed her again. During her time in their custody, her sister reported she had been placed in "about ten homes" and "has caused lots of trouble."[42] In the rush to accept a child deemed unfit for the Rose Orphan Home, the Glenn Home may have placed out a child who would have been better served by a specialized facility.

The state of Indiana received praise from national reformers for founding these boards and in 1899 granted smaller counties the ability to form a board, commonly known as the county board of charities. As these boards spread across the state they took on not just the needs of children but also the inspection of institutions like poor farms and jails, thus expanding the work beyond that of the CBOCG.[43] If local volunteers could oversee welfare work the state could avoid financial burdens like a state school or a visitor, and local control struck a compromise with those who wanted to maintain power over their own system. But without willing board members this assistance ended up unevenly distributed around the state. The county charity board members held no elected office, and when problems were identified, they publicized them and brought them to the attention of county officials who controlled the budget. This did cause conflict, and in 1900 the Marion County trustees aired their grievances under a headline reading, "Is Tired of Criticism: It is unable to carry out the recommendations of the county charity board." The charity boards could request improvements, including nicer buildings, but counties did not have to pay for such requests. Despite the growth of state oversight, many of these boards remained active through the 1920s, and in 1923, 65 county boards in Indiana helped manage 1,561 children.[44] While they proved effective in many places, unregulated volunteer visitors did not meet the standards for supervision expected to protect children. As a result, state boards demanded, and received, funding for professional visitors who reported directly to the state about the placement activities of institutions and charity groups.

State Visiting Agents

As the state boards worked to legitimize their expertise and county officials tried to improve the care given to dependent children, work remained to standardize care and encourage placements. State boards recommended a second initiative in addition to better oversight of institutional care to secure more placement homes and supervision for children. State visiting agents hired to supervise placed-out children first gained ground in Michigan following Lyman Alden's criticism of the local volunteer boards and his subsequent resignation. In 1885 Michigan hired a visitor who reported to the Michigan State Board of Control, which directly supervised the management of the state school.[45] Before this hire, only Massachusetts provided state funding for this type of in-placement supervision, which was made easier by the township structure where many children were placed and the shorter distances between locations for visiting. Trustee S. J. Hathaway from Washington County wanted Ohio to hire agents to help minimize the possibility of children being used "as cheap servants." As part of his explanation as to the importance of creating a state visiting position, Hathaway recounted, "You cannot always trust people who come after children . . . they will not send the child to school . . . they will work the little fellows too hard . . . they will abuse them at times shamefully . . . the cure for all this is the visiting agent." Hathaway had two concerns: if children stayed in an institution too long they could become institutionalized, but if placement was not done carefully it could do further harm to a child. Agents serving all the dependent children in a state could help with both problems.[46]

Once states authorized the expense of a visiting agent, the challenge became getting institutions to use the services of the agent. This was not a problem in Michigan and Minnesota because the agents worked for the state public schools, but Ohio's law hired an agent and then invited Ohio institutions to hire him for placement supervision. The institution contracting the state agent was responsible for paying a fee for the service, similar to paying a private agent. Those who believed they knew the best way to manage their own institution rejected hiring a state visitor and saw the state board of charities as an unwanted intrusion. While crediting this new position with the power to remedy bad placements, Ohio officials worried that not all institutions chose to use the provisions of the law. The need to pay for the service discouraged institutions from using the visitor, leaving many children unsupervised. Indiana agents complained that a majority of the forty-one children's homes in the state did not properly investigate applicants for children or engage in visiting because they lacked money and trained employees to do the job and did not want to hire the state agent.[47]

While hiring an agent to visit children might not have appealed to all institutional managers, the urgency with which placed-out children needed supervision could not be ignored. As national expert Homer Folks remarked, "The first duty of a state toward its dependent children is to know where they are"—easier said than done in many parts of the region.[48] Lyman

Alden recorded his assessment of this problem when he said, "It remains a serious fact that there are quite a number of children scattered over the state from whom nothing has been heard for quite a long time."[49] Recovering from decades of lax record keeping and supervision took time and money. Even though Michigan started the state visitor initiative, at first, the state only paid him to supervise the children from the state school, not all the placed-out children in the state. At the time, the single visitor was responsible for monitoring more than one thousand children scattered across the state, but he just handled placement cases. In his first 9 months, Galen Merrill visited 626 children, inspected the homes of 68 applicants for children, visited 44 counties, and traveled more than 7,000 miles. County volunteer agents, who previously bore the responsibility for supervising placed-out children, "[were] now obliged to visit children only when requested."[50] In other words, they could be used in the event the state agent could not get to a home, but would need to wait for his instruction. By 1900, Michigan county volunteers still assisted hired visitors in the supervision of 1,200 children annually. Using volunteers alongside state agents increased the number of visits performed and the number and quality of pre-placement screenings, causing Michigan's state agent to report that only 45 of the 1,200 children under the institution's purview could not be located.[51] While the state school children received this type of supervision, a mandate for the inspection of all other institutions or agencies placing children did not come until 1894.[52] Michigan gradually added members to the visiting staff, lessening the burden on a single individual but increasing the cost to the state. Merrill, after years as the visitor for Michigan, was hired by Minnesota to oversee their state public school, where he immediately required a visiting department be established. By 1900, that state employed four visitors and subcontracted two others to handle extra cases in the metropolitan areas.[53]

The job of the Michigan state agent and those in similar positions was to supervise children and find new homes for others. The Ohio state board encouraged its legislature to provide funding for a visitors' position after receiving reports from the Indiana board indicating better success with child placing.[54] Both states eventually dropped the payment requirement altogether to encourage supervision, but that left the entire cost to the state.[55] The small number of state agents initially hired in Ohio and Indiana did not immediately supervise all the placed-out children because there were too many children and not enough resources, so the assistance of county boards helped. Hiring state-employed visitors helped increase oversight for institutions and placed-out children and could reduce financial burdens for institutions that hired their own full-time visitor, but doing so ceded local power to state employees when it came to inspecting and finding placement homes.

In 1897, to launch Indiana's visiting program, Amos Butler declared that by hiring visitors, placed-out children would be visited at least once, if not twice, a year. He lauded the cooperation between newspapers that advertised children, township trustees, and county officials who wanted to save money by adopting placement. However, during the initial year State Agent W. B. Streeter did not manage to inspect every children's institution, let alone visit all the children in homes. He only investigated forty-eight applications for children and placed thirty-seven children at the cost of $265.[56] In the years that followed the start of state visiting, private charities continued to do more placements of children. As Butler reported, of the more than two thousand children eligible for visitation in 1900, only about four hundred of them had been initially placed by the state. In 1899, the state agents were outnumbered by charities two to one in the number of placements. Turning what could be conceived of as a negative for the state into a positive, Butler declared, "There has been much greater activity in placing children in family homes." He chose not to specify that charities accomplished much of the placing activity while the state handled supervision.[57]

During the transition from placements controlled by institutions to those handled by the state, some institutions opted for alternative methods. Those who did not want to cede power to state officials had two choices to improve supervision and increase placement numbers; they could hire their own agents, or they could contract with private placing services. In 1900, the Indiana "Child Saving Department," which employed visitors, vetted more than 300 applications for children, placed more than 150 children, and cost the state approximately $1.64 per child.[58] In comparison, the institutions of the state placed almost 600 children without the assistance of the visitors. Part of this contrast reflected the desire of institutions to keep the state out of institutional practices—if the institutions were placing effectively, perhaps the state would not come calling. This choice remained with the institution, but supervision of placed-out children was mandatory. The Lucas County, Ohio, children's home began with what it called the Advisory Board of Lady Visitors, headed by a Mrs. Stanley. In 1902, the expenses and per diem for visiting children totaled $173. By 1915, the institution retained paid visitors to supervise placements, and the expenses for that service totaled almost $700. During the 1910s, C. C. Ware, Mabel Coates, Grace Meyer, and Katherine Marshall all received stipends and travel reimbursements for visiting placed-out children. Ware worked previously for the Humane Society, filing reports about the supervision of children as well as animals in Lucas County. Everyone other than Ware hired by Lucas County indicates that women, while not a majority of institutional managers, did play an important role during the professionalization of visiting. The larger expense demonstrates how expensive a visitor could be, and that the cost was worth paying to ensure supervision was done professionally and locally.[59]

Privately managed groups also continued to assist with placements and visitation. The state visiting agents were modeled after privately funded visiting programs already in effect, like the one manned by G. T. Green in Cincinnati. Groups such as the Children's Home and Aid Society (CHAS), the Children's Aid Society state affiliates, and the Children's Home Finding Society received public funds to help with the supervisory burden. Not everyone was pleased with this hybrid system. In Illinois, State Agent Charles Virden launched a number of complaints about private charity tactics, including sending children to new homes wearing tags around their necks but having no adult supervision and private agencies that advertised in newspapers for homes. He faulted ads by private placing groups for encouraging abuse of the placement system, citing one that read in part: "a fine boy, nearly six years old, to be placed in a home . . . a farm home preferred . . . light brown hair, fair complexion . . . just the boy you need on the farm." By framing placement that way, Virden believed, "The tendency is for irresponsible foster parents to make the child a cheap hired man or girl."[60] His complaints marked a departure from the compatible relationships built between local governments and private agencies. But, having lagged so far behind in state oversight of dependent children, Illinois struggled more than others to gain some semblance of control. As late as 1914, state officials there asserted that binding out children had ended because it was a barbaric practice that resembled slavery, but in fact children all over the state, in both public and private institutions, were still being bound by indenture contracts.[61]

Private placing groups, despite criticisms, played a crucial role in placing more children and supervising them once placed. Groups such as the CHAS helped organize placements and visitation, often working as a middle man, charging a fee to move children from institutional care to a placement home.[62] Additionally, some groups that provided placement and supervisory services also operated their own institutions funded by parents who paid board for their children, endowments, and donations.[63] The CHAS/CAS national spokesperson (and Illinois leader) Hastings Hart claimed, "It is impossible to carry out the system of placing out children properly unless country and village homes can be secured. The system is vicious unless the selection of such homes is wisely and cautiously done. There is no reason why one such agency properly organized and administered should not carry on the work." In states like Illinois, the CHAS/CAS did about half the placing in the state, much of it to farm homes.[64] In Iowa, the superintendent of the CHFS placed 105 children with farmers and another 100 or so with other professionals combined. Even the courts referred children directly to private agencies when needed. Ohio counties, typically those with no institution for dependent children, also hired the Children's Home Society to place a child for approximately $30. Using such a service could be a substantial savings in the long term since counties without children's homes paid between $1 and $2 per day to other institutions for care. The average length of time a child stayed in an Ohio institution was around two years, so using the CHS could provide a substantial savings. Both Williams and Ross Counties used the CHS as an alternative to opening their own children's home. Contracting with a private group saved the trouble of communicating with multiple institutions and paying indefinitely for a child's board.[65]

Many of the private groups existed prior to state involvement in placing, and as a result private supervision and placement services outpaced state-run efforts. In Illinois between 1909 and 1912 the CHAS monitored almost 1,500 children per year.[66] These groups found homes like they always had, issuing specific requests, as in 1917, when the Illinois CHAS needed farm homes for boys ages ten to thirteen with these specifics: "will not be overworked; colored children placed who could be placed permanently; temporary free homes where children may be boarded to relieve temporarily distressed parents."[67] The Children's Home and Aid Society helped Illinois with placements and substituted for the state by sending trained social workers into rural counties, especially in the southern part of the state, to try and fill the need. The CHAS possessed more working experience in these remote parts of the state because they traveled there to place children.[68] Workers for the CHAS also encouraged county courts and local officials to keep children with parents when possible instead of automatically passing the children on to the privately funded organization for placement. During the 1910s, as it helped to implement direct aid, the group decreased their own placement numbers by almost half.[69]

In other states around the country private placement agencies stepped out in front of state boards in terms of new recommendations and care plans. On the West Coast, placement groups demanded formal relinquishment of children by parents so they could be legally adopted by new families. Groups across the country investigated biological families in an attempt to keep them together if possible. Even though the CHS of Washington state allowed people to choose between an indenture and an adoption until 1910, and allowed those adoptions to be returned, they, like their Midwestern counterparts, had more experience in the nuances of the family crises that caused childhood dependency and tried to help lessen the need for placement homes by introducing other options.[70] Instead of being an opponent of greater state involvement in placing, private placing groups facilitated better care when possible and enhanced the reach of supervision. By the 1920s, private agencies like the Michigan Children's Aid Society participated in "social service exchanges" as a way to circulate case records and avoid duplication of services. This rationalization of case files resembled the work of the COS in Indianapolis, which first developed a master case file for needy residents of the city.[71] Other groups did studies of the families and children before developing a comprehensive care plan that suited the needs of all interested parties. They also did physical and mental evaluations of children as a way to provide better care.

These private groups gained the trust of other institutions precisely because of their supervisory practices and because they often saved institutions money. State visitors, both men and women (although the department was almost always headed by a man), would take up similar tasks by traveling the state, checking in on children and their placement families. The reports filed by this new class of visitor supported the earlier, but more scattered accounts of problems. In more systematically cataloguing the widespread problems in rural placement homes, visitors exposed the myth of the perfect placement.[72] By the 1910s, visitors asked questions specifically trying to gain knowledge of the farm conditions that awaited placed-out children—how big was the farm, how many animals, was there hired help, and was there an explicit agreement that the child would attend school until sixteen after which time that child would be paid for their farm labor? These questions did not spontaneously emerge: they developed because of a more comprehensive understanding of the conditions for placed-out children on farms. One placement recommendation included this helpful advice: "A boy of 12 must not get up at 4 or 4:30, clean the stables, water the stock, milk the cows, and then get a hurried breakfast to go to school, and then return home in time for the same stable chores."[73] In the 1870s, this type of work bothered almost no one, but ideas about acceptable childhoods were changing by 1900, and increased investigations into conditions for children added to the growing worry that children placed on farms too often worked instead of attended school.

Depending on the state, there often existed a period of ten to twenty years where supervision for placements, and the placements themselves, were handled simultaneously by state and private agents. While initially private groups were not subject to the oversight of the state, that changed in the 1910s when states demanded better records from private charities. Although not required to stop using their own visitors, some private placing agencies and institutions began filing reports with states and using the services of state agents instead of paying for it themselves.[74] By the 1920s, not only did private placement agencies have to file reports with the states, they also had to be licensed. To start, six did so in Indiana, and they included the Children's Aid Society, which operated an institution in St. Joseph County. In spite of having only six licensed private placement groups, these charities placed hundreds of children each year.[75]

Moving toward full state supervision over placements was a long-term process, with most visiting departments starting between 1897 and 1910. In Indiana, state agents tried to work as a clearing house, receiving applications for children and finding children to fit the requests from institutions across the state. Each year state agents rejected approximately one-fourth to one-third of the applications they received based on a lack of references or on evidence that the child would be used as a worker. They took more requests for young children under the age of five, or children over the age of twelve, but not enough suitable children of those ages were regularly available. In Minnesota the same proved true. Agents believed the younger children stood a better chance of placement success and only approved 44 percent, or more than two hundred of the more than five hundred applications for children.[76] Like private placing agencies, Indiana's visiting department continued the practice of soliciting homes for children by advertising in farm publications. These ads directed those interested in taking in a child to contact the state board with their request.[77] Appealing to patriotic reasoning during World War I, the ads stressed that taking a child helped the state and the child and would bring happiness to placement parents.[78] The homes found by state agents followed the rural ideal; beginning in 1897, which was the first year of state visiting in Indiana, Agent William Streeter claimed, "Our special effort is to place the children on farms . . . to this end no effort is made to find city or town homes for them . . . the farm home . . . more effectually removes the child from familial surroundings . . . he will sooner learn the dignity of labor and sooner fit himself for his life of struggle there."[79] Almost twenty years later, state visiting agents continued to seek out farm homes above all others. Visitors who found a problem were authorized to handle the problem immediately and used local courts to aid them in their task.

Although the original intention of these advertisements was to increase the visibility of the state in placing, private agencies continued to perform the majority of the work for placing children on farms while the state agents provided most of the supervision. The use of agents helped increase placements and improved supervision by ensuring that children received a visit, but finding good homes for children in the country challenged private and public visitors alike. Each year Indiana's agents re-placed more children than they placed. Between 1897 and 1920, Indiana's state agent supervised 4,200 children, resulting in 7,825 placements and re-placements. The increased supervision by visitors made it possible for them to better assess the overall success of rural placement and what they learned was troubling. In 1912, Indiana agents visited 3,300 children but found 259 children "in unsatisfactory condition." Another ninety-four visits revealed that the address given no longer belonged to the placed-out child, and those children were lost. In addition, agents made 561 "unclassified" visits that included investigations of complaints, reports of mistreatment, and other business.[80] Until 1920, children placed by other means, such as the Children's Home Society, accounted for more than four times the number of children placed/re-placed with families by the state.[81]

Approving applications from people requesting a child took up valuable state agent time. Instead of following traditional methods of reference letters as proof of competency, potential families received a state agent visit before approval. In the words of one agent, "the self-confidence of some applicants is truly wonderful. They expect that all they have to do is to ask, and as many children as they want will be turned over to them immediately."[82] At the Minnesota State Public School, contradictory letters of recommendation showed why such a limited system did not do a satisfactory job of vetting applicants. Using the evaluation of an applicant who received one positive letter, the state quoted the second letter at length, "If you have a girl that you must dispose of, take her out and shoot her, don't let this woman have her."[83] By utilizing a more centralized, labor-intensive method for screening homes, applications requesting children like one received from a man recently released from the county poor farm, could be vetted.[84] Performing a pre-placement inspection sought to fix the problem of institutional workers not possessing the time or financial resources to make inspections or verify references. Superintendents with an institution to run could not be expected to travel to homes for screenings and visits. Inspections by state visitors tried to prevent problems that occurred because of local corruption or the equally dangerous tendency of allowing people to drive up and select a child from the home without leaving their name or address.

In addition to a pre-placement inspection, newly placed children needed to be visited more often until it was determined by a visitor that the home was satisfactory. The necessity of that plan became clear when visitors recorded problems during unannounced visits shortly after a placement was made. In Indiana, a visitor arriving just a few days after a child moved in found that a couple recommended by local businessmen kept their child in rags and in need of food and water. When they visited children in Minnesota, state agents spoke to children alone, arrived unannounced, and checked to make sure that nothing was being done to stigmatize the child as dependent, for example, verifying that the child was clothed in the same manner as the family and the other children in the neighborhood.[85] Agent Frank Lewis also stressed the importance of follow-ups, noting that children close to their time of severance needed special attention, with children informing the visitor of their plans for the future and the visitor offering assistance when possible. "Occasionally one desires to leave the farm, and engage in some other business. In such cases the agent is able to help," offering to aid in finding the child a new position.[86] In 1908, Minnesota's state school children all finally received annual visits with the work of four state agents and two localized agents in the St. Paul/Minneapolis, area. Despite a better system for supervision, re-placements of children continued, demonstrating the challenges of making the right fit for children in the best situations. In Minnesota, agents improved their placement persistence during their second decade of work, but still re-placed almost half the children. They observed that while children could be mischievous, placement parents, too, bore a share of the issues by expecting too much work and giving too little affection. Priscilla Ferguson Clement correctly notes that while this once-a-year visit may seem inadequate, given the rural placements and the travel required to reach farms across large Midwestern states, these agents worked diligently simply to make one visit per year. Other state agents in the region faced similar challenges to accomplish the same task.[87]

To visit each placed-out child across the state even once a year took massive amounts of travel, which cost money. In 1900, Minnesota had one of the most effective visiting plans in the region, but Superintendent Merrill, a former state agent himself, still felt the need to defend the expense of such a program: "Adequate supervision of the placed out children is economy, as it gives advice, and sometimes warning to foster parents, help and encouragement to the children, and prevents the return to the school of many who would be returned but for such supervision."[88] Merrill thought investing in supervision at the outset saved resources from being used for multiple re-placements. Minnesota agents rotated through the regions of the state, so that the children received visits from different agents and their observations could be combined to make a more complete case file of the home and child in question. They did this for more than one thousand children annually.

In other states, agents struggled to meet all the goals of their job because of a lack of finances. The need for visitation was so great in Indiana that state visitors could not focus on finding homes for children, leaving much of the placement home finding to the institutions and agencies across the state.

State visitors had to visit institutions as well as placement homes, which left little time for the process of home finding. Going to children's institutions they looked for treatment that encouraged children to be "industrious, rather than industrial" and looked for conditions affecting health, all with an eye to encouraging healthy children to be placed out.[89] Illness and death were common problems with institution life, and epidemics swept through buildings, affecting a large number of children. There was good reason to assign state visitors to this task in addition to their other duties, which often included visiting other types of institutions such as prisons and poor farms. As late as 1910, children living in the Illinois Soldiers' Orphans' Home did not have toothbrushes or their own beds. The uniforms at this institution often became infested with mites. In the 1910s, the new superintendent expressed his disdain at the lack of warm outerwear and demanded all the children be given shawls, coats, and hats.[90] The constant bad publicity generated from negative visits by inspectors finally helped to remedy some of the worst conditions of the Illinois Soldiers' Orphans' Home. These problems gave further incentive to remove children from institutions and find new rural homes more conducive to healthy childhoods. But removing children from an institution and placing them with farm families did not alleviate the work of the state agents.

The massive amount of work to be done meant that institutions, state visitors, private agencies, and the courts all needed to work together. In this hierarchy, institutional management ceded power to local officials and state visitors. The network of placing grew increasingly complicated. During 1912, Illinois recorded forty-eight county courts that joined private institutions, police matrons, associations, almshouses, and reform schools in placing 1,800 children. A total of 97 separate placers were listed in the report for that year, most presumably seeking out farm homes for children; a few had placed just one child, while one placed as many as 208. In order to use the Illinois state agent to assist with placements, institutions had to agree to allow visitors to inspect their facilities—and given the poor track record of several of those institutions, not all wanted the attention. The Springfield, Illinois, Home for the Friendless decided to consent to these inspections so that the state agents would visit the children placed out from the institution, saving an expense for the children's home.[91] Miami County, Ohio, started using outside assistance more heavily in the 1910s. With options that included not just the state's visitors but also separate institutions for children with problems, the institution called in help. When children were difficult to place, the institution referred them out to the state visitor or to the Children's Home Society. Edna, who returned to the county after four years in a placement because she was "acquiring habits that would eventually cause them [placement parents] trouble," was first re-placed by the county but returned because the wife in this second home did not like her. In 1916, the county surrendered Edna to the CHS for placement, giving her to another agency in the hopes they would have better luck.[92]

Institutions did not just rely on state agencies for help; many groups continued the practice of finding homes for children elsewhere. What seemed like a good way to separate children from bad influences became a supervision nightmare. Long-distance placing of children was a popular notion that complicated supervision. Some placers believed that removing children from their place of origin was a way to prevent parents from involving themselves and to deter them from using institutions. Illinois Agent Charles Virden complained about the continuing practice of out-of-state placements; in 1910, more than eight hundred Illinois children lived beyond the state with placement families.[93] Virden's workers visited as many of those placements as possible, while attending juvenile court hearings, investigating special cases, transferring children to juvenile facilities, keeping an eye out for truancy, and visiting more than one hundred institutions across the state. During a single year more than three thousand Illinois children were eligible to be visited in their placement homes.[94] In-state cooperation helped agencies work to visit children, but out-of-state cooperation of the same type did not come as easily. Placing children in another state made proper supervision for those children nearly impossible unless they lived in a neighboring state. In 1911, Minnesota Agent H. J. Jaeger made a "long trip" through Wisconsin, Iowa, Illinois, and the Dakotas to visit "children who had not been visited in some time owing to the great distance away." Although these children were either with relatives or former Minnesota residents who had moved, Jaeger recommended finding ways to transfer their supervision to a local agency as a way to save money and time.[95]

Most social workers were based in towns and cities, as were most of the visitors hired by the states. Social workers based in towns had to make a real effort to reach children placed on farms, and these were the children most in need of visiting. Hastings Hart, who became the director for the Department of Child-Helping at the Russell Sage Foundation, claimed, "No children need more faithful watch-care and guardianship than those who are placed in the homes of strangers who receive them with a view to the advantage that may be gained from their services."[96] In general rural caseworkers had harder jobs because of larger territories, bigger caseloads, and a lack of financial support. The Children's Bureau claimed that "cases were not handled so efficiently, nor were local conditions well understood, if an investigator's work extended more than 30 to 50 miles at most from her headquarters."[97] In addition to potentially not understanding or relating to the people they supervised, they had to travel long distances and deal with the challenges of travel in remote areas. Increasingly social workers were women, and those women hired by the states to supervise placed-out children faced the challenge of covering enormous amounts of territory and visiting hundreds of children annually, while enjoying few conveniences and experiencing difficult travel conditions in rural areas. Mary Allen Davies, a Minnesota state agent, assessed her rural work in Iowa, Wisconsin, and southern Minnesota with an interesting summation: "A person traveling by team so constantly has many experiences, some disagreeable and some very amusing." In 2 years she visited 609 children in 31 counties and 3 additional states.[98]

To increase placements and handle the caseload states increased their visiting staff. Despite their attempts at thorough work, outside events sometimes prevented agents from visiting every child. Legally, Indiana agents were required to visit all children placed out inside the state, but with a limited budget and a handful of employees the agency could not fulfill this demand. In 1912, the budget increased enough to hire one additional agent—marking the first year all eligible children received a visit.[99] It took fifteen years to accomplish the goal initially espoused by the state board. By 1914, Indiana employed eight full-time agents and during the 1920s they made more than three thousand visits annually, costing the state more than $21,000. Slightly more than two hundred children were placed for the first time, or into a different home each year by agents, with the bulk of the placement work still being done locally or by private groups.[100] Once multiple visitors were employed, a head state agent compiled and presented all the visiting data to the board of state charities, while the other agents performed work akin to that of social workers by keeping standardized case files. These tactics closely followed centralized and rationalized record keeping that marked Progressive Era ideology.[101] Agents' jobs were to keep as many able-bodied children out of institutional care as possible.

With states supervising between three thousand and five thousand children a year, boards needed more official administrative power. In 1913, Ohio altered its departments to consolidate all institutional and supervisory efforts under the Ohio Children's Welfare Department. To head these efforts the state hired two managers from outside the state, causing an outcry of concern from institutional managers who were worried that the new staff would order a closure of county children's homes. After a conference with panicked institution superintendents, the new goals of the Children's Welfare Department were better articulated. The welfare department encouraged the following goals: state oversight of institutions and children, using county homes primarily for children whose parents paid some board, and placing all other children in family homes with proper screening and supervision.[102] The Children's Welfare Department included the state visitors and as such continued to solicit homes for children using newspaper articles. An article for Perrysburg mentioned the need for a home, or homes near each other, for a trio of siblings, and enticed people to volunteer by playing on the sentimentality of needy children as well as the utilitarian prospects of inviting a needy child into one's home: "These children need REAL fathers and mothers who will give to them that love and sympathy for which they have an infinite longing. They will reciprocate with their services as they are able."[103] Citing the improved Children's Code that Ohio passed in 1913, readers were also informed of the new powers contained in the welfare department. Now, the juvenile courts could commit children to the state agent, whose office was now a facet of the welfare department. County children's homes could ask for assistance in placing children, but they were all, institutions and children, under the supervision of the state board for the first time. The new Children's Code also allowed children to be placed using boarding payments not to exceed $3.50 per week. With these legal changes to the powers of the state board and the responsibility of the courts and state, Ohio became the first state with a comprehensive oversight plan.[104]

While Ohio made critical changes to the administrative side of visiting and supervising, Indiana's board of state charities complained that the continuing existence of local children's homes resulted in far more children abandoned to public responsibility than would normally occur. The much hoped for reduction of the number of children inside institutions had not materialized despite more placement activity. Parents continued to use local children's homes during times of need because it kept their children close. Counties and state agents had not been as successful with rapid placements as originally touted. The help from state visitors to increase placements was not enough for those who wanted all "normal" children placed with families.[105] Over time, however, the number of institutions shrank, even if the number of institutionalized children did not. Wabash County, Indiana, closed its home in 1903 after officials determined it was cheaper to pay to send children to a private institution. According to State Agent J. A. Brown, other counties were interested in closing their children's homes, but some kept their institutions open simply because they could not find another institution with the space for additional children.[106] During the 1910s, the number of county institutions in both Indiana and Ohio decreased, with approximately twenty county children's institutions remaining in Indiana and about fifty in Ohio. H. L. Hurst, a county commissioner for Fayette County, Indiana, explained the decision to close his county's children's home by providing a cost analysis. Operating a children's home cost anywhere from a few thousand dollars a year to more than $10,000, depending on the number of children and the upkeep and repairs required. After Fayette County closed its home it sent children to a nearby private institution where all but three were reportedly placed in good homes. The county went from an entire facility to manage to paying board for a few children. World War I prevented institutions from making needed repairs, leaving some of them dilapidated and not able to provide good educations or medical care for the children. With the emphasis firmly on placing out, Indiana counties began searching for alternative care options so they could shutter their children's homes.[107]

World War I increased hardships for visiting agents as well. Agents were particularly challenged as they struggled with wartime visiting. Costs for transportation and lodging increased beyond their normal budget, and workers left public service for wartime employment. By the end of World War I, Supervisor of Field Service (formerly referred to as the State Agent) J. A. Brown noted the diminished amount of successful placement. In addition to the higher travel costs of visiting children, he linked declining successes with the lack of desirable children inside institutions. As he noted, the selection of the "best" children left only those who were difficult to place because of their "defectiveness" or their age (between five and twelve).[108] A combination of factors resulted in fewer children being available for placement. The increase in placements succeeded in keeping some children home with family because their parents did not want to see them sent away from the institution, while other distressed parents tried to pay board to keep children there.[109] Almost 15 percent, or four hundred children, living in Indiana institutions in 1915 returned to their parents during that year.[110] State institutions took some of the most challenging behavior and health cases out of smaller institutions. Even the Children's Home and Aid Society visitors, whose livelihoods depended on placing, found many situations in which, with a little public assistance, children could remain with their parents instead of being placed in a placement home or institution. They encouraged the use of outdoor relief in order to maintain viable families.[111] The return to direct aid marked an important turning point in farm placement practices, and the increase in the use of the courts helped administer the change.

Direct Aid and the Courts

As states became increasingly involved in the lives of placed-out children, they developed departments and new jurisdictions for the purposes of supervision. Among the first steps to increasing the role of the judiciary in child welfare decisions were the appointments made by judges to county boards. Between 1900 and 1920, when states increasingly included judges in placement decisions, the courts, specifically the juvenile and family courts, made more decisions about whether or not children should be institutionalized, be placed, or remain at home. The courts relied on the expertise of caseworkers and visitors to provide information for decisions. Using the courts took additional control away from institutional management. An example of the changes occurred in the Rose Orphan Home case of George Johnson, age twelve, whose parents died, leaving George and his brothers to live with relatives and neighbors. George lived for three years with John Hall, "a poor farm laborer," before being removed from that home by order of a judge because of the impoverished conditions—as the case record noted, "Hall has five or six children of his own and is nothing more than a poor farm laborer himself." Judge Mack received this case when the county board requested permission to remove George from the Hall home. Mack sent the child to the Rose Orphan Home, where he arrived on a cold day with "nothing on but a thin pair of pants, a cotton shirt and cap." George tried to run back to his former home and siblings, and for the next two years intermittently ran between placement homes on farms and his brothers. In 1894, George was out on his own when he stabbed another boy and was arrested.[112]

George's case is not just sad, it also illustrates the power shared between judges and boards. The institution played a minor role in George's case, accepting him from the court and then trying to find him a different placement. The Rose Orphan Home had a good reputation for helping children, but that did not guarantee success. George was removed from a home that he apparently liked to be jostled through an institution and various homes before struggling into adulthood.

Clara Baxter lived in four different homes before her fifteenth birthday. One she left because she became dissatisfied, one she left because a neighbor made trouble, another failed because she became too fond of boys, and yet another reported she slipped out to converse with young men. The Rose Orphan Home went so far as to place her in Kansas City, Missouri, to keep her away from the negative influences of her Indiana acquaintants, but nothing worked. Between Terre Haute and Kansas City, correspondence about what to do with Clara included the superintendent of the Rose Orphan Home, an officer of the court, a reverend, her placement mother, and two judges—one in each state. Finally, it was determined by the judge in Missouri that Clara would go to a convent in Indianapolis. Twenty years earlier all the decisions about Clara might have been made by the superintendent of the Rose Orphan Home, but when county boards, state agents, and judges gained a foothold, other people needed to be consulted about her care.[113] With all the people in positions of power involved in Clara's case, she was not one of them. Instead, the decision of the judges directed where Clara spent the final years of her childhood.

When the courts began placing children into institutions, they faced familiar problems. In Illinois, the courts could bypass institutions and order children directly into placement homes at the suggestion of local officials.[114] These children, although ordered into a placement by the courts, still needed supervision from a visiting agent. In the Illinois counties of Warren, Madison, Woodford, and St. Clair, court records indicate that children remaining in poor farms avoided formal indentures after the court system became involved in their cases and ordered paid foster care instead.[115] When available, courts used consultations from social workers and child psychologists to make decisions. In Indiana, judges made changes to procedures for placements, including a mandate that both adults in the home sign the contract to accept responsibility for the child. The altered contracts ensured that most children received a financial reward at the end of their term.

States also authorized the court system to play an increasing role in the determination of dependency. The increased activity on behalf of dependent children was another piece of administration that took control of local aid away from trustees and superintendents by deciding which families to maintain with aid. Like George Johnson, Harry Lang was admitted to the Lawrence County, Ohio, children's home with his siblings because his widowed mother could not support them. The court refused to grant her enough direct aid to keep her family together. Once admitted, Harry was then taken by the state agents to be placed on a farm near Columbus, severing his ties with his county and his family because of a court order. Without the judge the case might have ended the same way, but his refusal tied the hands of local officials who might have been inclined to maintain this widow in order to keep her children at home. Judges also relied on the expertise of county visitors, and in a 1913 case where a father tried to demonstrate he could support his two children, the county visitors and the court disagreed with him and institutionalized the children over their father's protests.[116]

Juvenile courts received help from other benches like the circuit courts; probate courts in Ohio took on cases in places where no juvenile court existed. Often these judges determined when children should be sent to institutions or a reform school or into indentures, or when mother's aid should be distributed.[117] Advocates of the juvenile court idea thought that better supervision was needed so that placement families "be not permitted to utilize and abuse the privilege" of having a child in their home. Used as intended, juvenile courts could help with supervision, adoptions, and finding new homes—they did not just work on cases of delinquency.[118] This legal control seemed like a move in a modern direction, but participants at the Ohio Board of State Charities meeting worried that too much court supervision might discourage people from taking in placement children because dealing with the courts would be more complicated than interacting with an institution or agency. Yet others voiced concern that children's homes might close because courts could move children into other institutions or place them with private agencies, showing a preference for certain facilities. These worries underscored the substantial changes taking place in placement and institutional care. All participants worked to meet similar goals but worried that certain types of intervention could diminish returns.

The courts participated in separating families, but they also bore responsibility for administering aid to keep them together. Although it did not work for Harry Lang's family in Ohio, the formation of policies to encourage family preservation grew in popularity after 1909, when the White House Conference on Dependent Children formally advocated the change in policy from placement to preservation. But even before 1909, child welfare workers suggested and acted on the idea that families should not be separated simply for reasons of poverty, forcing all those involved in placements to consider new options for keeping children in their parents' homes.[119] The 1903 NCCC Committee on Needy Families in Their Homes blasted the year's worth of debates about the miniscule details of charity and bluntly framed their work this way: "In order that our government or social life should attain to that perfection which is necessary for our common welfare, it is essentially necessary that the families composing it should possess the normal characteristics intended by nature . . . We arrive at the logical conclusion that the greatest and noblest labor which may claim our attention is the preservation of the normal unity of the family."[120] Courts in some places around the region were already putting that idea into practice. The probate court in Lawrence County handled family-related issues during the 1890s, and Chester Young was admitted to the institution through this court; however, through the consultation of the township trustees and the judge, Chester went first to his grandfather and then back to his remarried mother after she petitioned the courts for his return.[121]

If children were to stay with parents, then those parents would need financial assistance. Prior to the White House meeting, states took steps to monitor biological families as well as placements; the first county boards were specifically charged with this task. At the state level the new responsibilities for children as well as families were encompassed under the Department of Welfare that could aid a family before they turned to an institution for help. States and counties might benefit in the long term from less institutionalization, and visiting agents would have less work. States began featuring "moral relief" as an alternative to institutional reliance, and formed new groups to provide this relief.[122] In 1905, the Illinois Department of Welfare was created to interact with families as well as institutions and placed-out children. Maintaining a child with his or her parent(s) cost money but allowed caseworkers to enforce behavior regulations that sounded slightly like the supposed benefits of rural placement: "social workers monitored . . . maternal behavior to ensure their children learned 'lessons of thrift and industry, the principles of good citizenship and a spirit of loyalty' to city, state, and country."[123] If children could learn these values in their own homes, they would no longer need to be sent to a farm.

Providing direct aid to families and mothers became part of the plan to keep children out of institutions and by extension out of placements, but it did mark a reversal of the decades'-long trend to rid the nation of this type of relief. Mother's aid reinvigorated direct aid, reversing a position about aid payments that claimed, "its' evils are many and manifest."[124] Although many counties and charities had not totally stopped giving direct aid, the official practice of mother's aid began in Illinois in 1911, marking a sharp departure from Illinois's previously heavy reliance on private charities to handle the welfare needs of dependent children. Assistance to women with children supplemented the income of working children or those women whose work kept them out of the home and therefore outside the range of acceptable middle-class notions about family structure. States did not mandate a minimum amount of relief, nor did they require counties to provide mother's aid. As a result, those pensions often failed to provide enough to substitute income for missing male breadwinners and children in school, a condition referred to as "neglected widowhood." States did, however, set their own maximum amounts, and they varied widely. Indiana generously allowed for no more than seventy-five cents per day.[125]

Direct aid did not act as a magic bullet to stop the need for placement homes, but its use did contribute to their decline. As Molly Ladd-Taylor describes, mother's aid worked best in counties willing and able to fund the program, and a lack of participation was a problem across the Midwest. According to S. J. Kleinberg, the Children's Bureau "estimated that fewer than one-third of those eligible for pensions received them." Kleinberg attributes the lack of rural participation in women's pension programs to the belief that poverty, and child poverty specifically, was an urban problem, and he notes, "States that authorized assistance for country dwellers typically did so at a rate lower than that for urban residents."[126] The county population limits on Illinois's maximums reflect that notion. Illinois capped its counties under 300,000 people at $15 per month for a single child. While this was a step toward prioritizing family maintenance, along with the southern states, Indiana provided less than 42 percent of eligible women a pension.[127] Ohio counties had no population limits, but their aid varied widely all the same.[128] By 1916, Knox and Butler Counties ranked third and second behind Hamilton (Cincinnati), respectively, in average amount given to mothers. By spending approximately $14 per month on each approved case, Knox County officials determined "not to take on so many mothers that the pension would be so small as to not do none of them any good," although they admitted there was a waiting list. In the same report, other counties confessed paying as little as $2 per case, which was also the standard in Iowa—not enough to support mothers or children.[129] Knox County managed to maintain approximately eighty children with their mothers by making use of this type of aid.[130] By comparison, in the early 1920s, the Michigan Children's Aid Society capped its boarding payments to foster parents at no less than $3.50 per week and no more than $7, making boarding comparable to well-funded direct aid.[131] By 1919, Lucas County's Juvenile Officer Patrick Purcell recorded just twenty-four children living at the county children's home, fifteen in placement homes, and one with the state board of charities; almost twice as many children stayed with their mothers than lived in a placement or institutional setting.[132] Lucas County's superintendent credited the 1915 mother's aid law with keeping some children out of the institution who might otherwise have been admitted.

The states utilized existing systems of oversight to determine who received aid and varied in their methods for raising the money needed for mother's aid. Responding to the new possibilities for local and state officials to work together, the Indiana state board encouraged "boards of children's guardians to cooperate with other local agencies and with the township overseers of the poor, for the enforcement of laws for the protection of children from evil influences and for the relief of good mothers from financial burdens which break down their health or threaten to disrupt the family circle." The boards wanted local areas to provide more direct aid, but that could only be accomplished if local boards worked with the courts and elected officials to implement state laws.[133] Children deemed neglected or dependent by the courts, or who were recommended to the courts by the county boards, could instead be kept at home with aid. While Illinois and Iowa granted the ability to levy a tax for the purpose, Indiana's funds came from the county budget, which helps explain the state's low levels of participation. Michigan provided state matching funds to counties but did not do so until 1922; Minnesota had a provision to cover one-third of the counties' cost but failed to make an appropriation. For distressed families living in areas with children's homes but given insufficient direct aid, family separation continued to be a reality. Other eligibility restrictions such as divorce, race, intemperance, or lack of church attendance could disqualify parents; Minnesota retained a clause that could require English to be the primary language of a home receiving aid.[134] Historian Steven Mintz estimates that around 60 percent of counties offered no mother's pensions, and those that did were not legally obligated to provide the maximum amount allotted under state laws.[135]

Regardless of how states organized their aid, keeping more families intact was the intended goal. The nationally renowned social worker Mary Richmond wanted to replace the "Save the Child" cry with "Save the Family." As historian Leroy Ashby notes, the holiday of Mother's Day was also a product of the 1910s, further supporting the idea of a special and sanctified role. By 1921, forty states provided some funding to help keep children with their parent(s).[136] The increase in laws regarding school attendance, maximum labor hours, women's wage work, and mother's aid sought to keep more children with their mothers and out of an institution, but the restrictions of residency, widowhood, and the low amount of payments hindered the application of the laws. Had the laws been applied liberally and financed fully, they might have helped more families, but institutions remained open even with this supplemental income intended to increase familial preservation. This rapid adoption of the practice is the original inspiration for Skopcol's "competitive emulation," in which interstate rivalry encouraged reform measures. That can certainly be seen in the Midwest, where states rapidly followed each other through the processes of not just mother's pensions but also institutional building and placement supervision.

The problems associated with more stringent supervision of children in rural areas generated one of the most striking changes in child welfare policy: the adoption of paid foster homes. Trained social workers played a role in many of the stages of state supervision and intervention in placements, direct aid, and eventually foster care. They were hired to implement direct aid to women, perform supervisory visiting of children, and keep the case records necessary to determine the fitness of households. Experts in the developing field, such as Mary Richmond, emphasized the family as the "cornerstone in the development of society."[137] This idea did not contradict placements, which provided families to children, and it tied in well with programs like mother's aid and eventually foster homes. This can be seen as an extension of the partnerships required to institute women's pension programs, with funding needing to be established, and the courts and social workers determining the fitness of the recipients. Determining who might be equally as fit to receive a payment to care for a child marked the next transition. The first steps to this process took place in Massachusetts, which became the first state to pay people to take in dependent children. Social workers, who already stressed the importance of maintaining home ties if possible, helped facilitate the transition to foster homes. Foster homes in the context of the early 1900s indicated a payment, made to a foster family, to cover the expenses related to taking in a dependent child. Essentially it was placement with a payment; the payment was intended to cover the expenses of the child so that the child did not need to work for the family.

Foster Care

The growing influence of women's groups has been credited with the meteoric rise of federal concern for children and widows, and by extension the growth of familial preservation, but placement workers enthusiastically endorsed such plans as well, noting the prominent role poverty played in breaking apart families and sending children into placements.[138] In most places, accepting mother's aid meant accepting potentially invasive visits and critiques from "experts" about child rearing and housekeeping. Based on the variety of legislation passed to enact direct aid to women, official visits from the county, the state, or the courts could determine the fitness of the mother and gauge how much aid she deserved. One of the long-term consequences of accepting payments and allowing for state supervision of the home was that the practice became more acceptable for other methods of care like foster homes.

The practice of paying for care was previously limited to people who took in large numbers of children, disabled children, or sometimes the very young, and was dismissed as a large-scale option because of the expense. Small-scale examples of boarding existed before larger trends moved in that direction. In 1901, Medina County, Ohio, boarded its children with local families. According to the report sent to the state, the county paid between $1.00 and $2.00 per week per child.[139] Medina was the only county in the state doing this, but by 1920 boarding out children was the new trend in child welfare. Paid foster care did not initially appeal to everyone. In the 1890s, when meeting attendees at the NCCC discussed Massachusetts's practice, many believed it to be unnecessary on account of the large number of good homes in need of children. In 1915, the Ohio state board rejected calls for foster payments because of the cost.[140] In 1920, having experienced problems placing children and keeping staff members, State Agent L. H. Millikan reported that the Indiana Agency for Dependent Children was struggling to do its full job of visiting and placing, leading to changes that grew to eventually include psychological examinations for institutionalized children and payments for care.[141]

Using foster homes, like placing out, did not always attract the most well-intentioned adults, but with a shortage of good free placement homes, paying people to take in children served an obvious need. In fact, the Children's Bureau believed that "perhaps the very obstacles encountered in finding [free] foster homes will be an indirect means of forcing attention to the need of setting up better standards of family life than now exist, such as better health and housing conditions, better-regulated employment, more supervised recreation, more individualized education, and better social legislation." Finding boarding homes required as much time and energy as locating placement homes, but the distance for visiting and supervising could be lessened.[142] That it helped make supervision easier was one of the advantages of paid foster care. Foster homes could be located closer to populated areas, making visitation by social workers and court appearances easier and more cost effective, as demonstrated in Massachusetts.[143] Paying people to care for children gave caseworkers access to those children and homes in a way that placement parents complained was invasive.[144] One writer referenced the debate about proper levels of supervision in free placement homes and said, "It is contended on the one hand that it is not fair to the family giving a free home to a child for the society to direct his upbringing in any detailed way."[145] Making foster homes beholden to supervision like women were for mother's aid was viewed as one of the benefits of making the change to payment for care. As Midwestern states began to make the change to paid foster homes as an alternative to free placement homes, rural households lacked the advantages of more accessible locations, increased schooling, and labor-free homes.

The increasing use of paid foster homes during the 1920s can also be interpreted as another way to assist with family preservation. Boarding payments helped siblings remain together and could be used for relatives to take in children they might not be able to afford otherwise. Foster homes also potentially allowed children to maintain ties to their parents. In sharp contrast to farm placements, in which children were discouraged from family contact so that they could better become members of new families, during the 1920s, child welfare workers agreed that allowing foster children contact with their own families provided numerous benefits. Included in the supporting arguments were giving incentives to parents to recover children quickly, sustaining the bond of responsibility on the part of parents for their children, and reassuring children that they had not been abandoned by family. The inclusion of parents in this process also increased the acceptability of parents paying board for children with the intention of reclaiming them in the future. Both of these types of contact with family were virtually unheard of in the placement system of the late 1800s but encouraged and in use by the 1920s.[146]

Using the broad network of social workers, visitors, courts, charity groups, and state and county boards, states gradually took over the role of supervisor and policy maker for dependent children. However, the involvement of state agencies did not prevent private agencies from also participating in placement and supervision; rather, the two worked together. In Indiana, for example, when agents fell behind in placements, private groups picked up the slack—placing 452 children in 1920 compared to state agents' 174.[147] Some of this partnership was necessitated by the sheer volume of work assigned to state boards once they gained power; states became more inspection oriented and less placement oriented by necessity. Ohio, according to historian Hamilton Cravens, became a model for the transition from child saving to child studying. He bases this conclusion on the content of the 1912 constitutional rewrite that included aid for children, a State Board of Administration to manage the state institutions, and juvenile courts.[148] Along with the Children's Code, this legislation updated laws for the management of public and private children's homes and provided uniform services and legal protection for children. Issuing licenses, which required a state inspection, became a part of this increased state involvement. These efforts developed into State Departments of Welfare and Departments of Children and Family Services.

The collusion of these changes, particularly those at the state level, affected all facets of dependent child care. The Ohio Department of Public Welfare refused to give a permit to new institutions or agencies unless a need for their services could be shown; it wanted available money spent for families in distress. Illinois refused to open any county children's homes because the state wanted care for children to be specialized based on their individual needs.[149] In Indiana, where keeping track of dependent children in institutions did not even begin until 1895, the State Agency for Dependent Children possessed multiple departments, including one for the licensing of institutions such as maternity homes. In 1911, Amos Butler, always the optimist, noted that in Indiana, "the opposition of a few institutions, at one time quite noticeable, has in all practical regard passed away."[150] The diminished resistance might have been due in part to the fact that counties in Indiana were rapidly shuttering their children's institutions, relying on private groups and state services instead. In 1919, the Indiana legislature denied another request from the state board for a centralized state school but did mandate an increase to the daily rate counties paid to children's homes to around fifty-five cents. The mother's pension rate would be capped at seventy-five cents, making it unlikely that any county would pay more to a mother for aid than it would to its own institution for child maintenance.[151]

Other options provided by the states helped alleviate even more children living inside local institutions. Operating specialized institutions for delinquents, epileptics, and the blind and deaf, among others, allowed more transfers between institutions, which resulted in the state providing care for the children who needed special assistance. County children's homes took advantage of this and sent the state difficult, handicapped, or troubled dependents, allowing some of them to close. In 1920, thirty-two county homes remained open in Indiana, but more than eighty county boards of guardians existed, showing that to be a more popular and affordable option than operating an institution.[152] However, even with all the improvements to supervision and partnerships between charity and government designed to protect children, not all children received the training or family environment envisioned for them. In 1922, the CHFS tallied 872 kids in free homes, board being paid for 273—and Illinois still struggling, with no "well developed program for the care of neglected children. Consequently the shameful neglect of children is common in many sections of the state."[153] It would be this neglect that helped move states toward paid foster care in locations where children could be better supervised.

As these states turned to a system of care that involved specialized institutions, caseworkers based in cities and towns, and preserving the family through direct aid, the usefulness of rural placement faded. With fewer small, local institutions and agencies to place out in the country, and with resources spent on visiting children who could be easily reached, the prominence of the farm placement idea—which had served thousands of children—diminished. The increase of government involvement and supervision of children was not the only force working to dissolve rural placement. Nationally, the problems associated with farm life, farm labor, and a growing emphasis on middle-class ideals altered the way child welfare workers thought about homes on farms.

Few in the child welfare system doubted the need for better supervision, but organizing the system required for such an undertaking took decades. States created a bureaucracy that stemmed from the earliest attempts to regulate public institutions, the state boards of charity. In conjunction with these boards, counties also improved their methods for placement and dependent child supervision. By centralizing the supervision with state visiting agents who were helped by private charities to locate homes for children, states realized that supervising children placed onto farms created logistical problems for travel. Constructing a model more like the supervision given to mother's aid recipients would be easier if placements were closer to supervision and if parents were obligated to permit frequent visiting. Children needed to be moved closer to visitors and social welfare agencies, and placement parents needed to be more accountable. In addition to these changes, other factors began to shed new light on farm homes and displayed them in less complimentary ways.

5. The Farm, the Federal Government, and the Decline of Placement

> "The farmer is a slave, and his wife is the slave of a slave . . . harp all you will about the pure air . . . but account, if you can, for the generally stunted physical and mental growth of country children."
> —Sarah Burns, *Pastoral Inventions*

Hastings Hart provided a blunt assessment of farm placement when he discussed how the farm affected children: "Take a boy of good parentage, with natural refinement, good features, small bones, small hands and feet; put that boy on a farm, where he will have to get up at five o'clock in the morning, milk five or six cows, attend a district school, with meager opportunities, and where he will be associated with people who lack refinement; and one of two things will happen: the boy will either deteriorate and go backward, or he will become discouraged and a complete failure . . . place that boy in a village home and he will be a complete success." The boy best suited for the farm, according to Hart, was "a rather dull and backward but strong and good natured boy." The virtuous American farm, once the savior of dependent children, served only as a good refuge for children for whom proper schooling or intellectual stimulation would be a waste.[1]

In the scenario Hart laid out, the bright boy needed to stay in a good home with interesting influences; the dull but otherwise healthy boy could be placed on a farm; and children for whom a normal home would not do because of disability could stay in an institution. Crucial changes in the national discussion of child welfare helped push Hart's hypothetical scenario into a reality. The 1909 White House Conference on Dependent Children made prominent existing suggestions about the importance of family preservation, and in 1914, standards recommended by the National Conference for Charities and Corrections further accelerated the turn away from farm placement by suggesting multiple annual visits by placing agents, with an emphasis on homes "restricted to distances within ready supervision of the organization legally responsible for the child."[2] States like Indiana had just managed to get children a visit at least once a year, so moving toward multiple visits would require a massive increase in resources. As one directive for placements explained, "Formerly it was supposed that nearly all the best available homes would be found on farms, and placement in towns and cities was not specially advocated or magnified. Experience has demonstrated that many of the best homes are in populous centers, and probably more children are now placed in towns and cities than on farms." Paid foster homes ensured that homes within easy distances could be located and that the job of foster parent went to urban or suburban dwellers of the working class, where they remained into the twenty-first century.[3]

The increased amount of state and local regulation for the care of dependent children brought change to rural placement, first by increasing the supervision placed-out children received and then by reducing the number of placed-out children through family preservation, paid boarding, and specialized institutions. This change happened at various times, with private, urban institutions in Chicago, for example, halting their farm placement programs in exchange for placements closer to the city during the early years of the twentieth century, the orphan trains ceasing in 1929, and a few institutions continuing to place children into work arrangements as late as the 1940s.[4] Regardless of the time frame, the motivations for ending farm placements tended to be the same. Alongside the challenges with supervising children in the country were the problems with farm life for children and the failings of farm families to live up to the lofty expectations placed on them in earlier decades. Two separate federal efforts, that of the Country Life Commission and that of the Children's Bureau, provided justifications for finding a substitute to farm placement. While not always directly aimed toward dependent children, the erosion of the reputation of the farm as highlighted by the Country Life Commission made it clear that the farm no longer provided the best living conditions for children. The Children's Bureau worked toward a range of reforms, including those of importance to farm placement—child labor, placement practices, and conditions of life and work on American farms for women and children.

Both the Children's Bureau and the Country Life Commission utilized aspects of Progressivism. By studying their subjects, identifying problems, and employing experts to resolve those problems, the two groups met with mixed results. The Children's Bureau had a much larger audience, dealing not just with rural issues or issues of childhood dependency, but working for all mothers and children. The Country Life Commission and the movement it later produced, while popular with those who participated, met with resistance from some farmers (and farm women) who resented the urban and academic pontificating of reformers. The commission's goal was to identify problems and offer suggestions, and the group cited the issues of economic unprofitability, unequal development, and a lack of comforts—all of which incidentally countered the supposed benefits of farm life for dependent children.[5] Despite their differences and limitations, both groups publicized shortcomings of farm life that had repercussions for placement. Neither group set out to accomplish this, nor did they focus solely on the needs of placed-out children living on farms, but their work reinforced what state and local officials had already discovered through increased supervision: the system of farm placement did not align with desires to send children to school, give them a loving family life, and prevent them from overly rigorous work; and farm homes did not resemble comfortable middle-class homes. The suggestion that a farmer slaved away at work while enslaving and damaging his own family did not resemble the healthy family labor previously associated with farm life. People trying to determine what to do about placement children had a decision to make: Were the powerfully nostalgic notions about the integrity of the farm still true, or had farm families been passed by? If they no longer lived in the best environment for raising a family, what should be done for dependent children in need of a new home?[6]

The Country Life Commission and the Children's Bureau disseminated decidedly middle-class notions about appropriate living conditions and advanced the visions of middle-class reformers. The expanding influences of middle-class ideals helped dependent children get included in what historian Viviana Zelizer calls the "economically worthless child." During the course of the nineteenth century as children became economically worthless to the middle class, who required they stay home and attend school, they became increasingly emotionally priceless; but working-class and dependent children lagged behind because of their tangible and needed work contributions to families on the brink of poverty. Zelizer notes that the 1930s marks the decade when working-class children were legally included in the idea of an economically costly childhood, and the same is true for dependent children.[7] Although no child labor law covered farm children's work, farm children came under scrutiny and were marked as different from their middle class peers and even from children whose work was regulated by law thanks to the efforts of reformers. Patricia S. Hart connects the growing popularity of adoption instead of placement homes to the two main motivations for middle-class involvement in dependent children's lives: "The middle class only became interested in homeless children when it had a need for their labor or desire for them to complete childless families." Hart marks the move toward adoption as a move away from this middle-class desire for laboring children. These ideological changes related to the place of children in the family, and for an increasing number of Americans, children were an investment instead of a form of income. Even though farm children maintained tangible financial value to their parents as workers, dependent children's value came to be seen as more akin to that of nonfarm children.[8]

Growing federal involvement in rural life and the formation of the Children's Bureau provide examples of the "demise of local, personal, and often religious forms of charitable assistance" in favor of what many scholars refer to as "scientific philanthropy."[9] This studying of the causes of poverty and family breakup, the case record keeping, and the tracking of aid recipients required the type of centralization discussed in chapter 4. Of primary importance for rural placement, these desires to reform affected not just child welfare but also the family farm. Farming techniques, rural roads and schools, and rural homes were studied and improvements were recommended; placement children were being sent out to the same farms and homes that needed intervention from experts. Experts studying farm life by the early 1900s claimed that "the ideas about farm life and rural conditions which have been preserved in the minds of the American people, not living in the country, are as erroneous as they are ideal, representing to those who possess them a sort of Garden of Eden condition of perpetual happiness."[10] As Hal Barron explains, the changes to society challenged the place of agrarianism in America and interfered with the local control long enjoyed by rural people. Philosopher Paul B. Thompson claims that by the mid-1920s, even agrarian philosophy was "in retreat" in the United States as intellectuals increasingly targeted the farm as backward and believed the roots of hyper-nationalism could be found in the agrarianism of the period. Clifford Anderson notes that while the moralizing component of the farm myth was fading during the 1920s and 1930s, the farmer-as-economic-engine myth remained. The dispelling of myths and the tenacity with which some held on to them had consequences for farm placements because the farm as an economic base was not nearly as compelling as the farm as the moral compass for a nation.[11]

Farm Problems and Farmer Activism

Agricultural historians mark the time between the late 1890s and the end of World War I as a "golden age" for farmers. While this proved to be a brief interlude in the otherwise difficult balance between production costs and profits, it did allow Midwestern farmers to continue the process set in motion during the Civil War to increase acreage, make mechanical investments, and focus on commercial production. Despite improvements, by the end of the nineteenth century, the American farm was being absorbed "into the industrial vortex, endlessly sustained by capitalism, science, and machinery."[12] As historian David Danbom notes, "To live in the countryside in 1900 was to have the sense that the nation was passing you by, leaving you behind, ignoring you at best and derogating you at worst."[13] Philosopher James A. Montmarque concurs, and refers to the farm's reputation during this period as potentially being left behind in a "perpetual dark closet of rural ignorance and boredom."[14] This sense of stagnation affected farmers, their families, and impressions about farm life for dependent children.

The reputation of rural people changed during the early decades of the twentieth century. Hal Barron analyzes a number of silent films that often depicted rural people as behind the times but showed the landscape in a positive light. These films downplayed the hazards of rural work and played up the benefits of the rural environment, with characters being reinvigorated by the landscape before returning to the city. Increasingly, Barron argues, rural America became a nostalgic memory on film—particularly as a part of childhood—but no longer served as a "touchstone for American values." Urban values and middle-class values, which increasingly became American values, marginalized the self-employment and productivity found on farms in favor of increasing consumption and professionalization.[15] Rural people themselves felt this change in status. As James Shideler notes in his examination of the decline of the rural ideal in the 1920s, "farm family expectations for a middle-class-level good life were dashed" by the decline in crop prices and the declining national status of farm life.[16]

Farmers themselves publicly identified problems with their profession, their diminished position in the nation, and the struggles they faced. The best known acknowledgment of trouble on farms occurred during the 1890s, when the Populists and their affiliated organizations such as the Farmers' Alliance directly challenged the rural ideal by articulating the challenges facing family farmers. Populists argued that farmers should earn a fair wage for their labor, particularly since their hard work put food on the tables of people in an increasingly urban nation. While appealing to farmers in most sections of the country, Populism as a political force found the most success in the Plains, the West, and the South, where farmers were not as well established as in the Midwest.[17] As farmers and their families politicized grievances about the monetary system, big business, and shrinking opportunities, their complaints illustrated the imperfections of rural life but did nothing to stop placement practices. In the Midwest, in addition to Populism, farmers' organizations such as the Grange or the Patrons of Husbandry represented similar interests. As discussed in chapter 1, while the group did not gather national political momentum like the Populists, it and others like it shared a desire to unite farmers socially and aided rural Midwesterners in a variety of projects such as granaries and cooperatives.[18] Regardless of location or longevity, farm organizations had a history of voicing a common concern: farmers needed help dealing with changing circumstances that favored big businesses, commercial exploitation of farmers, and the growing urbanization of America.[19] With the formation of the National Farmers Union in 1902, a revival of the Grange, and the rise of the Farm Bureau in the 1920s, membership in farm organizations increased considerably during the period of federal attention to farms. Farmers believed the Grange might be able to provide vital assistance to the business side of the farm through better production methods, cooperative buying and selling, and education, as well as for social uplift as the centerpiece of communities and a way to stem the tide of outmigration.[20] In general, farmers used these various associations to advocate for services they believed would improve their profits and their lives.[21] Organizations like the Grange worked to keep the farm as a focal point of American life because without the elevated status, the farm could fall further in influence.

In their discussions of the diminishing influence of the farm, farm people held themselves partially responsible but also lashed out at those they saw as darkening the farm's good reputation. In 1904, editorialist C. L. Northrup complained that popular authors "make farm life undesirable and city life the one thing to be desired . . . ninety-five percent of our fiction either ignores farm life or represents it as coarse, vulgar, and undesirable; that to escape from it is like an escape from slavery." Northrup blamed the agricultural press for not doing more to combat the negative associations promoted in literature.[22] Part of the need for better publicity came from the growing concern, among farmers and experts alike, that the brightest young people and the best workers rejected the farm for better opportunities, leaving behind the less talented to work the farm. What would become of the democratic spirit, work ethic, and moral guideposts provided to America by its farm population if the talent they produced left? This question worried farmers, farm organizations, reformers, and the federal government.

In the defense of those who left, there had long been incentive to go; as early as 1879, farm workers in Illinois, Indiana, and Ohio made about $20 per month while farm workers west of the Mississippi earned wages almost $3 higher.[23] Farm papers and newspapers thought it necessary to remind farmers to treat their workers with respect and pay them fair wages. A Cleveland newspaper advised farmers to pay workers in installments rather than once a year and to foster good relations in any way possible. As one female guest editorialist commented, "How any wife can be contented to have her husband toiling . . . for wages that will just permit them to live . . . I do not see."[24] Writers noted that adult and young laborers alike rejected farm work. One commented, "We think now that no intelligent young American with a fair education could labor faithfully at hard farm labor one whole long year for a miserable stipend that would give him about $100 for his years work."[25] That amount might have looked appealing to a placed-out child who could labor for an entire childhood for the same amount. The situation did not improve markedly over the next few decades. Hired hands earned as much as $30 per month but faced seasonal unemployment. Adult laborers found new industrial jobs in cities and on the railroads, and there was the potential for the ownership of their own farms farther west.[26] Wages for children finishing an indenture, on the other hand, remained the same, earning them between $50 and $150 for terms that ended at 18 or 21 years of age.

It was not just wage laborers who abandoned farm work. Children working for their own families suffered from the burdens of farm labor and a lack of personal freedom. A letter to the *Ohio Farmer* began: "There is not a doubt that one of the principal reasons why so many of our farmers' sons grow up with an absolute distaste of farm life, is because they are kept so constantly employed in some petty choring and drudgery." "Boy life on a farm isn't in many cases boy life at all—it is a workingman life."[27] Editorials in the *Indianapolis Times*, for example, told farmers to treat their own sons with respect. One columnist believed that boys who grew up with the limited conveniences of the farm often tried to escape by misbehaving in town. These same farmers' sons showed a dislike for those who possessed more than they did. A farmer should "show him [the son] he is not a slave who gets nothing in return for his work."[28] If farmers' own children faced such daunting problems, the situation for a child indentured to a farmer could not have been much better. The social and economic conditions of the farm might be altered, but little could be done to change the amount of work required to keep a farm operational.

While the quality of life affected people's decisions to leave the farm, the effects of increasing production efficiency, increasing startup costs for new farms, and the variety of opportunities off the farm became decisive factors for a rural exodus. Farm work at least allowed children to get outside, but that lost some of its appeal when taken alongside the loss of school attendance, the dangers, and the long hours. Reformers came to understand that it was not just the constancy of the toil and drudgery that made children working on farms unseemly, it was also the potential for injury. Pamela Riney-Kehrberg has found multiple cases from the Wisconsin state school of placed-out children being injured through their work. Former resident Edward, age thirteen, died in 1899 after he "fell from a load of hay and wagon ran over him . . . Causing injuries from which he died next day."[29] Another Wisconsin ward was killed in 1892 after being kicked by a horse. Both these boys, young teens at the time of their deaths, did not come from farm homes originally, and perhaps their inexperience on a farm contributed to their accidents; however, such things were not uncommon for farm children raised all their lives on the land. This explanation by naturalist John Muir of his life on his parents' Wisconsin farm indicates the arduous, industrial-type work he performed as a child:

> The summer work . . . was deadly heavy . . . the chores were grinding scythes, feeding the animals, chopping stove-wood, and carrying water up the hill . . . We stayed in the field until dark, then supper, and still more chores, family worship and to bed; making altogether a hard sweaty day of about sixteen or seventeen hours. I was put to the plough at the age of twelve . . . We were all made slaves through the vice of over-industry.[30]

Placement children routinely did work as described by Muir, and "over-industry" came in a variety of forms. James, a child hired out from his placement home to a mill in Kansas, died after being crushed between the rollers. James's injuries included a broken neck, jaw, arms, and shoulders. Mill operators could not say for sure what happened because James had been left alone with the machinery.[31]

As an additional problem, children trained for farm life found themselves with few practical skills for a life in industrialized America. Those not inheriting a farm could work as seasonal or hired laborers, try to rent their own farm, or move to town and find off-farm work. Basic training as a farm hand did not promise a prosperous or stable life. These problems illustrate a major contradiction between the praise attached to the placement of children on farms and the struggle to keep young adults in rural areas. One placement home superintendent noted that those who disliked farm work and rejected the rural lifestyle would eventually make their way back to cities for employment in factories, stores, or trades. Yet, he maintained that "the best preparation for success in city life is a preparatory period in the country."[32] Few people expressed concern about how an environment said to be beneficial for dependent children was one that other young people sought to escape.[33]

Even though the work performed by children on farms clearly required long hours and some exposure to danger, federal and state lawmakers chose to distinguish between family farm labor and industrialized agriculture practiced on large truck farms and other commercial operations. When reformers examined children laboring on farms, they directed their attention to employers like the Sanilac Sugar Company, which brought 125 boys between the ages of 7 and 15 from Detroit's Home of the Friendless Orphanage to work on their company farm and gave them a small payment and clothing in exchange for their work. Sugar beet labor, which reformers thought resembled factory work because of the physical hardships and low wages, garnered the attention of child labor reformers, while the work of children on a family farming operation would go unchallenged at federal and state levels.[34]

The exclusion of the family farm from child labor laws legitimized the work as healthy and necessary for family success and came after aggressive campaigning from farmers' organizations.[35] The total significance of child labor on farms was not slight; in 1900, 60 percent of working children labored on farms but were excluded from protective legislation. Government researcher J. R. Dodge reported that five-eighths of all farm workers were under the age of twenty-five and that one-tenth were under fifteen.[36] More than one million children labored in agriculture at the time of the 1910 census, and approximately 260,000 children worked on farms not owned by their parents. Placed-out children should have been included in this group, but no distinction was made for them as a category, and as a result, they were considered exempt from child labor laws even though they were not technically working on their own parents' farms. Ten years later, children working on farms remained an important source of agricultural labor; 61 percent of all working children between the ages of ten and fifteen worked in agriculture, with 88 percent of those children working on their parents' farms.[37]

One of the reasons farmers' children did not get included in child labor laws, aside from the vigorous lobbying by farm groups, was that even the Children's Bureau, which argued in favor of regulations, struggled to separate the myth of the rural ideal from reality. One bureau researcher fantasized that the prairie held mystery and charm for its young residents. Professors working for the agency continued to claim that there was no better place to raise a child than on a farm; strong character still came from working the soil. As historian Kathleen Mapes effectively argues, manufacturers like Sanilac played on this impression of "the mythic association of agriculture and democracy by priding themselves on turning 'waifs, orphans, and homeless children from heartless parents, city slums who were on the general road to ruin' into 'boy farmers' and 'useful citizens.'" This image building met with little resistance from groups such as the Grange, which fought the Children's Bureau on child labor regulations that dealt with farms. Midwestern politicians aided this effort, with Indiana Senator Albert Beveridge, who supported child labor regulations, proclaiming, "I do not for a moment pretend that working children on the farm is bad for them. I think it is the universal experience that where children are employed within their strength and in the open air there can be no better training." The distinction made by Senator Beveridge about children working on farms as opposed to in industry typified the categorization of the farm as a place of healthy and traditional labor. In addition, the Grange argued effectively that farmers struggled to find qualified and affordable workers, so family members had to work in order to guarantee the operation of a farm.[38]

The Commission

The timing of the Country Life Commission and the movement that followed is one of the great ironies of the early 1900s because the political turmoil of the 1890s was over and the buying power of farmers was increasing. Farmers' attempts to draw attention to the economic and social ills of their profession met with mixed results, but in the midst of a supposed "golden age," issues on American farms seemed serious enough to warrant a full-scale federal investigation. In 1908, the relationship between the food commodities produced on farms and the "industrial vortex" that required affordable food, along with his personal concern about the loss of rural values because of rural to urban migration, prompted President Theodore Roosevelt to form the Country Life Commission. Its members possessed academic expertise in agriculture and rural life. The commission studied the problems affecting rural people with the specific goal of improving the efficiency of farming and the standards of farm living in order to maintain a stable rural population, thereby solving two concerns at once: food would remain affordable and the American values propagated through farm life would be preserved and not siphoned off to the cities.

Instead of focusing only on farmers' calls for competitive advantages in the marketplace, the Country Life Commission's efforts centered on the efficiency of farms and farm homes, the conditions of schools and transportation, and the declining parity between rural and urban residents. The recommendations of the commission helped form what came to be known as the Country Life Movement, a Progressive effort to act on suggestions made by the federal report. The commission's report also influenced later legislation that funded programs designed to benefit the farm in bills such as the Smith Lever Act, which funded extension and 4-H; the Smith Hughes Act, which funded agricultural and home economics education in public schools; and the Purnell Act, which funded economic and social research through experiment stations.[39] As David Danbom points out, the simple existence of such a movement and commission indicated that the position of rural Americans and their way of life was going through a substantial transition that required outside intervention. It reflected the larger changes taking place in the nation; where once the typical American had been a farmer, now farmers were "objects of concern," and rural America, despite being in a "Golden Age," went from "backbone to backwater."[40]

The commission's perspective on the farm problem encouraged "nothing more or less than the gradual rebuilding of a new agricultural and new rural life."[41] Several of the major dilemmas motivating this rebuilding included population loss of young adults, increasing tenancy, increasing farm value (cost of land), and a decreasing economic price parity. Despite improving profits not all farmers prospered equally. Due to rising production costs, a number of families lost their farms, especially those on less productive land. Like others before them, these people faced a critical choice: they could become farm tenants or seek work elsewhere. By 1900, Illinois recorded a farm tenancy rate of 39 percent. The number of owner-operator farms decreased while the value of farms increased, making it more difficult for young or new farmers to become owners.[42] For the entire history of the nation, a majority of Americans had farmed, but after 1910 the number of farmers in Ohio, Indiana, and Illinois rapidly declined. An increasing number of people living in rural areas worked off the farm in pursuits such as agricultural-related factories, schools, sawmills, and construction. Those farmers who did prosper did so less than other Americans. Industry was rapidly replacing agriculture as the primary business of the nation. Farm residents carried debt, continued to lack basic services found in cities, and their homes did not keep up with middle-class standards.[43] Additionally, the increasing productivity on American farms did not improve the quality of life for farm families; efficiency in the field did not necessarily mean better living in the house. The commission faced a challenge in trying to bolster the futures of rural Americans.

Roosevelt and others, such as Country Life Commission chairman Liberty Hyde Bailey, worried about the numbers of young people leaving rural areas for other employment. The commission attributed part of the youth exodus to the gap between urban and rural standards of living. Pamela Riney-Kehrberg concurs, saying, "More rural youth were choosing what they perceived as the comforts and pleasures of the city over the stresses of rural life."[44] The telephone and rural free mail delivery were two of the improvements that reformers thought represented steps in the right direction toward making farm life less isolated and better for emotional satisfaction.[45] Liberty Hyde Bailey explained that to counteract the lure of the city and diminish the effects of hours of labor, farmers needed to be "awakened" to a new appreciation for their connection to nature and science.⁴⁶ Bailey joined his message of rural improvement to dependent child welfare when he participated in the National Conference for Charities and Corrections. In 1908, his linking of rural life and social welfare unintentionally contradicted the supposed benefits of rural placement when he claimed: "[Rural people have a] lack of real personal initiative . . . of enterprise that gets things done. This is due to the lack of contact with fellows, to the arrested development that results from individualism, and to the sterilization . . . the removal of centers of interest."⁴⁷ The isolation and stoic individualism that used to be praised as a benefit for dependent children was now a liability. Bailey's paper not only dealt a blow to the rural ideal, he also went on to foreshadow a problem that contributed to moving dependent children off farms in favor of urban and suburban foster homes. When discussing the need for social services he said, "The good social worker [in rural areas] should be a farmer, rather than a missionary, charity organizer, officer of correction, or philanthropist. The work should be established in real rural regions . . . The worker must be a resident the year round."⁴⁸ At the time of his talk, almost no full-time social workers lived and worked exclusively in rural districts in the Midwest and therefore were not available to supervise placed-out children or provide other services.

The lack of social services in rural areas was not just a problem for placed-out children; it came to be viewed as a negative and sign of backwardness for all residents. By 1925, the American Country Life Association, a more permanent manifestation of the commission's ideals, maintained a Committee on Rural Social Work. They defined the nature of the work undertaken by country social workers this way: "Broken or incapable families requiring aid; abused, neglected, dependent, delinquent and otherwise handicapped children, requiring care or protection by others than their parents; care of the aged dependents; care of feebleminded and mentally diseased persons; prevention of juvenile delinquency and crime; school attendance and child labor; housing conditions; community organizations for any social welfare movement." In other words, rural areas possessed the same problems as urban areas but with the added complication of distance and a lack of support services.⁴⁹ Rural social workers would need to be versed in the new field of rural sociology and have to be willing to, according to the social work leader Henrietta Lund, "bunk with the squatter's family in the one room shack if need be."⁵⁰ Although private groups such as the Red Cross increased their rural outreach during the first few decades of the twentieth century, many rural people living outside of town were "unreached." Social workers trained for rural work claimed that some of their clientele denied problems existed, and those not trained for rural social work held their clients in contempt.⁵¹ Others experienced loneliness and isolation from the rest of the field.

It is not surprising that child welfare reformers stopped viewing farm placement as the only solution for dependent children around the same time that the problem of supervision and services became a topic of professional discussion, but other issues relevant to placement also captured the attention of reformers. For example, youth flight from rural areas received federal attention, but the more farm children who left the farm, the more farmers needed laborers. Placers did not run out of applicants for children, instead they exhausted the idea that a farm work ethic was the way to make dependent children productive members of society. A USDA study in Minnesota showed that almost 30 percent of farmers' daughters over the age of twenty-one moved to cities, compared to 22 percent of boys. The children of farmers increasingly turned down a life fraught with difficult work and little relaxation or social stimulation, and soon child welfare advocates would do the same.⁵² Reformers acknowledged this when the Children's Bureau indicated changes to placement practices: "Isolated farm homes were used less frequently than formerly, since however desirable the family itself, such homes were not likely to afford either the educational or the recreational facilities needed by growing boys and girls."⁵³ The investigations of placement homes and the attention paid to subpar services and activities helped encourage reformers to find a new option for dependent children.

Farmers themselves dismissed much of the Country Life Movement because they "disliked being criticized by self-styled experts and urban outsiders," but reformers did draw attention to the problems associated with farm life, the lower standards of living, and the myth of farmer self-sufficiency.⁵⁴ The social work publication *The Survey* regularly printed missives about the diminished capacities of rural areas. Katherine Piatt Bottorff tried to explain how dirty and unhealthy rural villages could be in her 1912 article about Indiana residents living in hovels and slums. In 1911, Canadian child placer J. J. Kelso, a regular participant in American discussions about social conditions, skewered services in rural areas. He claimed, "Without doubt, the worst cases of immorality, incest, cruelty, and neglect of children . . . have been in the country. In the cities and large towns there is a strong Christian sentiment and greater social activity. People are better educated in right living." He went on to indicate that the lack of good schools, churches, and an understanding of the law actually made rural people degenerate.⁵⁵ This sort of criticism, while potentially exaggerated for effect, completely disassembled motivations for farm placements. Although largely rejected by Congress and therefore not supported with immediate federal action, the shortcomings identified through the commission's work were similar to those identified in *The Survey* and suggested ways to improve rural life while at the same time inadvertently giving reformers more indications that life in rural America no longer met the same standards it had when placement practices began for dependent children.[56] In a telling indication that farm standards no longer represented American ideals, some of the findings of the commission stressed that farm families needed to be brought up to urban, or middle-class, standards. In response, farmers tried to combat the notion that they overworked wives, lived with fewer entertainments, and suffered from second-rate schools.

During World War I, when farming played a pre-eminent role in the nation's war effort, farming publications boosted the morale of their readers by assuring them that "there can be no better place to start child life than on a farm," "from the farm home comes a strength and power our nation can well boast about." Although reassuring farmers that their wives stayed younger longer, their children received excellent educations, and the farm home was keeping up with urban standards, evidence suggested that these notions did not match the reality of conditions.[57] Farmers' wives reported staying home from church and social functions because of the material and cultural divide between themselves and the ladies from town; women reported feeling underdressed and burdened with other responsibilities that made it hard for them to attend regular activities.[58] In these ways farm women more closely resembled working-class women than middle-class housewives.

Emphasis on Education

The commission tried to address ways to encourage young people to make modern farming their vocation. At the core of their recommendations were better schools that focused on farm-related material. The follow-up efforts from the Country Life Movement tried to develop ways to provide better educational opportunities to rural children. Land grant schools and vocational training that included home economics were promoted to make better farmers and farm wives who would embrace technology for convenience. Agricultural education for farmers through outreach programs and the extension service attempted to help the older generations of farmers become better, more scientific producers, and ultimately higher earners able to improve their standard of living. While taking a positive tone about the improvements to make rural education more relatable to farm life, author W. S. Jennings admitted that rural people paid teachers less, suffered more illiteracy, and sent fewer children to high school than their urban counterparts. Further,

Jennings traced some of the inefficiencies back to a National Education Association study that showed that almost 80 percent of rural schools had not yet consolidated, leaving those teachers to instruct multiple grades in one room. Conditions in buildings were poor—open stoves and outhouses abounded, and one district sent an account of cows using the school house for summer shade and delaying the start of the term when they refused to leave.[59]

Even with efforts toward improvement, schools exemplified the diminished opportunities for children in rural areas. As early as the 1890s, the National Education Association issued a statement publicly acknowledging the poor quality of rural schooling.[60] In 1912, discrepancies between town and "admittedly poor" country schools were noted in Minnesota, and farmers in turn blamed schools for feeding children's minds with dreams of the city and subjects irrelevant to the farm.[61] Apparently little reform took place in the state during the 1910s, because in 1918 Minnesota county superintendent Julius Arp claimed, "There is no defect more glaring today than the inequality that exists between the educational facilities of the urban and rural communities. Rural education in the United States has been so far outstripped by the education of our urban centers, that from an educational standpoint, the country child is left far behind in the struggles of life."[62] This issue of poor schools struck at the heart of rural placement because sending placed-out children to local schools had always been a priority; if farmers' biological children could not get a decent education, neither could placed-out children. In her research about the Minnesota State Public School, Priscilla Ferguson Clement confirms that three-fourths of the children placed from that institution went to farms, and that the children in farm homes most likely to get an education were biological children and not the placement children.[63]

Education reforms became a priority for both the Country Life Movement and the Children's Bureau, and Progressive Era attempts to legislate compulsory education were complete by 1918, when all states had at least some type of law on their books. Enforcing minimum school attendance required the help of the courts, but enforcing the schooling terms of farm placement contracts proved to be more complicated. Minnesota State Agent J. H. Jaeger claimed that the school law made his job at enforcing attendance easier because he no longer had to "scold and threaten to secure four and five months schooling," but he thought that resistance from farmers to the new law would result in a change for full-time attendance only until the age of fifteen.[64] Bureau investigators discovered that a variety of reasons kept farm placement children away from school.[65] Above all, work on the farm and work in the farm home were the main culprits. Visiting agents were instructed to view children's school records as a way to gauge their treatment. In those school records, the agents found the following notations: "Lost schooling at beginning and ending of year for work"; "work on farm"; "attended irregularly, weather bad, and needed for work"; "work, late registration—withdrew in spring"; "probably work—absence in fall and spring"; "placed in home in March—out for work probably"; "frequently kept home for work"; "most of absences in Spring—work."[66] The 71 percent of placement children who attended school for at least the 120 days required by their indenture did not necessarily meet attendance regulations. In Wisconsin, a standard school year required 160 days, and only 19 percent of the placement children surveyed attained that amount.[67] For children interested in continuing their education in high school, a new problem emerged because farmers lived prohibitively far from high schools, and bureau agents believed this to be a major factor as to why so few placed-out children attended school past the eighth grade.

Farmers discussed the problems of rural schools in their own publications. L. N. Hines, Indiana State Superintendent of Instruction, claimed that "if there are to be any country people in the future there will have to be better schools in the country than there are now." Not only were schools poorly run and maintained, adults needed to follow attendance laws and send their children. In 1898 alone, Indiana spent $35,000 to employ 237 truancy officers, which resulted in 32,000 children being added to school attendance.[68] By 1920, when the state's Department of Visitors saw 1,600 children (of the 3,000 in family homes) they determined that of those children, only 123 were not attending school. State Agent L. H. Millikan made clear the changing goals of his agency when he summarized, "We frequently hear the statement that such children are desired in family homes only for work and their education is sadly neglected . . . The Board is always desirous that children who are capable, continue their school work as long as possible. They need it."[69] If dependent children needed as much schooling as possible, then perhaps the farm, where children struggled to advance past the eighth grade, was not a good option.

Farm children working on their parents' farm fared better in studies of attendance than the children of tenants and migrants but still missed more school than nonfarm children. Fewer of them tested at or above their normal grade level, and the more years they spent doing farm work, the further behind they tended to fall.[70] Although groups like the National Child Labor Committee focused most of their attention on the schooling missed by the children of migrant laborers, in 1920, Gertrude Folks asserted that farm work was "the greatest causation of irregular school attendance."[71] State workers made a similar correlation between farm placements and poor attendance. State Agent Mary Allen Davies noted, "As the majority of our children live on farms, it is not always easy for them to get the full time in school."[72] Both distance from schools and the need for their labor contributed to this problem. State Agent Frank Lewis of Minnesota believed that most placement parents intended to comply with schooling requirements, but like most rural people in the state, they did not know what the law required. As of 1899, children between the ages of eight and sixteen were to attend at all times when their district was in session. Lewis reported that most placement children, like other rural children, probably did no better than half this attendance. On examination of one boy's records, the visitor discovered that while he claimed to have attended five months of school, his attendance during those months was inconsistent, and he actually received less than two months of total schooling during the year.[73] The placement parents of Frank, the Cincinnati child who almost lost his placement home when a neighbor caused trouble, admitted that because he was on a six-month trial, they would not spend the money for his school books until they were sure he would remain in their home.[74]

When child placement first emerged as a leading care option, rural America stood as a pillar of strength and tradition against the ills of an industrializing and urbanizing nation, but reformers came to understand farm work as simply a different type of drudgery—particularly for children, who often missed school to accommodate farm work. In discussing the changing image of rural placement, Solomon Schindler, superintendent of the Leopold Morse Home for Infirm Hebrews and Orphanage, disputed the idyllic image of rural life as "a boy standing beside a cow." Instead, he charged, "Are there not unwritten histories of unhappy lives which are never published unless some especially flagrant crime against childhood has been committed?"[75] It was just such "flagrant crimes" that drew state intervention. But Schindler was right, many children simply languished in farm placements, not suffering "flagrant crimes" but dealing with not enough schooling and too much work.

Although they focused much of their efforts on children working in industry, the school attendance of farm children did receive attention from the Children's Bureau. The bureau commissioned a North Dakota study, which concluded that rural children's education sometimes suffered because of their workload. Worried that this new agency might extend its child labor activism to farms, American Farm Bureau Federation representatives urged Congress to restrain its involvement in children's agricultural labor, particularly on family farms, and instead press for better enforcement of school attendance laws.[76] The efforts of the National Child Labor Committee pressed on with their own farm labor concerns, but encountered opposition from southerners who depended on child labor in mills and on farms. Overall, children working in agriculture—particularly on family farms—regularly received legislative exemptions from child labor restrictions, and while increased schooling laws did extend to farm families, rural districts continued to set their own terms.[77]

Concerns over the quality of farm life did not diminish the desire to bring rural values into the lives of American children; however, reformers increasingly sought different ways to achieve that goal—methods that did not involve farm placement. The School Gardening Movement provided opportunities for urban children to experience the best part(s) of rural life: the growing and nurturing of new life and time spent in the outdoors. Such opportunities meant that children did not necessarily need to be placed on farms to experience the benefits of farm life. Children living in town could get the chance to go to more modern schools and still maintain contact with the soil because gardening encouraged "industriousness, skills, and self-reliance; taught orderliness, cleanliness, and punctuality . . . ; and prevented moral degeneration." These lessons formerly associated with rural life could now be found elsewhere.[78] If children could connect to these values living anywhere, the farm needed a renaissance that required federal assistance. If placing children in town made it easier to supervise them, what purpose did it serve to send dependent children to farm homes? Increasingly, urban residents found ways to access nature without the drudgery of a farm. According to Blaine Brownwell, people increasingly believed that their support for cities as the modern cultural standard of the country was in no way incompatible with their desire for natural spaces. The values attributed to rural people, "thrift and frugality, hard work, regular routine, progress, law and order, a respect for the family unit, and the ownership of property," also described the urban middle class. Since this group shaped policy for dependent children, it increasingly reflected their appreciation for the "superiority of the city." More ways to enjoy a healthy environment without country living meant fewer reasons to place children on farms.[79]

The Country Life Commission documented the apparent demotion of farm families as their quality of life was surpassed by urban and suburban workers, but other federal departments also worked on the rural problem. In 1919, the USDA formed the Bureau of Agricultural Economics to study rural sociology and farm life with the intention of advancing the lives of farmers and families.[80] The combined efforts of the federal government did not stop the emigration out of the countryside but did succeed in encouraging farmers to mechanize and consolidate when possible. Between 1870 and 1945, the farm population declined from 75 to 17 percent of the total population, and the number of people working in agriculture declined from 53 to less than 15 percent of the working population. As Alfred Griswold notes, "These figures show at a glance the extent to which the total structure of American democracy had outgrown its agricultural foundations."[81] The federal government did not remedy this growing gap between quality of living in cities and on farms. Land owning farmers, who were often associated with the middle class, found that their urban counterparts lived an increasingly better lifestyle. While city residents gained indoor plumbing, electricity, libraries, and entertainments, rural areas lagged behind. Around the time of World War I, the health and workload of farm residents earned criticism. In 1915, the *Journal of Home Economics* noted that farm women in Indiana and Illinois worked thirteen hours per day year round, far more than deemed acceptable for middle-class women.[82] Additionally, the work of farm children marked them as different from their urban counterparts, who were subjected to new industrial child labor laws, mandatory schooling rules, and notions that play should replace work. It was not just the work that began repelling people from the rural idea. Jon Lauck reviews a variety of post–World War I intellectuals who attacked the "Midwestern domination of American life and values" and made the region "'a convenient whipping boy . . . for all that was wrong with American life.'" These attacks, from notables such as H. L. Mencken, continued well into the 1920s when the region and rural life were blamed for being backward and overly traditional.[83] A general feeling of urban-rural conflict pervaded the country.

Faith-based organizations echoed the concerns of other groups. In a "Statement of Social Ideals" in 1925, Protestant groups "identified land security, lower distribution costs, better social, cultural, and recreational opportunities, and cooperative organization as the major needs of rural Americans."[84] Despite the willingness to identify problems with rural life, the myth of the rural ideal did not entirely expire: "While urban liberal Protestant thinkers achieved admirable prophetic insight into the rural plight, that insight was sometimes blurred by a confusion between immediate social and economic problems and a nostalgic ruralist ideology."[85] They were not the only ones confused, people wanted to improve farm conditions but it remained to be seen whether the farm could be returned to its rightful place in the hierarchy of the nation.

Child Labor and the Children's Bureau

The efforts of the Children's Bureau marked the beginning of a concerted effort for child protection on the part of the federal government, which included child labor, family preservation, and mother and child health.[86]

The bureau itself was the product of the 1909 White House Conference on Dependent Children, called to address the needs of the nation's children. As historian Kristie Lindenmeyer points out, the White House Conference of 1909 actually committed federal attention to reinforcing ideas about child welfare that were already being used across the country, having been proposed and acted on previously by state boards and discussed at the NCCC.[87] The recommendations of the White House Conference directed attention to dependent child welfare issues and increased federal involvement for all children. The ideas of note included increasing the number of foster homes and preserving families. One other recommendation was amended in an interesting way—the point that noted that "there should be frequent visitation of placed out children" was changed to read "adequate visitation," a problem that the Children's Bureau took issue with at a later time.[88] However, as Lindenmeyer emphasizes, the conference did not mandate that states unify their systems of care for children under a federal agency; a variety of methods continued after the conference and during the time of the bureau.[89]

The national conference attendees who helped shape the goals of the bureau included renowned Progressives such as Julia Lathrop, Florence Kelly, and Lillian Wald, who recommended keeping children with their families when possible and moving institutionalized children into smaller, more specialized institutions.[90] The federal government's foray into dependent child welfare began in earnest with the development of the Children's Bureau. The beginning of this agency is often seen as a watershed in the development of public policy and influence on policy from a national level. In spite of the recommendations to preserve family homes made at the meeting, the number of children's institutions increased in the decade following, and the decline of placements is more complex than previously understood. The Children's Bureau, not particularly the conference, did a great deal to uncover the problems with rural life and rural placement.[91]

The Children's Bureau began work in 1912 and charted a path aligned with Progressive efforts to encourage states and the federal government to intervene on behalf of children. Although child labor laws met with strong resistance from the Supreme Court, mandatory education laws succeeded in keeping more children in schools instead of at work. Working conditions that denigrated children's intellect and their physical well-being were already a target of action for Progressive reformers as they sought to enact child labor legislation across the country.[92] Urban children previously engaged in industrial work benefited most from labor regulations, but a majority of working children labored in agriculture. Although reform efforts during the 1910s sought to keep all children in school more and working less (and hoped that increasing farm efficiency could decrease farm child labor), as many as 60 percent of children between ten and fifteen years old employed in 1920 still worked in agriculture. Despite being referred to as an "increasingly anachronistic practice," the indenturing of children to farms continued during this period. Children working in a placement or on their family farm may have seen their labor decrease—but not dissipate—alongside advancing mechanization.[93]

One of the largest investigations of children laboring on the farms of others happened in the sugar beet industry. Kathleen Mapes shows that sugar beet farmers in places such as Michigan altered their family farming operations in order to take advantage of new opportunities to grow the sugar beet, but that change required enormous amounts of hired labor. The difficulty of the work combined with low wages did not attract local hired hands to sugar beet fields. In fact, the beet fields of Michigan so countered the notions of agrarian independence that child labor reformers targeted beet producers as exploiters of children and referred to them as a "factory without roof or walls."[94] Ultimately, growers drew in immigrants from across the country; entire families moved to the beet fields during the early decades of the 1900s. Once there, they attracted attention from child labor reformers who worried about the thousands of children in beet fields, considering them to be working in "industrial agriculture." In the process, as Mapes notes, reformers "directly confronted the myth that all agricultural child labor was good for the children, because it built their morals and character, and good for the nation, because it ensured future generations of hearty and wholesome citizens."[95] Reformers noted that children on these farms were contract laborers and not just helping their families. Grace Abbott, chief of the Children's Bureau, determined that children at work on sugar beet farms "could not be compared with the traditional farm child labor" because that "led to a 'sense of family solidarity' and 'real training.'"[96] Lost on Abbott and others were the contracts of placed-out children who labored on the farms of others. Although placement children were not included in the discussion of sugar beet children, the iconography of the Midwest did come under scrutiny; working families on these farms did not get to enjoy the touted benefits of abundance, democracy, and the yeomanry of generations past.

Although the Children's Bureau and the National Child Labor Committee took up the charge on child labor laws, they provided exclusions for children working on family farms. The 1924 proposed constitutional amendment banning various forms of industrial child labor drew the ire of groups such as the Ohio Farm Bureau, which protested the loss of parental control and blamed reformers for the intrusion. Religious associations, in turn, took offense with the notion that Congress was overly inclined to "listen so attentively to social uplifters." As noted by the *Herald of Gospel Liberty*, issues of rural truancy and overwork affected people across the country, and religious reformers believed that rural children deserved the same benefits as those living in cities.[97] As reformers argued, Grace Abbott advocated on behalf of the child labor amendment thusly, specifically trying to quell the fears of farm associations:

> Although evidence of exploitation of children in certain kinds of agriculture is not lacking, it is generally believed that a better enforcement of school laws will reduce interference with school attendance, which is the most serious evil in rural child labor. As the employment of children in agriculture is usually on the home farm and is seasonal and out of doors, it is much less objectionable ... Moreover, many of the farm children help their fathers with the farm work just as the girls help their mother with house work. If not too arduous, the work is, of course, valuable to boys and girls for the training it gives and the sense of responsibility which it develops.[98]

Since child labor on farms varied according to region and family prosperity, some children performed less labor-intensive tasks than others, but the general notion of outside work alongside one's parents helped encourage legislative exclusions. In the Midwest, where grain farming dominated the agricultural landscape, as many as two-thirds of all children over the age of twelve helped in the fields.[99] Children working on their family's farm were excluded from most labor regulations, but technically any child working under a contract might be subjected to new child labor restrictions. The indenture or placement contract, like a contract for children working on commercial farms, linked children to labor for commercial production. By not including children who labored under indenture contracts, reformers categorized those children with farm children instead of as children laboring on the farms of others, despite decades of evidence that suggested many were taken only for their work.[100]

World War I

The challenges of child farm labor and the generally low wages paid to farm workers were a problem that spread beyond the purview of a single government agency. During World War I the federal government increased its involvement with farmers for labor and production. The Committee on Industrial Relations examined working conditions for laborers and determined that "rural life smelled of rot by the First World War."[101] The rise of immigrant and migrant labor on Midwestern farms affected this perspective since it was seen to ruin the so-called "classless and homogenous place of family farms."[102] Farmers, desperately clamoring for laborers during the war to keep pace with increased demand and increased acreage, sought help from machinery, the government, and laborers from the South and as far afield as Mexico. In an effort to attract workers to farms during the war, Assistant Secretary of Labor Louis Post encouraged increasing farm labor wages to $45 per month with room and lodging. Despite attempts to get more workers into the fields during the war, shortages remained and farm families often worked harder, longer hours to maximize production and profit, which meant placement children may have been working harder than usual. Before and during the war, reformers spoke of child labor in factories, mines, and mills, but not on Midwestern farms.[103] In fact, children were solicited to pitch in for agricultural work. The Boys Working Reserve, housed in the Department of the Interior, recruited boys to work in the fields during the war and encouraged them to do their patriotic duty.[104] At the war's end, farmers clamored for the return of sons and laborers, citing concerns that planting would be drastically delayed if men were not immediately released from service and claiming "the matter of returning farm boys is being overlooked."[105] During the conflict children working on farms were viewed as a matter of national security.

The war played an important role in altering the policies of child placement. At a time when placed-out children could expect to receive between $50 and $100 at the end of their contract, older children realized that wartime wages made their labor far more valuable on the open market. Children complained to their visitors that they were working for free.[106] As one Indiana caseworker recorded, "They [the children] are becoming restless and are asking why they do not receive wages."[107] These complaints reached the National Conference on Social Work (formerly the National Conference of Charities and Corrections), which endorsed paying older children in placements wages but failed to establish a plan to implement this recommendation.[108]

Resistance from children because they were being robbed of wartime earnings only added to the already present problems. Historian Jessica Ramey suggests that children themselves helped dismantle placement, and provides examples of placed-out children expressing their displeasure with placement arrangements that did not allow them the opportunity for urban experiences, relevant work training, and schooling.[109] As early as 1904, agents from the Minnesota state school reported that "the scarcity of farm help has fostered a spirit of jealousy or envy on the part of some of the neighbors, who have unwisely gone to the boys with offers of wages, thus making them feel that they were not being justly treated by their foster parents."[110] In later years, the agents recommended that farmers pay the older children wages, especially during the busy season. Priscilla Ferguson Clement notes that these children resented the lack of schooling and boys understood that their peers who worked for farmers made as much in a single year as they could make from their entire indenture; during the war it might have been possible to make almost as much in a few months.[111]

In addition to not being paid regular wages at a time when wages were high, the type of work required of children on farms—and, in fact, farm workers in general—came under attack. At a meeting of the International Workers of the World, a union known for reaching out to unskilled laborers, the mass of seasonal farm laborers struggling for recognition were described in a way that could have been used for placed-out children: "[They are] the necessary product of conditions under which they have been raised. They were taken out of school at a tender age, and all the physical development they got was hanging onto the handles of a plow, and the most inspiring scene before their eyes was the rear end of a mule, and now reduced to premature old age, with vitality sapped and form bent earthwards, [their] ambition [is] blasted and hopes blighted."[112] This description would have been unrecognizable to the placers who vigorously promoted placement in the 1880s and 1890s, but national opinions about child labor were changing the way such work was viewed, and more policy makers agreed that vitality-sapping work was no longer the right choice for dependent children.

The Bureau and Rural Health

During the war the Children's Bureau launched "The Children's Year" in which the bureau worked to reduce the rate of infant mortality, to improve the health of urban and rural families, and to educate women on sanitation and child rearing techniques.[113] Picking up on Country Life concerns, the bureau used data from studies done in the 1910s to support the claim that farm life contributed to the poor health of rural women and children, who suffered higher instances of infant mortality and postpartum death. Other evidence from dependent children in the Midwest corroborates those claims. The Allen County, Indiana, children's home received children from the city of Fort Wayne and from the outlying rural areas that covered most of the county. In 1913, administrators complained about health problems of the rural children admitted to the institution. Rural children arrived with the most "defects," including bad teeth, adenoids and tonsils, and venereal diseases. In certain cases, these children were labeled defective and faced transfer to state-operated institutions for delinquents or the mentally challenged. These "defective" children from rural areas gave institutional managers clear evidence that conditions in the countryside were falling behind the standards of urban areas.[114]

During World War I, the Children's Bureau conjectured that "country life is no longer a guarantee of good morals."[115] The bureau argued that rural areas needed more financial assistance from federal and state governments to aid people whose local governments lacked the funds to improve the standard of living. The agency was "concerned with the problem of bringing to the mothers of country children (who comprise three fifths of the children in the United States) a reasonable amount of help, and of insuring to the 18,000,000 girls and boys living in rural areas a fair chance of growing into happy, useful citizens."[116] The poor health of farm youth volunteering for World War I service encouraged the Children's Bureau to act. In justifying their expenditures, the bureau stated, "The lack of resistance shown by our country boys in the cantonments and under forced physical strain, and the reports of recognized authorities as to the relative prevalence of defects among rural as compared with urban children, are too significant to be ignored."[117] The bureau described the physical symptoms of a hard farm life: "Winged scapulae, rounded shoulders, and a contracted chest are typical of the rural child; and the average parent, who has accepted this as an inherited and inevitable trait, receives with interest the suggestion that swimming, or daily exercise . . . might improve the position of the pliable little shoulders and incidentally increase the breathing capacity."[118] Until the bureau began these studies, the generalized problems recorded by the Country Life Commission lacked specificity. Armed with new evidence about the health of rural people, the bureau targeted reform measures and federal intervention to assist through efforts such as "The Children's Year." The doubts about the healthiness of the farm environment added to the criticism mounting against placements.

In 1922, the Children's Bureau strongly supported the passage of the Sheppard-Towner Act, a measure designed to reinforce the health and education goals of the bureau. The short-lived programs funded by Sheppard-Towner benefited white farm women more than any other group.[119] They received health information like prenatal care and assistance to purchase modern equipment meant to sanitize the home, including screens for doors and windows. In that same year, the Red Cross also sponsored rural child health clinics in states such as Kansas, where nurses documented that farm parents believed their children to be in the best of health because they lived on a farm. Further examination showed that based on the standards of the time, only 24 percent of the children in one county measured as "normal" in size, teeth, eyes, and overall health.[120] Cooperation with local areas proved important, and when the Child Welfare Special—a health clinic in a vehicle—roamed the countryside during 1919 and 1920, the bureau encouraged residents to petition for their own local resources, such as a public health nurse, instead of relying on future visits from the bureau itself. As the report on the effort summarized, "In no county [visited] had there been any expression of municipal obligation concerning the well-being of their children, or any effort made to insure proper physical or mental development."[121] The lack of social services and health care placed rural people behind other groups once again.

One of the intentions of the Children's Bureau was to learn about the status of children across the nation and provide mothers with scientific information about healthy child development. Doing so included child study and research, which increased the need for professional training, investigation, and scientific methods to determine the best care for the so-called normal child. According to Hamilton Cravens, this move toward science and professionalism inverted the priorities of Progressives from child saving to child research. The Children's Bureau evolved further, from research, to promotion of what Michael Katz calls the "semi-welfare state."[122] By supporting family preservation efforts through direct aid to provide a "normal" home life with the mother staying home to care for children, the bureau discouraged placements and encouraged familial preservation. Mother's aid, as one existing way to make this goal a reality for families who might have placed children in an institution in previous decades, became a cornerstone of federal child welfare policy. In 1921, ten years after the implementation of mother's aid began, the Child Welfare League of America commissioned a study of 150 rural children. They discovered that children were removed from their parents when the application of direct aid might keep the family intact. Such cases went uninvestigated for lack of staffing, and local people were unaware of the aid options available to them through the state and county.[123] Although the attention to the shortage of mother's pensions in rural areas may have helped, areas continued to struggle with the lack of direct aid resources available to rural people in need.[124]

The Bureau and Placement

While the Children's Bureau made efforts to improve rural conditions for children and encouraged tactics that helped to preserve biological families, it also studied placement. In the first large-scale research project directly targeting placed-out children, conducted in 1923 and published in 1925, the

Children's Bureau hired seven trained agents to follow up with hundreds of children placed out from the Wisconsin State Public School between 1913 and 1917. The study summarized what decades of child placement already established: farmers were the most likely to take in placement children, and they did so because they needed the labor. The $50 due an eighteen-year-old for serving out the length of his or her contract was profoundly less expensive than seasonally hiring an adult.

The bureau agents immediately discovered problems with the methods being used by the Wisconsin State Public School, which had been placing children for almost forty years. With five hundred children to oversee annually in placements, "It is obvious that two agents can cover the entire State inadequately. According to the annual reports of the school the children placed in indenture homes for the first time have averaged 180 per year . . . in view of the fact that many of the children are placed in several homes in the course of their indenture histories, it is evident that the number of indenture homes to be looked up in a year is extensive."[125] As bureau agents tried to track down children placed almost a decade prior, they sought to visit the children's biological homes, all the placement homes in which the children lived, and the children themselves if possible. Their efforts at information gathering exceeded the state's efforts at supervision, which fell woefully short of what the bureau's workers believed it should be, even with an allowance for the children placed in remote locations.

Despite all of the efforts to keep children safe and select good placements, children had few places to turn once out of state view. In Wisconsin, "many children . . . apparently gained little through the aid given by the State except maintenance." The training they received in placements gave them experience on farms and in homes, and little else. Children specifically said they wished for a chance to attend vocational training of some kind but often remained in the neighborhood working for other farmers. Of 127 young people surveyed in Wisconsin, farm work for men and marriage and housework for women accounted for the largest occupations. Other employment included the military, factory work, telephone operator, and railroad worker. Federal investigators criticized the state of Wisconsin for providing little or no guidance to children as they aged out of placements. Children and their placement parents reported that they did not know what to do when the child turned eighteen; they expected someone from the state school would contact them with information or assistance.[126] Wisconsin children were not alone in these issues of job training; Galen Merrill at the Minnesota state school lobbied his legislature for funding to better help children gain vocational training and for more funds to keep children with their parents when possible.[127]

Farms featured prominently in the report; a few children came from rundown farms, but more often they were sent to farms. Of the 768 indenture homes used during the study period, the investigators knew the location of 655; 79 percent were farm homes, 3 percent were in villages, and 18 percent were in cities. The personal visits to more than five hundred of these homes resulted in investigators classifying almost half of them as "detrimental" to the child's welfare. The Children's Bureau study repeatedly noted that homes were not carefully selected, children who needed extra assistance were hastily placed and re-placed, and "sometimes a farmer or his wife in poor health might apply to the State public school to get a strong boy or girl to do the work. This happened in numerous instances and resulted in the overworking of the children and in lack of proper recreation."[128] The bureau took issue with almost every aspect of the placement system, including the pattern of separating siblings: "It is extremely difficult under the indenture system to keep members of the same family together . . . the solution undoubtedly lies in providing boarding-home care for groups of children who should be kept together."[129] This study gave more comprehensive evidence for the anecdotal reports of problems, and the authors' recommendations supported the newer emphasis on sibling preservation through foster care.

Although Country Life efforts tried to improve the lives of rural people through community engagement and education, the bureau study showed that few areas possessed so much as a "calf club" at the time the subjects lived in their placements, and that in most homes "the reading matter was limited to farm papers."[130] In two rural school districts, investigators found that state school children were discriminated against for being "queer" or "decidedly inferior to other children." Some of the children released from their indenture contracts still labored on farms in the area, and locals recounted they were "about as good as you could expect from the State School."[131] The stigma of dependency, which placers long assumed would be overlooked by kindly farm people once children were made part of a new family, clearly lingered.

The bureau was not alone in trying to determine the effectiveness of rural placement. In 1912, the Children's Home of Cincinnati, long considered such a successful placing and supervising institution that other counties sent their children there, produced a report updating their statistics about child placement. Two decades earlier in their first official collection of data, the home's superintendent Meigs Crouse reported that his institutional visitor G. T. Green tried to find as many farm homes as possible for children because the homes of laborers would not do. In 1909, the year of the survey, the home tried to contact the approximately 1,600 children placed in families between 1864 and 1880. Three hundred and sixty-two children could not be located, 46 were dead, 90 were insane, and 69 were listed as a "bad credit" to the home. However, more than 1,100 former placement children gave responses to the survey that prompted the institution to list them as a "good citizens." In 1915, the institution sent out another 750 questionnaires, and almost half were returned with positive feedback about their experience in the institution and subsequent placement.[132] By 1912, the institution still placed approximately 45 percent of its children with farmers, but more than half of the children went to nonfarm families. Forty-nine percent of these children were under the age of six, making them not as useful for work and better candidates for adoptions. Between two and three homes on average needed to be found for those children who were removed from their first placement. Almost 90 percent of the children who needed to be re-placed were over the age of six, and 89 percent of adoptions were for children under the age of six. In total, between 1904 and 1912, the visitor for the home traveled almost 200,000 miles. What these numbers indicate is a slight but significant change in the way this institution operated. It placed more young children and fewer children on farms, and it relied more heavily on adoption for younger children.[133]

The issue of increasing adoptions in Cincinnati helps develop an important aspect of Children's Bureau recommendations, which sought permanent homes for children whose families could not be saved. Reformers had high hopes for increasing legal adoptions. In Minnesota, the state school hoped for adoptions, but gained few. No more than 20 percent of its residents were adopted, and most of those were the youngest children.[134] The same was true elsewhere, with only the youngest children finding adoptive homes. The failure of adoptions to take place indicated a larger issue with the plans of placement in general. Children were not finding permanent homes the way reformers intended. Free placements created as many problems as they solved—children not adopted needed visiting over long distances, they were not included as members of the family, and they worked hard to earn their keep, which in turn kept them out of school.

In its study of Wisconsin placement techniques and results, the Children's Bureau linked together the various attempts at improvements to the placement system and indicted the farm as part of the problem, not part of the solution. The researchers summarized their findings:

> No doubt it has been the thought of the state authorities that a dependent child is better off on a farm than in a city, and in many cases the life on the farms undoubtedly may have been an improvement upon the conditions from which the children were removed. But ... a considerable proportion of the homes into which children were indentured fell far short of providing good training for future citizenship.[135]

A single report did not generate dramatic nationwide changes, so in the late 1920s, complaints about indenturing children to farms continued. Researcher Neva R. Deardorff repeated worries from decades prior when she categorized indentures as "a survival of the days when slavery and serfdom were tolerated . . . the bound out boy or girl is still in a state of semi-servitude." Although it suggested that little came of the bureau's research, studies continued to indicate that children being adopted were those under five, and that finding people to take an older child required board or the promise of a labor exchange.[136]

Katherine P. Hewins and L. Josephine Webster, both experienced child welfare workers, performed the field work for a second bureau study, this time of larger geographic scale. During 1922 and 1923, the women examined ten child-placing groups to determine what, if any, national standards existed; they found none. Far from seeing an end to placement, they found changes happening in the application of terms such as "foster care." A few of the 198 groups participating in placement indicated a payment for foster care, while a majority still referred to finding free homes for children. In their section about rural services, the researchers claimed, "Methods have been developed more slowly for the rural sections of the country than for the larger urban centers, and it is only in the last decade, perhaps since the World War, that interest has focused on bringing social service to children handicapped by their very isolation."[137] This handicap could be remedied by moving placement services closer to towns and cities. The report went on to single out rural areas for their lack of social services: "The work of several societies was very uneven, some of it being of much higher quality than the rest. This was especially noticeable as between the work in the large cities which was usually good, and that in the more rural sections where for a variety of reasons the work often fell below standard."[138] Despite two decades of increased state involvement in dependent child welfare, care practices did not meet the standards of the bureau, nor had rural areas invested in improvements.

The Children's Bureau investigators assembled enough information to paint farmers and placement in a poor light. Bureau workers reported that farmers, mistaking them for state school agents, asked if they had any children available for work because "hired help costs so much" and "I could use a good girl right now." Some wanted to take in state school residents to relieve their own children of farm work burdens, giving those children the opportunity for more schooling and less labor. The payments, to be provided by placement parents to the children after their indenture ended, increasingly seemed an archaic practice. For child welfare workers, those payments represented an inappropriate expectation of work, but farmers interested in taking children commented as late as 1923 that "they had to get at least the equivalent of the $50 in work," and several complained that the children went back to the state school "just as they were beginning to be of some value." In earlier decades placers viewed this attitude as a facilitator for finding children farm homes, but in the 1920s when an increasing number of American children went to school, played, and did light chores, bickering over a $50 payment for months—and perhaps years—of work, was no longer acceptable.[139] By the 1920s, a "considerable proportion" of former placed-out children chose not to work on farms and immediately sought out work in more urbanized areas; the training of the farm and the farm home did not serve children as well as industrial vocation work or other more specific training.[140]

Among the agencies studied in 1922, the Michigan Children's Aid Society demonstrates best the changes happening in states and counties across the region. This group, while not trying to duplicate the work of the Michigan State Public School, increased its work among "normal" children because the state school had been accepting more difficult children from the courts. These children could not easily be placed in family homes. Thus, the aid society took the normal children with distressed families and accepted reimbursement for their care from family members instead of sending them through the state school. This had been a key part of its work since its founding in 1891; it provided professional services the state school did not. In addition to housing children whose parents kept guardianship by paying board, the agency specialized in the adoption of infants and toddlers. The bureau research into the training and work of staff at these placing agencies indicated that most were "eligible for either full or junior membership in the American Association of Social Workers," which required field experience or higher education.[141] Throughout the region, the older institutions, especially the state-operated institutions, were increasingly being used for the specialized care needs of disabled or delinquent children, and the placement, foster care, and other dependency cases were being referred to private groups like the Michigan Children's Aid Society. In 1917, for example, the Minnesota Board of Control took over the state public school, and children admitted to the institution now came through the juvenile court system. More disabled children than able-bodied ones began arriving, and those considered healthy and normal were placed through agencies specializing in foster care.

Demonstrating the changing practices, these bureau investigations happened as the long-time leader of the farm placement movement, the CASNY, was in the process of moving its own efforts to a boarding home program that focused on finding suburban homes for children. Started in 1923, the program intended to help children transition back into the homes of their parents. In 1926, the organization's department for placements changed its name to focus on the role of boarding home, adoption, and placement locators. In 1931, the department went through a final evolution, calling itself the Department of Foster Care.[142] The CASNY joined other private groups in this effort. The Michigan Children's Aid Society, which until 1921 was called the Michigan Children's Home Society, spent as much as 25 percent of its budget to board children. States in which boarding was adopted early, particularly those on the East Coast, spent a larger percentage of money on boarding.[143] While Wisconsin had to answer for the scathing review that revealed a lack of modernization in the way it cared for dependent children, institutions, charities, and state agencies were adjusting their care methods to lessen the number of children in farm placements. Of the children studied by the bureau in 1922–1923, at least two-thirds of them did not need placing services and were cared for using other methods.

As suggested by the bureau's report, finding paid boarding homes for siblings, temporary placements, and children with special needs would be safer and more effective. Keeping families together but monitored using direct aid methods helped children avoid the trauma of placement and separation and allowed social workers access to homes. Institutions, formerly a gateway to placement, were now a refuge for delinquents and special needs cases. Ideally, normal children could go to school, work less, and be moved around fewer times, and trained social workers could visit easily and record their progress in their own homes or in foster homes. To highlight the ways caseworkers and social workers positively improved child welfare, the Children's Bureau noted, "Formerly, it was thought that placing-out visitors whose main business was the supervision of placed-out children could investigate applications from prospective foster families in their odd moments." With more care options available, including paid foster homes, direct aid to families, and specialized institutional care, more attention to the needs of children and parents was paid.[144]

Increased federal research revealed compelling evidence suggesting that placement homes did not offer the best choice for dependent children. The Children's Bureau report of 1925 criticized not just the existing system, which came under special censure for putting too many special needs children in placements and failing to understand the unique needs of children as individuals, but the entire foundations of farm placement homes. "Indenture, even in its modified form, is a direct inheritance from the old form of binding out . . . the whole stigma of binding out remains . . . The whole relationship of the State, the foster parents, and the child rests on a false basis. The interests of the children ... require ... a fundamental change in the system."[145] A fundamental change did come, and not just to the methods by which children found new homes. As an educator on the importance of healthy homes, school attendance, and appropriate social welfare methods, the Children's Bureau made strides for advancing the cause of child welfare. The suggestions from the 1925 report encouraged states to give more direct aid and rely more on foster care. When Nettie McGill studied children working in agriculture in 1929 for the bureau, she found conditions similar to previous reports. Children missed school due to work, their working hours and conditions varied widely, and little could be done to diminish their labor except to enforce school attendance.[146]

By the 1930s, one of the things intended to help dependent children were more New Deal benefits for family maintenance that further discouraged large numbers of placements but did not stop them all together. Because no reform effort could consolidate dependent child welfare under one recognized code of practices, states, and especially institutions, provided whatever type of care they deemed appropriate. This meant that even though much changed with the use of foster payments, adoption of younger children, and family preservation, some children still went out to homes under a free placement system.

One such child, Curtis Beireis, was placed by the Miami County, Ohio, children's home during the 1930s after his mother died. His son, Robert, remembered his dad recounting the experience:

> Children, usually boys, were sent out on indenture as often as possible as this reduced the burden on the County, and the local farmers could use them as [a] source of low cost labor ... The Williamsons were only interested in obtaining free labor, as he was not paid, and his food and board were given begrudgingly. He was overworked (he was approximately 14 at the time), and his glasses were taken away from him out of a misplaced fear that he would lose or break them. He was near sighted, and needed his glasses full time. He was also beaten because he could not see well enough to perform his chores on the farm. Finally he had enough, and early one morning he ran away and returned to the Home on foot, a distance of about 30 miles. He told me that life at the Home was preferable to that at the Williamson house.

Curtis was the second generation of his family to be placed from the Miami County home. In 1898, his own father, John Herbert, was admitted after the death of his mother. John Herbert went into three placement homes before disappearing from the records. When his wife died during the 1930s and his own children went to the same place where he spent part of his childhood, John Herbert suffered a mental breakdown, spending the rest of his life in a state hospital.[147]

The funding and influence of the Children's Bureau waned in the late 1920s, but the bureau, the Country Life Movement, social workers, and various state, local, and private agencies all played a role in removing free farm placement homes from the care options for dependent children.[148] Each piece of information about the status of farm households, the issues of school attendance and farm work, and the lack of social services in rural areas chipped away at the foundations on which farm placement was built. What began as new expectations for the supervision of placement children living on farms revealed two separate problems. First, the farm itself suffered from a declining position in American society by not keeping up with middle-class standards increasingly being set in urban and suburban areas where amenities were available to improve the quality of family life. Second, supervising children placed on distant farms made it challenging to meet the new standards for visitation in placements, which made placing children closer to visiting services more appealing.

The work done by both the Children's Bureau and the Country Life Commission gave evidence to these problems. By way of Progressive Era studies and analysis, reformers deconstructed the rural ideal that provided the original foundations for farm placements. Poor health and educational opportunities demonstrated the decline of farm life when compared to middle-class life elsewhere. In addition, the increasing emphasis on child labor reform acknowledged the hard work children performed on farms, but did not include them in legislation if they worked on a family farm. Placement children got caught in this exclusion because while they did not work on their own families' farm, they also were not considered to be workers on an industrial farm. World War I influenced policy changes about placement because older children wanted to be able to participate in a competitive labor market. Finally, the studies completed by the Children's Bureau in the 1920s gave low marks to practices of placements to farms, and as demonstrated by the story of the Beireis' children, these studies did not change any situation immediately, but they indicated gradual changes to state and local practices that acknowledged the problems with farm placements and sought to rectify them with paid foster care and familial maintenance.

There is a sad sort of irony in the changes to dependent child policy that moved away from farm placements. Farm placement existed because people initially believed farmers to be a special, and in fact exceptional, kind of good. But because they were regular people and not superheroes of the fields, some met those expectations while others fell far below. When it became clear that farmers suffered from their own problems of social and economic backwardness, reformers determined that farmers could not be givers of as well as receivers of aid. In their place, urban and suburban Americans were viewed as the new saviors of dependent children since through their acceptance of a foster payment, they also accepted the intervention of the state.

Epilogue

"The great drama of childhood"

> "It is too apt to supply a home with a child instead of a child with a home."
> —"Children Indentured by the Wisconsin State School," Children's Bureau Publication

In 1920, Indiana State Visiting Agent Millikan mused, "And now another year has passed in the great drama of childhood, but the curtain must rise again and let us see that the stage is properly set for the coming months." During the 1920s, setting the stage properly meant relying on a variety of care practices that included placement homes, foster homes, and institutional care. During the 1920s and beyond, states placed greater emphasis on paid foster homes and family preservation.[1] In 1922, the Ohio Department of Welfare reported that 71 percent, or 1,400 children, remained in free homes, while almost 600 children, or 29 percent, were being boarded in foster homes. Decades before, almost no children were cared for in foster homes, and those numbers ultimately inverted with more children being cared for in methods that were not free placements.[2]

The decline of the farm home as a symbol of American prosperity, the appropriate levels of work and education for children, the expense of placement, the problems with supervision, and efforts at family preservation all affected child welfare policy changes. The farm, which featured so prominently in the arguments for free placement out of institutions, featured prominently again in the arguments to adopt other methods. The decisions made during the Progressive Era to rationalize, study, centralize, and professionalize institutionalization and placement permanently altered the methods of care for dependent children in the United States. The effects of these changes are still a part of twenty-first–century life as family and juvenile courts, state departments for health and human services, welfare assistance, and caseworkers all continue to work on behalf of dependent children.

The placement system did not change simply because middle-class Americans changed their minds about the role of children in society. It also changed because the farm itself was in transition. In the 1920s, the profile of the rural ideal remained intact, even as agriculture was diagnosed as a "sick industry" in need of permanent federal policies in part to make sure the "greatest and fundamentally the most important of our American industries" survived.[3] Historian A. Whitney Griswold, himself no believer in the connection between farming and democratic strength, noted in the 1940s, "[The] ideal of democracy as a community of family farms has lived on to inspire the modern lawmakers and color the thoughts of their constituents when they turn their minds to rural life."[4] But, in practice, by the end of World War I, it no longer served the best interests of the nation to place children somewhere they would fall behind and that failed to give them training for the modern industrial nation. Education, not work, became the hallmark of American advancement, providing what children needed to succeed as adults. As children became more economically useless, it became harder to place them in families for "free." The foster home system, where adults were paid to accept children, responded to that problem directly and also opened the way for more people in urban areas to take in children. Increasingly, people willing to take in children for free wanted young children available for legal adoption.[5]

The family farm, once the seeming salvation of dependents, ultimately needed salvation of its own. The efforts to increase efficiency on farms reduced the number of farmers needed to produce cheap food products, a situation that undermined other efforts to keep farmers and their children on the land.[6] After New Deal programs such as the Agricultural Adjustment Act and the Farm Security Administration targeted farmers for assistance, price supports of the 1940s and 1950s helped solidify the interdependence of the federal government and farmers. The policy changes begun during the Progressive Era evolved into crop specialization, rationalization, and the consolidation of the 1970s, leading to the farm crisis of the 1980s. This dependence on single crops and subsidies made farmers wards of the state, a reversal of fortunes for the group of people who used to be trusted with caring for wards of the state. Instead of farmers helping the nation by taking dependent children, eventually the nation needed to help farmers retain their livelihoods.

The idea that "the family farm is the final stronghold against oppression, whether economic or political, and no tyranny or 'ism' will ever thrive in a country that grounds its agriculture on that base" remains a potent idea in the twenty-first century.[7] Even the topic of child labor on farms continues to provoke controversy. In 2012, the Obama administration suggested changes to child labor laws in order to ensure that children did not perform potentially dangerous work if they were employees on a farm, but immense pressure from groups like the Farm Bureau and the public outcry that followed, which claimed an attack on the family farm, derailed any attempt at reform. Weighing in on the manufactured controversy, former Alaska governor and television personality Sarah Palin wrote, "If I wanted America to fail, I'd ban kids from farm work." In response to the misleading publicity, the White House issued this statement, "The Obama administration is firmly committed to promoting family farmers and respecting the rural way of life, especially the role that parents and other family members play in passing those traditions down through the generations." When paired with the traditional idea that farm work is healthy for children, any attempt to intervene on the farm remains a politically charged move.[8]

The 1930s brought New Deal policies and increasing numbers of social welfare agencies, but the rise of foster care did not eliminate the need for institutions, a goal long sought after by reformers. To the contrary, farm placement declined, but the Depression worsened, and the number of children living in American institutions increased. By 1933, 102,000 children lived in foster homes, 140,000 lived in orphanages, and 220,000 remained with family members using benefits including mother's pensions.[9] Direct aid proved incapable of handling the needs of such an economic crisis. Only half of U.S. counties provided any mother's aid in 1931, and the counties participating paid out small sums. Nationwide the country spent only 0.04 percent of gross national product on this type of aid. These paltry efforts reflected not just the financial dilemmas of the time period, but the patriarchal control of the court systems that awarded aid and the concern that women might be less dependent on a male bread winner if mother's aid became too readily available.[10] Although the spending for mother's aid varied widely, the states of the Midwest participated more than any other region outside the Mid-Atlantic. In 1931, Ohio, Michigan, Wisconsin, and Illinois were all giving some amount of aid to more than six thousand families.[11] Alongside this problem, the increase in juvenile legal codes placed more children in reformatories. Despite efforts to ensure that "normal" children stayed out of institutional care by increasing support to keep them in homes with their parents, in areas with few social services or insufficient mother's pensions, dependent children continued to go to an institution.[12] The initial intention of the farm placement system had been institutional removal, but more children than ever before found themselves living inside a public or private institution.

Dependent children did benefit from increased New Deal relief provided in the form of the Federal Emergency Relief Act (FERA) in 1934 and Aid to

Dependent Children (ADC), a component of the Social Security Act (SSA) of 1935.[13] FERA turned direct aid for women over to the federal government, which provided an increase in the number of women who received funds, but the SSA placed more emphasis on old age insurance and other forms of aid, leaving funding shortages for women and children. Children's Bureau leaders such as Grace Abbot lobbied on behalf of ADC and ensured it resembled mother's aid, but because the program gave money only for children and none for mothers, families could not be maintained on ADC help alone. The habit of cutting women out of this program reflected similar tactics in Social Security, which focused on male workers. Not until 1939 was the program revised to give death benefits to women and children. As Linda Gordon notes, categorizing some benefits as earned and others as unearned led to a stigma regarding ADC and later Aid to Families with Dependent Children that remains in the twenty-first century.[14]

Unfortunately, the foster home proved to be unsuccessful in ways alarmingly similar to the practice of farm placement. Today, children's advocates point to startlingly reminiscent problems with dependent child care policy; social workers struggle with too many cases, while foster parents sometimes exploit the payment system by neglecting children and profiting from government money. Current policy has rekindled the pattern of moving children in and out of different homes, causing them to miss school and lose connections with family and friends. Siblings still face separation in foster care, and parents find that direct aid is sometimes not enough to maintain their family. The current system of foster care allows a wider variety of working-class Americans to participate by providing funds to offset the costs of care but prevents some foster parents from adopting those children because of a loss of financial support. The increased involvement of state and federal governments and the professionalization of social workers have proved incapable of handling the multifaceted issues of dependent children. Private charities still exist to care for children and to try and keep families together, but they continue to struggle with chronic shortages of funding.

As social welfare policy stagnates in the United States, dependent children find themselves at the mercy of a system that suffers from understaffing, funding cuts, and a myriad of ideas regarding the correct course of action. Today's foster children are trapped in a web of bureaucracy that undermines conscientious foster parents from being able to parent since everything from bike riding scrapes to haircuts must be approved by the placing agency. Historically, placement parents were able to parent as they saw fit; the problem was that many of them did not view themselves as parents. Foster parents must clear every decision with a social worker and sometimes a judge, while other children are lost inside the system. This vacillation between hyper-supervision and carelessness is not necessarily more effective than the neglect faced by placed-out children who received no supervision at all. Additionally, in foster care of the twenty-first century, children's safety and stability is compromised because of conflict between foster parents and agency workers who demand documentation and compliance over parenting skills, causing children to be moved in and out of homes when these adult issues result in foster parents quitting or children being removed from homes for issues of noncompliance with policy as opposed to mistreatment of any kind.[15] Children leaving abusive homes fail to get the mental health care they need and are sometimes placed into abusive situations. In the 1990s, acknowledging the vast problems with foster care, former Speaker of the House Newt Gingrich, himself a former dependent child, angered many when he suggested a return to orphans' homes in order to eliminate the problems of foster care. As anyone who studies institutional care knows, it came, and still comes, with its own set of hazards and problems. There seems to be no easy or perhaps affordable solution to the problems of dependent child care in the United States.[16]

Although losing local control of dependent child care became one of the largest changes over time, some local care options persisted into the mid-twentieth century. States continued to fund specialized institutions for children. Industrial schools, schools for the blind and deaf and feebleminded, and state orphans' homes remained vital components of state care for children.[17] Other institutions remained by changing the type of children whom they served. Counties and private charities also kept some children's institutions open. The Lucas County Children's Home not only still operated during the 1940s, it also continued to place children for light labor. As one prominent local family's request stated, "We don't wish to adopt a girl, however, we would appreciate having someone to live with us and help with the housework." The social worker who visited this home had the following to say about their fitness: "Parents too young but friends have girls from Home and they are determined to do so, too. It might work but Visitor is not certain, and since they are neighbors Home cannot very well refuse." The visitor also indicated that the two adults in the home seemed lazy, hinting that their status as members of a prominent local family might allow them more leisure than typical. Even though they could obviously afford hired help, a thirteen-year-old girl was placed in their household. During the 1940s, local farmers also asked to foster children from Lucas County. One owner-operator of a fifty-four-acre farm requested a boy between one and five years old because he and his wife had no children of their own, while another owner of a larger farm asked for an older high school age boy to help with light work on the farm. He and his wife had two small children in the home and came with excellent references.[18]

The Perry County Children's Home in Ohio also remained open until the late 1960s. In 1965, a sixty-eight-year-old man brought $100 to the home. In the ledger entry from 1900 it showed that as a three-year-old he had lived there for a single day before a family member came to claim him. His two siblings were placed with other people. He said the money was meant to repay the home for the care they provided him and for that of his sisters. He said he hoped it would help the superintendent provide for the children who remained in his care.[19] For this man, and tens of thousands like him, the web of local, state, and private institutions and agencies working to provide for dependent children faced a variety of challenges when trying to give children housing, training, and removal from bad influences; for more than fifty years, the farms of the Midwest helped meet those needs.

Notes

Introduction

1. Indenture Records, 1870, Montgomery County, Ohio, children's home, OHSL. Children's names and those of their placement parents have been used in cases where their information is open to the public, has been previously published, or digitized for the use of genealogists and researchers. Otherwise, the names from previously unpublished cases, like those from the Lucas County Children's Home, whose records were closed in 2013, have been shortened or omitted altogether.

2. Crenson, *Building the Invisible Orphanage*, 60.

3. Holt, *The Orphan Trains*. The Children's Aid Society name was used in other states by groups unaffiliated with the CASNY; O'Conner, *Orphan Trains*; Gordon, *The Great Arizona Orphan Abduction*.

4. *Laws Related to Interstate Placement of Children*.

5. Cmiel, *A Home of Another Kind*, 3.

6. Statistics used in Reef, *Alone in the World*, 54. A quantitative examination of census records to establish how many children were categorized as nonfamily would be a contribution to childhood, labor, and agricultural history, but that is not within the scope of this project.

7. Katz, *In the Shadow of the Poorhouse*, 14–15; White, "The History and Development of the Illinois Children's Home," 3.

8. Hammack, *Making the Nonprofit Sector in the United States*, 76. See also Franklin, *The Autobiography of Benjamin Franklin*, 135. The decline of the apprenticeship system in the United States has been attributed to a number of factors, including the lack of strong guild participation, land availability and expansion, and the problem of runaway apprentices; Elbaum, "Why Apprenticeship Persisted in Britain." They left the arrangement with one horse bridle and saddle, $10, and one set of clothing. See

Henry County, Indiana, Early Deed Records, Henry County Genealogical Services, www.hcgs.net, accessed January 31, 2008.

9. O'Conner, *Orphan Trains*; Holloran, *Boston's Wayward Children*, 32–35.

10. Rooke and Schnell, *Discarding the Asylum*.

11. Wall, "'My Constant Attension on My Sick Child,'" 162; Herndon and Murray, eds., *Children Bound to Labor*.

12. Mapes, *Sweet Tyranny*, 171.

13. First meeting in 1874 under the name Conference of Boards of Public Charity and operated by state board members, the NCCC adopted its new name in 1880 and began increasingly including private charity workers as opposed to state board members. In 1917, it became the National Conference of Social Work.

14. *Annual Report*, IBSC, 1891, 90.

15. Lyman Alden, "The Shady Side of Placing Out," NCCC, 1885, 202.

16. *Biennial Report*, MSPS, 1882, 43–44.

17. Swartz, "Mothering for the State," 585.

18. Riney-Kehrberg, *Childhood on the Farm*, 169.

19. Hindman, *Child Labor*, 31.

20. Riney-Kehrberg, *The Nature of Childhood*, ch. 1; idem, *Childhood on the Farm*, 51–54.

21. *Home Life for Childhood*, no. 4 (July 1919), RJDL. See also *Home Life for Childhood*, no. 5 (1917): 10, which defined dependent children as "any male child who while under the age of 17 years or any female under the age of 18 is for any reason destitute homeless or abandoned or dependent upon the public for support or has not proper paternal care or guardianship or habitually begs or receives alms or is found living in any house of ill fame."

22. Folks, *The Care of Destitute, Neglected, and Delinquent Children*, 102.

23. F. M. Gregg, "Placing Out Children," NCCC, 1892, 415.

24. Holt, *The Orphan Trains*, 62, 24, 7. Holt does not claim that indenturing ended with the CASNY. Trammell, "Orphan Train Myths and Legal Realities."

25. Zelizer, *Pricing the Priceless Child*, 172–182; Folks, *The Care of Destitute, Neglected, and Delinquent Children*, 29.

26. Huron County Infirmary Records, CAC-BGSU; 1860, 1870 U.S. Census, s.v. "Josiah Sutherland," Ruggles Township, Ashland County, Ohio. All census records accessed via ancestry.com.

27. "Farm Law," *Michigan Farmer*, Detroit, July 1, 1884, 5.

28. Only Massachusetts used payments for the care of dependent children with regularity before 1900. The state used these payments as a way to place children who could not be expected to contribute to a household income.

29. Tiffin, *In Whose Best Interest?* 98.

30. Hart, *A Home for Every Child*, 14, 87.

31. Carp, ed., *Adoption in America*, 9.

32. Book 1, MCCH; 1910 U.S. Census, s.v. "John M. Reeder," Bethel Township, Miami County, Ohio. The specific records for each child are organized by name.

33. Book 1, MCCH; 1920 U.S. Census, s.v. "Ella Schnell," Troy Ward 4, Miami County, Ohio; Book 1, MCCH; 1930 U.S. Census, s.v. "William A. Crowell," Newberry Township, Miami County, Ohio. William and his parents lived with his grandfather and he was listed as "adopted grandson." In 1943, Roy lived in Piqua with his wife and worked as a painter; see Piqua City Directory, 1943, accessed via ancestry.com.

34. Correspondence dated September 17, 1943, Lucas County Children's Home, CAC-BGSU. The Lucas Co. Children's Services Records, including those of the institution, were closed in 2013 and remained closed. The archive requested that the box numbers of the collection not be printed, and I have honored that request.

35. Mintz, *Huck's Raft*, chs. 8–9; Zelizer, *Pricing the Priceless Child*, ch. 1.

36. Effland, "When Rural Does not Equal Agricultural," 489.

37. Katz, *In the Shadow of the Poorhouse*, 85.

38. Riney-Kehrberg, *Childhood on the Farm*, 170.

39. Katz, *In the Shadow of the Poorhouse*, 122–124.

40. Hart, "A Nation's Need for Adoption," 182.

Chapter 1. The Rural Ideal

1. "Letter from E.I.R.," *Annual Report*, MSPS, 1884, 79–80.

2. C. D. Randall, "Michigan: The Child, The State," NCCC, 1888, 264; Bellingham, "Institution and Family."

3. Cayton, "The Anti-Region."

4. M. M. Southworth, "Homes for Children Wanted," *Ohio Farmer*, Cleveland, May 2, 1895, American Periodicals Series Online, 352, http://search.proquest.com/docview/137266205?accountid=7116.

5. Welle, "'Things which I was never interested in,'" 12.

6. Byron C. Matthews, "The Duty of the State to Dependent Children," NCCC, 1898, 371.

7. Quoted in Hagenstein, Gregg, and Donahue, eds., *American Georgics*, 9.

8. Griswold, *Farming and Democracy*, 30–31; P. Thompson, "Thomas Jefferson and Agrarian Philosophy," 118–139.

9. Kindell, "Washingtonian Agrarianism"; Hofstadter, *The Age of Reform*, 25.

10. Demos, *Past, Present, and Personal*, 58–59; Reid, "The Agrarian Tradition and Urban Problems."

11. Danbom, "Romantic Agrarianism in Twentieth Century America," 1; Barillas, *The Midwestern Pastoral*, 37–50; P. Thompson, "Thomas Jefferson and Agrarian Philosophy," 44–48.

12. Quoted in Brownwell, "The Agrarian and Urban Ideals," 576. Although ownership increased the ideal conditions of rural life, for the placement of dependent children, ownership of a farm was not a requirement. In the census of 1880, approximately 20 percent of Midwesterners claimed to be tenants or renters, but the percentages vary—in Michigan, for example, only 10 percent of farmers claimed tenant status.

See Heller and Houdek, "Farm Tenants and Landlords," 598. For a brief summary of labor and tenancy data from the 1900 and 1910 census, see Coulter, "Agricultural Laborers in the United States," 40–44.

13. C. Nelson, "The Orphan in American Literature," 79–91.

14. Baum, "The Burden of Myth"; James Whitcomb Riley poem text "Little Orphan Annie," www.poetry-archive.com/r/little_orphant_annie.html, accessed March 13, 2012.

15. Montgomery, *Anne of Green Gables*; Erisman, "Transcendentalism for American Youth." Kate Douglas Wiggin also discussed the role of kindergarten education at the 1888 NCCC meeting held in Buffalo.

16. Bowen, *Abby Blake*.

17. Morris, *Farming For Boys*; Nelson, *Little Strangers*, 44.

18. "Deliver Us From Evil," *Ohio Farmer*, Cleveland, August 10, 1893, 113.

19. J. E. Sanford, "The Hope Farm Man," *Forum*, New York, July 1916, 209.

20. Luther Burbank "The Training of the Human Plant," *Home Life for Childhood*, no. 4 (July 1919), RJDL.

21. Mrs. William Sullivan, "Our Boys on the Farm," *Michigan Farmer*, January 19, 1907, 71.

22. Burns, *Pastoral Inventions*.

23. Dorn, "The Rural Ideal and Agrarian Realities," 58.

24. Hagenstein, Gregg, and Donahoe, eds., *American Georgics*, 166.

25. Hagenstein, Gregg, and Donahoe, eds., *American Georgics*, 170.

26. J. L. Irwin, "The Health of the Farm Boy," *Christian Observer*, Louisville, August 7, 1901, 19.

27. Babener, "Bitter Nostalgia."

28. Brace, ed., *The Life of Charles Loring Brace*.

29. Nelson, *Little Strangers*, 22.

30. Ross, "Society Children," 115.

31. Tiffin, *In Whose Best Interest?* 89.

32. Quoted in Burns, *Pastoral Inventions*, 311; Askeland, "'The means of draining the city of these children.'"

33. Charles Loring Brace, "The Best Method of Founding Children's Charities in Towns and Villages," NCCC, 1880, 232.

34. Atack and Bateman, *To Their Own Soil*; Argersinger and Argersinger, "The Machine Breakers," 397–398.

35. Brace, "What is the Best Method?" 23.

36. Crenson, *Building the Invisible Orphanage*, 211. Some of Brace's farm-bound children actually ended up working in industry along the Mississippi. See Hindman, *Child Labor*, 125.

37. Meigs V. Crouse, "Methods," in *Fifth Annual Ohio State Proceedings of Conference of Charities*, 22.

38. "Boys in the West," *The Youth's Companion*, Boston, August 21, 1879, 280.

39. George J. Manson, "The Farm as a Means of Reform," *Christian Union*, New York, August 8, 1889, 156.

40. *Annual Report*, IBSC, 1912, 143.

Notes to Chapter 1

41. "The Industrial School," *Cleveland Morning Daily Herald*, March 6, 1873.
42. Bush, *Who Gets a Childhood?* 33. See also Ashby, *Saving the Waifs*, 24.
43. http://dlib.nyu.edu/findingaids/html/nyhs/childrensaidsociety_at.html.
44. *Children's Home Farm Book*, vol. 24, CHLA.
45. *Annual Report of the Trustees of the Illinois Soldiers' Orphans' Home for the Year 1893*, 12.
46. Lucas County annual reports, 1915, 1902, CAC-BGSU.
47. Brownwell, "The Agrarian and Urban Ideals," 577.
48. Cmiel, *A Home of Another Kind*, 70.
49. Ramey, *Childcare in Black and White*, 28, 56.
50. Charity Organization Society of New York, *The Survey* 32 (1914): 487; *Annual Report*, OBSC, 1892, 358. Foundations and other charities funded trips to the rural countryside for poor children. By 1891, 94,000 children from New York City had participated in fresh air trips. The practice continues today with New York's Fresh Air Fund. See Holt, *The Orphan Trains*, 17.
51. See Keppel, "The Myth of Agrarianism"; Kohlstedt, "'A Better Crop of Boys and Girls.'" The Salvation Army also sent people to farms by way of "farm colonies" for unemployed urban residents. See Danbom, *Born in the Country*, 163; Riney-Kehrberg, *The Nature of Childhood*, 70.
52. Crenson, *Building the Invisible Orphanage*, 39; Riney-Kehrberg, *The Nature of Childhood*, 6.
53. Holt, *Indian Orphanages*, 102, 209, 190.
54. *Biennial Report*, MNSPS, 1919, 10–11.
55. Beito, "Mooseheart," 64.
56. Beito, "Mooseheart," 85.
57. "Incorrigible Children and Reformatories," *Ohio Farmer*, September 25, 1902, 228.
58. Mennel, "The Family System of Common Farmers," 148; Bush, *Who Gets a Childhood?*
59. Hyde Bailey, *The Country Life Movement*, 20.
60. Brilla H. Cartwright, "The Blessings and Needs of a Farm Home," *Coleman's Rural World*, St. Louis, January 2, 1901, 6.
61. *Annual Report Cincinnati Children's Home, 1876*, CHLA, 31.
62. *Annual Report Cincinnati Children's Home, 1884*, CHLA, 9.
63. Longman, *Report of the Placing of Children in Family Homes*.
64. Langsam, *Children West*, 26.
65. Quoted in Zelizer, *Pricing the Priceless Child*, 179.
66. *Laws Related to Interstate Placement of Children*. In the early decades of the CASNY orphan trains, the state of Indiana accepted the most children. See the CASNY website, http://www.childrensaidsociety.org/about/history/orphan-trains.
67. Effland, "Agrarianism and Child Labor Policy for Agriculture," 285.
68. Lauck, *The Lost Region*, 39.
69. Cronon, *Nature's Metropolis*; Shortridge, *The Middle West*.

70. Mapes, *Sweet Tyranny*, 125.

71. Lauck, *The Lost Region*, 24.

72. In 1900, 5.6 percent of Indiana's population was foreign born, and blacks accounted for 2.29 percent of the population. In 1920, blacks still accounted for only 3 percent of the population, and the percentage of foreign-born individuals had dropped to 5 percent. Indiana was the "least ethnically diverse" state in the Old Northwest. Within Indiana in the nineteenth century both blacks and foreign-born were more likely to be urban than rural residents, a pattern that persisted throughout the twentieth century. Steinson, "Rural Life in Indiana," 229.

73. Mapes, *Sweet Tyranny*, 68; Gjerde, *The Minds of the West*, ch. 6.

74. Cayton and Gray, eds., *The Identity of the American Midwest*, 17.

75. Cayton and Gray, eds., *The Identity of the American Midwest*, 143.

76. For information on the adoption of agricultural technology, see Hurt, *American Agriculture* and *Agricultural Technology in the Twentieth Century*; Atack and Bateman, *To Their Own Soil*. Labor concerns are also discussed in Bowers, *The Country Life Movement In America*, ch. 1.

77. "Help Needed in the Country," *Ohio Farmer*, April 12, 1894, 290.

78. "Would make tramps work on farms," *Perrysburg Journal*, October 11, 1907, 3.

79. Fitzgerald, *Every Farm a Factory*; Wells, "The Changing Nature of Country Roads."

80. Argersinger and Argersinger, "The Machine Breakers," 396.

81. Argersinger and Argersinger, "The Machine Breakers," 402.

82. Nelson, *Farm and Factory*, 9. Priscilla Ferguson Clement points out that hired neighbor children were not typically treated like servants because they possessed parental supervision nearby and enjoyed the power to leave, even though they were probably hired out by their parents because of financial difficulty at home. See Clement, *Growing Pains*, 126.

83. Schob, *Hired Hands and Plowboys*, 218; C. Thompson and Warber, *Social and Economic Survey*, 5, 11–13. For a 1901 study that analyzed the various wages around the country for farm labor, see Dodge, *American Farm Labor*.

84. Atack and Bateman, *To Their Own Soil*, chs. 11, 13.

85. Danbom, *Born in the Country*, 167–175.

86. C. Thompson and Warber, *Social and Economic Survey*, 8.

87. Shover, *First Majority, Last Minority*, 123.

88. Cruse and Cruse, *History of the Children*, 339 . During World War I, Ed's twin brother, Fred, died in France and Ed worked at a grocery in Terre Haute. Eventually he married and moved to Kansas City.

89. Cruse and Cruse, *History of the Children*, 181; Book 1, MCCH .

90. Cruse and Cruse, *History of the Children*, 452.

91. 1880 U.S. Census, s.v. "Jacob Cramer," Madison Township, Hancock County, Ohio; Book 1, MCCH.

92. Although this placement father became the stepfather to Roy, that family environment did not prevent him from getting into trouble. He went to the reform

school and ended up in jail for rape. That conviction sent his two daughters to the Rose Orphan Home in 1930 by order of the court.

93. Higbie, "Rural Work," 64.

94. Book 1, MCCH. Ray was Roy's brother. Their father lived at the children's home in 1880 but ran away the same year.

95. "More about farm labor," *Cleveland Morning Daily Herald*, January 21, 1873. Some locations reported paying as little as $10 per month for a hired hand, but farmers still complained about the cost. For those not interested in paying this small amount, a dependent child provided an even better bargain. See Argersinger and Argersinger, "The Machine Breakers," 399; Dodge, *American Farm Labor*, 117.

96. Mapes, *Sweet Tyranny*, 71.

97. Riney-Kehrberg, *Childhood on the Farm*, 46–54; Holt, *The Orphan Trains*, 30.

98. Craig and Weiss, "Hours at Work," 23; Gillette, "The Drift to the City."

99. *Annual Report*, MSPS, 1878, 36.

100. Schob, *Hired Hands and Plowboys*, 200–201; Clement, *Growing Pains*, 130.

101. *Annual Report*, MSPS, 1874, 57.

102. Letter, June 2, 1884, vol. 53, General Protestant Orphan Home Records, 1849–1970, Mss 1043, CHLA.

103. Holt, *Children of the Western Plains*, 70.

104. Danbom, *Born in the Country*, 154.

105. McConnell, *The Decline of American Democracy*, ch. 1.

106. McMath, *American Populism*, 17; Griswold, *Farming and Democracy*, 144–145.

107. Riney-Kehrberg, *Childhood on the Farm*, ch. 1; see also Effland, "Agrarianism and Child Labor Policy for Agriculture," 284.

108. Sanders, *Roots of Reform*, 102; Cruse and Cruse, *History of the Children*, 460.

109. Wiggin, *Children's Rights*, 11–15; Mintz, *Huck's Raft*, 183–184.

110. Gratton and Moen, "Immigration, Culture, and Child Labor in the United States"; McGill, *Children in Agriculture*.

111. Gjerde, *The Minds of the West*, 150.

112. Sophie Minton, "Family Life Versus Institutional Life," in *Proceedings of the National Conference of Charities and Corrections*, 46–47.

113. Higbee, "Rural Work," 69.

114. Ross, "Society Children," 140.

115. *Biennial Report*, MSPS, 1882, 44.

116. Hall, *Youth*, 226, 31–34; Nelson, *Little Strangers*, 54.

117. Bowers, *The Country Life Movement in America*.

118. U.S. Country Life Commission, *Report of the Commission on Country Life*, 91–95; Peters and Morgan, "The Country Life Commission."

Chapter 2. "Qualify them for the duties of life"

1. William Doyle to Comfort Lewis, January 5, 1857, Huron County infirmary, CAC-BGSU; 1870 U.S. Census, s.v. "Comfort Lewis," Hartland Township, Huron County, Ohio; 1880 U.S. Census, s.v. "Comfort Lewis," Norwalk Township, Huron County,

Ohio. Huron County did similar indentures during the 1850s; in 1855, directors of the Huron County Infirmary bound Henry E. Underhill, age five, to Francis Briggs, a farmer with forty improved acres of land. Henry remained on the Briggs farm in some capacity until at least 1870.

2. Kleinberg, *Widows and Orphans First*, 61.

3. Katz, *In The Shadow of the Poorhouse*, 107–113.

4. Johnson, *The Almshouse*, 10.

5. Katz, *In the Shadow of the Poorhouse*, 109.

6. Gollaher, *Voice for the Mad*, 206; "Board of Health Report," *Daily Ohio Statesman*, June 22, 1867, image 3; "Ohio News: Happenings in the Buckeye State," *Perrysburg Journal*, May 17, 1907, 2. These write-ups included details of "vermin covered inmates" strapped to beds and the infirmary as a "nusance."

7. *County Poor Asylums—Construction and Management: Reports of Visits by Secretary, Statistics of County Poor Expenses* (Indianapolis: n.p., 1890), IHS.

8. *Annual Report*, OBSC, 1868, 23.

9. Van Wert Infirmary, 1885–1891, CAC-BGSU.

10. *Annual Report*, OBSC, 1888, 30. Julius Thompson, described as a "colored tramp," was convicted of setting the fire.

11. *Annual Report*, OBSC, 1867, 36. Although most Midwestern states had removal laws in place by the beginning of the 1890s, Illinois did not force total removal of children from poor farms until the 1910s.

12. *Annual Report*, IBSC, 1894, 11.

13. *Indiana Quarterly Bulletin of Charities and Corrections*, December 1896, 17.

14. Kleinberg, *Widows and Orphans First*, 61.

15. *Tenth Annual Convention of the Trustees and Superintendents of the Children's Homes in Ohio*, n.p., 1891, 19–20.

16. Katz, *In The Shadow of the Poorhouse*, 123.

17. Amos Butler, "Saving the Children," NCCC, 1901, 206; Homer Folks, "The Removal of Children from Almshouses," NCCC, 1894, 119–136; see also Hasci, "Orphanages as a National Institution," 233.

18. "The Miami County Home," http://www.thetroyhistoricalsociety.org/m-county/MiamiCountyHome/MiamiCountyHomeListings.htm.

19. Book 1, MCCH.

20. White, "The History and Development of the Illinois Children's Home," 5.

21. Rose Orphan Home Ledger 1, "Records," committee notes, 1874–1889, 12–15, VCPL.

22. Vigo County Board of Children's Guardians Report, 1896, 5, ISL; *Benevolent Institutions 1904*, 70. The Rose Orphan Home board of directors almost immediately changed its policy about full orphans after discovering there were not actually many children who fit that description. Further flexibility followed, but they did not admit all dependent children from Vigo County.

23. *Second Annual Report of the Northern Indiana Orphans Home*, 1884, ISL.

24. Cornelius and Kay, *Women of Conscience*, 54.

25. *Second Annual Report of the Board of Managers of the Northern Indiana Orphans Home*, 1884, ISL.

26. Cornelius and Kay, *Women of Conscience*, 52–65. They only received $3.75 per month per child from the county.

27. White, "The History and Development of the Illinois Children's Home," 6. In 1882, Illinois counted 589 children living in poor farms. The problem of children in Illinois poor farms remained. Between 1908 and 1920, the Fulton County, Illinois, poor farm housed more than eighty children. See also *Fulton County, Illinois Almshouse Register, 1908–1920*, IRAD.

28. *First Annual Report*, MSPS, 1874; Foster, "Preventative Work in Michigan." Kansas also operated a state orphan's home, but it began in 1887 as the Soldier's and Sailor's Orphan's Home before admitting dependent children from across the state two years later. After 1909, it was known as the State Orphan's Home.

29. Crenson, *Building the Invisible Orphanage*, 55–56.

30. Between 1898 and 1899, Ohio's poor farms contained approximately five hundred children. The Ohio Board of State Charities noted that these children lived there contrary to state law. The number of children living in Indiana poor farms between 1865 and 1900 is difficult to discern because some data are missing and residents went uncounted. An approximation of around nine hundred children living in poor farms remained steady throughout the region until the late 1880s. *Annual Report*, OBSC, 1885, 8; *Annual Report*, OBSC, 1891, 48. Stark and Columbiana Counties operated a single children's home known as the Fairmount Children's Home. It was located in Alliance, Ohio.

31. Joseph Byers, "The County Homes of Ohio," NCCC, 1901, 237.

32. *Annual Report*, OBSC, 1891, 48, 346. At the same meeting, the representative from Jackson County admitted that the commissioners in his county demanded that children remain in the infirmary, contrary to law.

33. *Proceedings of the Ohio State Conference on Dependent Children held at Dayton, Ohio*, 6.

34. *Annual Report*, OBSC, 1882, 39.

35. Sangamon County Poor Farm Inmate Records, 34.

36. Gittens, *Poor Relations*, 24.

37. Jeffers, "The Development in Indiana of Public Resources."

38. *Annual Report*, OBSC, 1890, 59. Not all of the children remaining in poor farms were considered "placeable."

39. *Annual Report*, OBSC, 1892, 18.

40. Homer Folks, "The Removal of Children from Almshouses," NCCC, 1894, 124.

41. Crenson, *Building the Invisible Orphanage*, 158. Ohio had enough children's homes in existence by 1881 that superintendents came together to found the Ohio State Convention of Children's Homes as a way to bring together superintendents, matrons, teachers, and other interested parties. In 1892, this group was subsumed into the State Conference of Charities and Corrections.

42. Hasci, *Second Home*.

43. *Tenth Annual Convention*, 20.
44. Ramey, *Childcare in Black and White*, 71.
45. Lucas County Children's Home, 1902, 15, CAC-BGSU.
46. Ramey, *Childcare in Black and White*, 110.
47. Cruse and Cruse, *History of the Children*, 152.
48. *Annual Report*, MSPS, 1877, 44.
49. "Letter from a fourteen year old boy, September 17, 1892," in *Third Triennial Report of the Rose Orphan Home for the Three Years Ending Sept. 30, 1892* (Terre Haute: C. W. Brown, 1892), 21, ISL.
50. Book 1, MCCH; 1910 U.S. Census, s.v. "Viola Madison," Piqua Ward 2, Miami County, Ohio; 1920 U.S. Census, s.v. "Viola Madison," Dayton Ward 1, Montgomery County, Ohio.
51. *Annual Report*, OBCS, 1890, 48.
52. *Annual Report*, MSPS, 1875, 38.
53. Lucas County Children's Home, 1902, 15–17, CAC-BGSU.
54. *Proceedings of the Ohio State Conference on Dependent Children*, 1914, 73.
55. *Annual Report*, OBSC, 1882, 33–35.
56. *Proceedings of the Ohio State Conference on Dependent Children*, 1915, 25.
57. *Annual Report*, IBSC, 1901, 121.
58. *Indiana Quarterly Bulletin of Charities and Corrections*, June 1907, 217; Hurley, *One Child at a Time*, 33. Other examples of farm training schools are included in Thomas Ring, "Catholic Child Helping Agencies in the United States," NCCC, 1896, 333.
59. Holt, *The Orphan Trains*, 89.
60. Holt, "The Orphan Trains," 213; Bellingham, "Institution and Family," S50–S51.
61. Book 1, MCCH.
62. Fulton County records, CAC-BGSU; 1900 U.S. Census, s.v. "Frank Snow," Clinton Township, Fulton County, Ohio.
63. Williams County records, CAC-BGSU; 1900 U.S. Census, s.v. "Bessie Bostater," Bryan, Williams County, Ohio.
64. Records of Indenture, 1880–1904, Miami County Children's Home (Knoop Children's Home), 67, OHSL.
65. Ledger, Belmont County, Ohio, children's home, 1881, OHSL.
66. Murray and Herndon, "Markets for Children," 363, 367; Dodge, *American Farm Labor*, 117.
67. Contract for boys and girls, Ledger, Greene County, Ohio, children's home, 36–37, OHSL.
68. Crouse, "Methods," in *Fifth Annual Ohio State Conference of Charities*, 23.
69. *Annual Report*, Lucas County Children's Home, 1896, 23, CAC-BGSU.
70. Book 1, MCCH; 1900 U.S. Census, s.v. "Peter Deweese," east half of Paulding Township, Paulding County, Ohio; 1920 U.S. Census, s.v. "Martha Deweese," Washington Township, Miami County, Ohio; "State News Items," *Perrysburg Journal*, November 8, 1889, 1.

71. 1880 U.S. Census, s.v. "David W. Bash," "Alice Walters," "Norman Johnston," "Emmet Deaty," Madison Township, Hancock County, Ohio. The same enumeration listed Christopher and Sarah Haugh as "keeping" five-year-old Della Lewis along with twelve-year-old Oscar Patrick, who worked on their farm. The enumerator did make distinctions; Sarah Bats is listed as adopted, seventeen-year-old Candace Kline was listed as housekeeper. Sarah's sister Bertha Bats lived with Dr. Benjamin Evans, who was "keeping" the seven-year-old.

72. 1900, 1910 U.S. Census, s.v. "Isaac Gruber," Pleasant Hill Township, Miami County, Ohio.

73. 1920, 1930 U.S. Census, s.v. "John Gall," Newton Township, Miami County, Ohio; Ohio Obituary Index, Robert V. Fahel, July 19, 1990, accessed via ancestry.com. Robert's biological parents were William and Ann Fahel (Grosse).

74. 1910 U.S. Census, s.v. "Anna B. Green," Piqua Ward 3, Miami County, Ohio.

75. Book 1, MCCH; 1900 U.S. Census, s.v. "Hattie Jefferson," Washington Township, Miami County, Ohio; 1920 U.S. Census, s.v. "Harriet Reiter," Piqua Ward 3, Miami County, Ohio. Hattie's uncle appears to have been unemployed in 1900, and her aunt worked as a laundress, which may help explain why they could not support her.

76. Zipf, *Labor of Innocents*.

77. "Home for Destitute Colored Children," *Friends' Intelligencer*, July 13, 1861, 276.

78. Cowger, "Custodians of Social Justice."

79. Book 1, MCCH; 1900 U.S. Census, s.v. "Howard Brady," Piqua Ward 5, Miami County, Ohio.

80. Loewen, *Sundown Towns*, 249. Loewen established that nearby Springfield, Ohio, had three distinct events—1904, 1906, and 1908—in which whites tried to drive African Americans from the city (92).

81. Book 1, MCCH; Kounse, *Annotated Lawrence County Children's Home Register*, 99.

82. Defiance County infirmary minutes, May 1, 1876, CAC-BGSU; 1880 U.S. Census, s.v. "Harvey Waters," Nobel Township, Defiance County, Ohio.

83. Defiance County infirmary minutes, May 1, 1876, CAC-BGSU; 1870, 1880 U.S. Census, s.v. "George Parry," Flatrock Township, Henry County, Ohio.

84. Loewen, *Sundown Towns*, 9.

85. Ramey, *Childcare in Black and White*, 127.

86. "Colored Families Attention," Lucas County Children's Home records, CAC-BGSU.

87. Miami County Children's Home records, loose papers from ledger, letter dated January 3, 1935, MS collection 5817 Record of Inmates, OHSL.

88. Gordon, *The Great Arizona Orphan Abduction*, 13; Crenson, *Building the Invisible Orphanage*, 41–44.

89. Creson, *Building the Invisible Orphanage*, 132.

90. "The Children's Home of Cincinnati," in Fulton, CO Correspondence, CAC-BGSU.

91. Putnam County Infirmary records, August 1899, CAC-BGSU; Kounse, *Annotated Lawrence County Children's Home Register*, 45.
92. Putnam County Infirmary records, 1906, CAC-BGSU.
93. Wyandot County Infirmary records, CAC-BGSU, 95; Pamphlets, Lucas County Children's Home records, CAC-BGSU; Morton, "The Transformation of Catholic Orphanages," 156.
94. Cruse and Cruse, *History of the Children*, 181; Folks, *The Care of Destitute, Neglected, and Delinquent Children*, 122.
95. *Biennial Report*, MNSPS, 1912, 332.
96. *Annual Report*, Lucas County, 1896, CAC-BGSU, 23.
97. Cruse and Cruse, *History of the Children*, 545.
98. Again, the complete records for Miami County are instructive. If known, the birthplace of the child was listed because Miami County did not want to care for children who were not residents of the county. But very few foreign birthplaces were listed, although sometimes a parent's nationality was noted. See also Riney-Kehrberg, *Childhood on the Farm*, 162.
99. Book 1, MCCH.
100. Crenson, *Building the Invisible Orphanage*, 80–81.
101. *Annual Report*, OBSC, 1891, 74–127.
102. During World War I, the Indiana Visiting Department consisted almost entirely of women; five women and one man reported to Field Service Supervisor J. A. Brown. See also *Annual Report*, IBSC, 1919, 164; *Biennial Report*, MNSPS, 1900, 4.
103. *Annual Report*, MSPS, 1877, 23; *Annual Report*, OBSC, 1891, 95. The terms of Highland County's arrangement with Cincinnati were that the county sent two suits of clothing, paid the rail fare, and paid $30 for each child.
104. *Annual Report*, OBSC, 1882, 9–10. Governor Foster also wanted this agent to help place rehabilitated prisoners.
105. *Tenth Annual Convention*, 1891, 19.
106. *Biennial Report*, MSPS, 1882, 55.
107. *Annual Report*, Children's Home of Cincinnati, 1866–1868, 13, CHLA.
108. *Annual Report*, Children's Home of Cincinnati, 1875, CHLA.
109. Anders, "The History of Child Welfare in Cincinnati," 140.
110. Crouse, "Methods," in *Fifth Annual Ohio State Conference of Charities*, 22.
111. Hurley, *One Child at a Time*, 53; *Annual Report*, Children's Home of Cincinnati, 1880, 7, CHLA.
112. *Annual Report*, OBSC, 1891, 320.
113. *Annual Report*, OBSC, 1883, 42.
114. Fulton County, CAC-BGSU.
115. *Biennial Report*, MSPS, 1882, 43; *Annual Convention of Trustees Ohio Children's Homes*, 1891, 54.
116. *Biennial Report*, MSPS, 1882, 28. Alden placed approximately 375 children during this biennial period, and 148 were returned to the school. *Annual Report*,

OBSC, 1892, 403; Hurley, *One Child at a Time*, 53; *Annual Report*, Children's Home of Cincinnati, 1880, 7, CHLA. Green also maintained contact with about 300 of the 2,500 children he visited through letters after their placements ended. *Annual Report*, Children's Home of Cincinnati, 1879, 10, CHLA. As an example, in 1880, Green personally visited 294 families with placed-out children.

117. Alden, "The Shady Side of Placing Out," NCCC, 1885, 202–207; Cruse and Cruse, *History of the Children*, 338.

118. Quoted in Robert W. Hebberd, "Placing out Children: Dangers of Careless Methods," NCCC, 1899, 172.

119. *Annual Report*, OBSC, 1892, 15.

120. *Biennial Report*, MSPS, 1884, 53.

121. *Annual Report*, OBSC, 1892, 32.

122. *Annual Report*, IBSC, 1898.

123. Crenson, *Building the Invisible Orphanage*, 151–154.

124. *Annual Report*, OBSC, 1892, 37; *Indiana Quarterly Bulletin of Charities and Corrections*, December 1896, 89.

125. *Indiana Quarterly Bulletin of Charities and Corrections*, October 1895, 7.

126. Holt, *The Orphan Trains*, 115. Holt used the year 1893 to determine an approximate number of children sent to Indiana.

127. *Annual Report*, IBSC, 1892, 61–62. Emphasis original.

128. Broadsides, New York Juvenile Asylum Train Records, ALPL.

129. Kidder and Clarke, *Orphan Trains and their Precious Cargo*.

130. Lucas County Children's Home collection, CAC-BGSU.

131. "Homes for Children Wanted," *Ohio Farmer*, May 2, 1895, 352. Hardin County did not have its own children's home and was almost entirely rural. Fairmount Children's Home was the joint institution for Columbiana and Stark Counties.

132. *Second Annual Report of the Northern Indiana Orphan's Home*, 1884, Children's Aid Society of Indiana, ISL.

133. *Report*, State Board of Administration, Illinois, 1914.

134. *Report*, State Board of Administration, Illinois, 1910, 1912, 1916.

135. *Report*, State Board of Administration, Illinois, 1913, 18.

136. Fulton County Poor Asylum Inmate Monthly Roll, 1910–1917, IRAD; *Report*, State Board of Administration, Illinois, 1913, 19.

137. Registers, Belmont County Children's Home, Series 3182, OHSL.

138. Hurley, *One Child at a Time*, 33.

139. *Annual Report*, OBSC, 1893, 363.

140. Kounse, *Annotated Lawrence County Children's Home Register*, 76, 162.

141. *Annual Report*, OBSC, 1892, 362. Between 1853 and 1865, Indiana accepted the largest number of orphan train children of any state, numbering approximately 1,326. See Holt, *The Orphan Trains*, ch. 1; Cook, "Experiences of Orphan Train Riders."

142. *Annual Report*, OBSC, 1892, 362–364.

143. *Proceedings of the Fifth Annual Ohio State Conference of Charities and Corrections* (Columbus: Westbot Co., 1896), 22.

144. *Biennial Report*, MNSPS, 1904, 20.

145. *Annual Report*, Lucas County Children's Home, 1896; *Indiana Quarterly Bulletin of Charities and Corrections*, December 1896, 19.

146. *Annual Report*, OBSC, 1891, 319.

147. *Indiana Quarterly Bulletin of Charities and Correction*, December 1895, 30.

148. Lucas County Children's Home, CAC-BGSU.

149. *Annual Report*, OBSC, 1892, 361–365.

150. *Annual Report*, OBSC, 1892, 401.

151. Crenson, *Building the Invisible Orphanage*, 156.

Chapter 3. "The hideous consequences"

1. Darke County, "Record of Inmates," OHSL; 1870 U.S. Census, s.v. "Ann Mosey," Harrison Township, Preble County, Ohio; 1860 U.S. Census, s.v. "Solomon Poe," Monroe Township, Darke County, Ohio.

2. Riley, *The Life and Legacy of Annie*, 6–11; "Annie Oakley," PBS *American Experience* transcript, www.pbs.org/wgbh/americanexperience/features/transcript/oakley-transcript/, accessed March 16, 2012. While it is possible that Anne was abused in the Bosse/Reynolds (Boose/Rannals) household, her naming them "Wolves" is interesting because living nearby were two large families with the surname Wolf. She may have been leased out to one of these families. See 1870 U.S. Census, s.v. "Jacob Wolf," "William Wolf," Harrison Township, Preble County, Ohio.

3. Pleck, *Domestic Tyranny*, 77.

4. Ohio law, Sec. 6984a, passed April 15, 1884; "The ABC's of Foster Care," 11; Pleck, *Domestic Tyranny*.

5. *Biennial Report*, MNSPS, 1900, 28.

6. *Biennial Report*, MNSPS, 1900, 35.

7. Solomon, the other Darke County half-orphan who lived with Anne at least briefly, went on to marry and have children, but lost his farm in 1881 to taxes and later remained in Ohio working as a butcher.

8. Pleck, *Domestic Tyranny*, 128; Rooke and Schnell, *Discarding the Asylum*, 143.

9. Gordon, "The Politics of Sexual Child Abuse," 57.

10. Gordon, *Heroes of Their Own Lives*, 9–11; Vandepol, "Dependent Children"; Pleck, *Domestic Tyranny*.

11. Tiffin, *In Whose Best Interest?* 208–209.

12. Gardner, "Home Placing," NCCC, 1901, 239.

13. Book 1, MCCH.

14. Meigs V. Crouse, "Methods," in *Fifth Annual Ohio Proceedings of Conference of Charities*, 23.

15. *Biennial Report*, MNSPS, 1900, 9, 17.

16. Longman, *Report of the Placing of Children*.

17. Record of Inmates, Champaign County Children's Home, State Archive Series 5344, OHSL; Miami County Children's Home, Record of Indentures, no. 371, State Archive Series 5816, OHSL.

18. Book 1, MCCH.

19. Cruse and Cruse, *History of the Children*, 456.

20. Folks, "Some Developments of the Boarding Out System," 143.

21. *Biennial Report*, MNSPS, 1900, 17.

22. Cruse and Cruse, *History of the Children*, 452. Lyman Alden, who placed Myrtle originally, died in 1904, and his son, Ernest, took over the management of the institution for the next forty years.

23. Argersinger and Argersinger, "The Machine Breakers," 395.

24. *Biennial Report*, MNSPS, 1890, 58; *Annual Report*, IBSC, 1900, 125.

25. Record of Indentures, 1886–1921, Brown County Children's Home, State Archive Series 3199, OHSL; *Annual Report*, MSPS, 1884, 64.

26. Admittance and Indenture Records, Clinton County Children's Home, State Archive Series 5376, OHSL.

27. Book 1, MCCH.

28. *Indiana Quarterly Bulletin of Charities and Corrections*, October 1895, 30–31.

29. LePage, "The Care and Training of Neglected Children," in *Fifth Annual Ohio State Conference of Charities*, 77.

30. *Indiana Quarterly Bulletin of Charities and Corrections*, June 1907, 219. Campbell's remarks can be taken in more than one way; being imposed on could also be a euphemism for sexual misconduct in the home.

31. *Biennial Report*, MNSPS, 1900, 34–35.

32. *Annual Report*, OBSC, 1892, 406–407.

33. *Historical Sketches of the Higher Educational Institutions*, 26.

34. "Report of the Committee on Child Saving," NCCC, 1897, 89.

35. "Debate on the Papers," NCCC, 1878, 238.

36. *Biennial Report*, MNSPS, 1890, 59.

37. Registers, 1880–1947, Belmont County, Ohio, children's home, April 1886, Series 3182, OHSL.

38. Cruse and Cruse, *History of the Children*, 449. "Flossie," as she was known, eventually went through eight placement homes before working for wages. The Rose Orphan Home recorded that she had an abortion in 1910 (reported via the Society of Charities secretary) and later married and divorced twice.

39. Cruse and Cruse, *History of the Children*, 287.

40. Cruse and Cruse, *History of the Children*, 464. Willie and his siblings shared success after their time at the Rose Orphan Home and in their placements. Three of the four children went west together to Montana, and eventually Arizona, Texas, and California. Sister Freda wrote in 1947: "A beautiful and very appreciative letter. Speaks of the Home as her dear old home and thinks that her life here laid the foundation for her entire future" (498).

41. *Annual Report*, MSPS, 1882, 59.

42. *Annual Report*, MSPS, 1877, 43.

43. *Annual Report*, MSPS, 1875, 60; *Annual Report*, MSPS, 1877, 43.

Notes to Chapter 3

44. Records of Indenture, 1880–1904, Miami County, Ohio, children's home, Series 5816, 67, OHSL.

45. Kounse, *Annotated Lawrence County Children's Home Register*, 117.

46. Letter, June 1906, *Cincinnati Convalescent Hospital for Children*, vol. 70, 1873–1910, CHLA.

47. Homer Folks, "The Child and the Family," NCCC, 1892, 422.

48. *Marietta Daily Leader*, Marietta, Ohio, June 15, 1897.

49. *Proceedings of the Fifth Annual Ohio State Conference*, 29.

50. Stanley Griffin, "Relative Functions of the State and Private Charities in Care of Dependent and Neglected Children," NCCC 1909, 57.

51. *Annual Report*, MSPS, 1875, 59.

52. Cruse and Cruse, *History of the Children*, 389. Anna's siblings also went through placement at the Rose Orphan Home. Her brother, William, wrote the institution during the 1940s and noted that he owned a small farm and berry-growing business. His 1943 letter included this comment: "I still thank the home for the training. It has slung to me down thru the years and has been a help in the rearing of our own children" (388).

53. *Annual Report Cincinnati Children's Home*, 1875, CHLA, 19; *Annual Report*, MSPS, 1875, 59.

54. *Annual Report*, MSPS, 1875, 60.

55. Kounse, *Annotated Lawrence County Children's Home Register*, 30.

56. Book 1, MCCH.

57. *Annual Report*, MSPS, 1878, 52–53.

58. Cruse and Cruse, *History of the Children*, 528. In 1931, Gertrude contacted Alden to tell him she was doing well and was investigating cases for a detective agency.

59. *Annual Report*, MSPS, 1877, 39.

60. Hasci, "Orphanages as a National Institution," 246.

61. Channing, "Illinois Soldiers' Orphans' Home," 106.

62. Book 1, MCCH.

63. Registers, Perry County Children's Home, 1895, Series 5938, OHSL.

64. Hood, *Foster Home Care for Dependent Children*, 157; Kounse, *Annotated Lawrence County Children's Home Register*, 82.

65. Streeter, "The Care of Dependent Children in Indiana," 741.

66. *Biennial Report*, MNSPS, 1912, 347.

67. Saksena, "Out of Home Placements for Abused, Neglected, and Dependent Children in Minnesota," 1025.

68. *Annual Report*, OBSC, 1869, 57.

69. Record of Indentures, Miami County Children's Home, March 14, 1902, Series 5816, OHSL.

70. Letter to Ellis Kerr, November 10, 1906, Cincinnati General Protestant Orphan Home, vol. 70, CHLA.

71. Indentures, Montgomery County Children's Home, 1868–1901, Series 5816, OHSL.

72. Record of Inmates, Warren County Children's Home, Series 6206, OHSL.
73. Hood, *Foster Home Care for Dependent Children*, 167.
74. Riney-Kehrberg, *Childhood on the Farm*, 167.
75. Kounse, *Annotated Lawrence County Children's Home Register*, 53.
76. Cruse and Cruse, *History of the Children*, 190.
77. Riney-Kehrberg, *Childhood on the Farm*, 167, 168.
78. Register, 1885–1918, Perry County, Ohio, children's home, OHSL.
79. Clement, "With Wise and Benevolent Purpose," 11.
80. *Biennial Report*, MNSPS, 1900, 75.
81. *Daily Commonwealth*, Topeka, Kansas, July 1, 1870.
82. *St. Paul Daily News*, February 27, 1892.
83. *Denver Daily News*, January 27, 1884; Jack Bacon, "Denver Historian Exposes Dark Side of Dispensing Justice in Colorado," *Denver Catholic Register*, 2002, http://www.archden.org/dcr/archive/20021127/2002112710ln.htm, accessed August 17, 2012.
84. *Akron Daily Democrat*, PM edition, March 3 and April 18, 1902. Cross was in prison at least through 1920.
85. *InterOcean*, Chicago, March 26, 1891.
86. *InterOcean*, Chicago, June 21, 1892.
87. *Valentine Democrat*, January 7, 1897, 2.
88. *Daily Tribune*, Bismark, North Dakota, April 14, 1892.
89. Book 1, MCCH.
90. Records of inmates, 1867–1912, Montgomery County Children's Home, 233, OHSL.
91. Hebbard, "Placing Out," NCCC, 1899, 183.
92. *Wichita Eagle*, June 15, 1889, 2.
93. *St. Paul Globe*, November 8, 1899.
94. *Sixth Triennial Report*, Rose Orphan Home, 20, Rose Orphan Home Collection (ROH), VCPL.
95. Letter, April 19, 1904, General Protestant Orphan Home Records, 1849–1970, Mss 1043, vol. 70, 1873–1910, CHLA.
96. Indentures, 1867–1908, Montgomery County, Ohio, children's home, OHSL, 344.
97. Cruse and Cruse, *History of the Children*, 112.
98. *Biennial Report*, MSPS, 1882, 58.
99. *Biennial Report*, MNSPS, 1900, 31.
100. *Annual Report*, IBSC, 1917, 183.
101. Cruse and Cruse, *History of the Children*, 460.
102. *Annual Report*, MSPS, 1878, 48–49.
103. Cruse and Cruse, *History of the Children*, 545.
104. *Annual Report*, MSPS, 1878, 48–49.
105. *Biennial Report*, MSPS, 1882, 56.
106. Book 1, MCCH.
107. Cruse and Cruse, *History of the Children*, 134.
108. Cruse and Cruse, *History of the Children*, 468.

109. Book 1, MCCH.
110. Riney-Kehrberg, *Childhood on the Farm*, 168.
111. Vl. 56, General Protestant Orphan Home Records, 1849–1970, Mss 1043, 152, CHLA.
112. Director's Minutes, July 1895, Guernsey County Records, Series 5558, OHSL.
113. "Children Cause Heavy Fire Loss," *Mahoning Dispatch*, Canfield, August 18, 1916.
114. *St. Louis Republic*, June 22, 1904.
115. *St. Louis Republic*, March 26, 1904; *St. Louis Republic*, April 1, 1904; *Valentine Democrat*, January 17, 1907.
116. *The Ohio Democrat*, Logan, Ohio, July 2, 1887.
117. *Indiana Quarterly Bulletin of Charities and Corrections*, December 1896, 17.
118. Hebberd, "Placing out Children," NCCC, 1899, 176.
119. Morgan County, OHSL, 1884, 8.
120. Gelle and Harrop, "The Risk of Abusive Violence Among Children with Nongenetic Caretakers," 78–79. This study reached no conclusions based on their results but did demonstrate that foster and adopted children were more likely than stepchildren or genetically related children to suffer abuse.
121. Orme and Buehler, "Foster Family Characteristics," 7.

Chapter 4. "The right of the state to interfere is unquestioned"

1. *Annual Report*, IBSC, 1893, 28; Hugh Fox, "The Relation of a State Board of Charities to Child Caring Societies and Institutions," NCCC, 1899, 385–386.
2. "Report of the Child Saving Committee," NCCC, 1897, 88.
3. Galen Merrill, "Some Recent Developments in Child-Saving," NCCC, 1900, 227–229.
4. White, "The History and Development of the Illinois Children's Home," 65.
5. "Discussion on Child Saving," NCCC, 1899, 381. Kelso was the superintendent of the Dependent and Neglected Children of Ontario.
6. Tiffin, *In Whose Best Interest?* 71.
7. Streeter, "The Care of Dependent Children in Indiana," 741.
8. "Discussion on Child Saving," NCCC, 1899, 380.
9. Ramey, *Childcare in Black and White*, 132.
10. Indiana Department of Public Welfare, *The Development of Public Charities in Indiana* (Indianapolis: Wm. Burford, 1905).
11. *St. Paul Daily Globe*, May 20, 1890. The newer states of North Dakota and South Dakota were well behind their regional affiliates in regard to the formation of boards and giving those boards oversight powers. When the Children's Bureau studied the two states in 1921, they discovered that in North Dakota, private institutions of the state were not under state supervision but under that of local judges instead. The state also made no provisions for children imported from other states or for placement supervision. South Dakota had slightly more structure. In this regard, despite their agricultural economies and placing-out practices, the two states do not necessarily fit squarely in the region.

12. *Annual Report*, OBSC, 1868, 59.
13. *Annual Report*, OBSC, 1885, 47.
14. Omaha Daily Bee, November 18, 1903, 3.
15. *Biennial Report*, Nebraska State Board of Charities and Correction, 1912, 46–48.
16. *Annual Report*, OBSC, 1884, 49.
17. Skocpol, *Protecting Soldiers and Mothers*, 55.
18. *Hocking Sentinel*, Logan, Ohio, July 17, 1884.
19. *St. Paul Daily Globe*, May 20, 1890.
20. *Indiana Quarterly Bulletin of Charities and Corrections*, October 1895, 35–36.
21. Channing, *Illinois Soldiers' Orphans' Home*, 70.
22. *Annual Report*, OBSC, 1891, 11–13.
23. "State Kills Charity Board," *Omaha Daily Bee*, January 28, 1908, 1.
24. *St. Louis Republic*, July 29, 1901.
25. Ernest Bicknell, "State Report," NCCC, 1897, 393.
26. "Byers is the Board," *Stark County Democrat*, Canton, Ohio, October 5, 1900, 5. J. P. Byers was the son of Reverend A. G. Byers, who also served as secretary of the board.
27. *Annual Report*, OBSC, 1868, 59. For information about the variety of tasks assigned to boards of charity, see "Report," NCCC, 1909, 397–413; "Minutes and Discussions," NCCC, 1887, 266–274; *Annual Report*, IBSC, 1890, 22.
28. "Orphans of this State," *The Independent*, Plymouth, Indiana, January 25, 1901, 2.
29. *Indiana Quarterly Bulletin of Charities and Corrections*, June 1907, 213.
30. *Annual Report*, IBSC, 1895, 36.
31. "Parents Claiming Children," *Indiana State Journal*, March 30, 1898, 3.
32. *Annual Report*, IBSC, 1900, 143.
33. *The Indiana Bulletin*, December 1896, 17.
34. Fulton County Infirmary records, CAC-BGSU.
35. *Proceedings of the Tenth Annual Convention of Trustees and Superintendents*, 1891, 47.
36. "Power of Trustees Over Children," Sec. 932, April 9, 1891: 88 v. 301. Reprinted in the *Proceedings of the Annual Convention of Trustees and Superintendents of the Children's Homes in Ohio*, 1891. The initial law allowing for county boards was passed in Ohio in 1882.
37. *Ohio Bulletin of Charities and Corrections* 7, no. 2 (June 1901): 44.
38. *Annual Report*, OBSC, 1891, 49.
39. *Annual Report*, MSPS, 1884, 77.
40. Butler, "Report on Child Saving," NCCC, 1901, 209. For social gospel influences and more information on the COS, see Curtis, *A Consuming Faith*; Ruswick, *Almost Worthy*.
41. Records: County Board of Children's Guardians, 1889–1939, Marion County Board of Children's Guardians, IHS.
42. Cruse and Cruse, *History of the Children*, 577.

43. Cruse and Cruse, *History of the Children*, 343–344; "1890," Marion County Board of Children's Guardians, Records: County Board of Children's Guardians, 1889–1939, IHS; "Report of the State Agent," IBSC, 1911, 160.

44. *The Indianapolis Journal*, January 19, 1901; Katz, *In the Shadow of the Poorhouse*, 126.

45. The Minnesota state school delayed hiring an agent until 1887, two years after the institution opened, because of a lack of funding. Between 1890 and 1904, the number of children needing visits increased five times, from more than two hundred to a little more than one thousand. The state went from one agent to four agents in a little more than a decade. The hiring of agents also increased the number of children placed and re-placed.

46. *Annual Report*, OBSC, 1891, 319.

47. *Annual Report*, OBSC, 1882, 9–10. Hathaway's suggestions dealt only with children. See *Annual Report*, OBSC, 1891, 317. *Indiana Quarterly Bulletin of Charities and Corrections*, June 1907, 141.

48. Fox, "Relation of a State Board of Charities to Child Caring Societies and Institutions," NCCC, 1908, 386.

49. *Annual Report*, MSPS, 1877, 23.

50. *Annual Report*, MSPS, 1885, 23–24.

51. J. B. Montgomery, "The State Public School Idea at its Best," NCCC, 1900, 234; Winfield Snodgrass, "The Michigan System for Caring for Dependent Children," *Christian Advocate*, August 1898, 34.

52. "Reports from States," NCCC, 1895, 356. This law also required a bond of $1,000 for each out-of-state child brought to the state for placement, providing that the child would never become a burden on Michigan resources.

53. *Biennial Report*, MNSPS, 1900, 21.

54. *Annual Report*, OBSC, 1899, 34; *Annual Report*, IBSC, 1897, 15.

55. S. J. Hathaway, "Children's Homes in Ohio," NCCC, 1890, 212.

56. "Indiana Child Saving," *Indiana State Journal*, June 14, 1899, 8.

57. *Jasper Weekly Courier*, Jasper, Indiana, January 25, 1901.

58. *Annual Report*, IBSC, 1900, 131, 137.

59. *Annual Reports*, Lucas County Children's Home, 1902, 1915, CAC-BGSU.

60. Board of Administration of the State of Illinois, *Sixth Annual Report of the Department of Visitation of Children Placed in Family Homes*, 14–15.

61. *Ninth Annual Report*, Illinois, 1914, 113.

62. Hastings Hart, "Common Sense and Cooperation in Child Saving," NCCC, 1903, 185.

63. Hewins and Webster, *The Work of Child Placing Agencies*, 18.

64. *Fifth Annual Report*, Illinois, 1910. The Children's Home and Aid Society was eventually renamed the Children's Aid Society of Illinois.

65. *Ohio Quarterly Bulletin of Charities and Corrections* 7, no. 2 (1901): 30–32.

66. White, "The History and Development of the Illinois Children's Home," 79.

67. *Home Life for Childhood*, no. 4 (1917), RJDL.

68. *Home Life for Childhood*, no. 2 (1917), RJDL.
69. White, "The History and Development of the Illinois Children's Home," 79.
70. Hart, "A Nation's Need for Adoption," 144–145, 200.
71. Hewins and Webster, *The Work of Child Placing Agencies*, 31.
72. Hood, *Foster Home Care for Dependent Children*, 24.
73. Hood, *Foster Home Care for Dependent Children*, 120.
74. *Indiana Quarterly Bulletin of Charities and Corrections* (June 1908): 100; *Annual Report*, IBSC, 1917, 177.
75. *Annual Report*, IBSC, 1920, 165.
76. *Biennial Report*, MNSPS, 1900, 20.
77. *Annual Report*, IBSC, 1896, 16.
78. "Homeless Children," *Indiana Farmer's Guide*, Huntington, Indiana, February 16, 1918.
79. *Annual Report*, IBSC, 1897, 37–39.
80. *Annual Report*, IBSC, 1912, 145.
81. *Annual Report*, IBSC, 1920, 180–181.
82. *Indiana Quarterly Bulletin of Charities and Corrections*, December 1896, 19.
83. *Biennial Report*, MNSPS, 1900, 21.
84. *Indiana Quarterly Bulletin of Charities and Corrections*, December 1896, 17.
85. *Biennial Report*, MNSPS, 1900, 28.
86. *Biennial Report*, MNSPS, 1900, 29.
87. Clement, "With Wise and Benevolent Purpose," 7.
88. *Biennial Report*, MNSPS, 1900, 23.
89. Welle, "'Things which I was never interested in,'" 12.
90. Board of Administration, *Department of Visitation of Children*, 50.
91. *Annual Report*, Springfield Home for the Friendless (Springfield: Press Illinois State Register, 1906), ALPL.
92. Book 1, MCCH. Patrick J. Ryan located cases of a few Ohio counties using the Juvenile Research Center as a means of removing certain children. See Patrick J. Ryan, "'Six Blacks from Home': Childhood, Motherhood, and Eugenics in America," *Journal of Policy History*, 19:3, 2007.
93. Board of Administration of the State of Illinois, *Sixth Annual Report of the Department of Visitation of Children*, 14–15.
94. Board of Administration of the State of Illinois, *Sixth Annual Report of the Department of Visitation of Children*, 14–15.
95. *Biennial Report*, MNSPS, 1912, 337–138.
96. Hastings Hart, "Admission and Discharge of Children" (New York: Department of Child-Helping Russell Sage Foundation, 1916), 9.
97. Hewins and Webster, *The Work of Child Placing Agencies*, 33.
98. *Biennial Report*, MNSPS, 1900, 30–32.
99. *Annual Report*, IBSC, 1912, 141.
100. *Annual Report*, IBSC, 1920, 173.
101. Katz, *In the Shadow of the Poorhouse*, 89.

102. *The Survey* 32 (April, 4, 1914): 63.

103. "Will you Adopt a Child?" *Perrysburg Journal*, July 2, 1914, 1; July 1, 1915, 1.

104. *The Survey* 30 (April 1913): 517–518.

105. *Annual Report*, IBSC, 1913, 160.

106. Woodward, *19th Century Care of Orphan and Pauper Children in Wabash County*, 170.

107. *Annual Report*, IBSC, 1900, 141; 1919, 162.

108. *Annual Report*, ISBC, 1919, 162.

109. Warren County, Ohio, records clearly show a decline in placements and an increase in parental reclamation after 1900. In Perry County a similar pattern emerges after 1910. Record of Inmates, Warren County Children's Home, 1874–1952, Series 6206, OHSL; Registers, Perry County Children's Home, 1885–1918, Series 5938, OHSL.

110. *Annual Report*, ISBC, 1915, 177.

111. *Home Life for Childhood*, no. 2 (1917): 6.

112. Cruse and Cruse, *History of the Children*, 227. George never again lived at the Rose Orphan Home but contacted the superintendent in 1924 when he needed documentation about his age and residency to apply for aid after the theft of his horse team.

113. Cruse and Cruse, *History of the Children*, 461.

114. *First Annual Report*, State Board of Administrators, Illinois, 1910.

115. White, "The History and Development of the Illinois Children's Home," 135; information compiled from Delinquent and Dependent Children Records, Warren County, Illinois, IRAD; Poor Farm Records, Woodford, County, Illinois, Normal, Illinois, IRAD; Poor Farm Inmate Registers, Madison County, Illinois, Carbondale, Illinois, IRAD; Poor Farm Registers and Quarterly Reports, St. Clair County, Illinois, Carbondale, Illinois, IRAD.

116. Kounse, *Annotated Lawrence County Children's Home Register*, 82, 156.

117. Indentures, 1867–1908, Montgomery County, Ohio, children's home, 43–47, OHSL.

118. Julian Mack, "Juvenile Courts as Part of the School System of the Country," NCCC, 1908, 371.

119. Mangold, *Child Problems*, 326; Katz, *In the Shadow of the Poorhouse*, 85. Lindemeyer, "A Right to Childhood," also establishes that the 1909 meeting served as more of a marker as opposed to a watershed moment.

120. Causes of Poverty, NCCC, 1903, 275; Cohen, "Child-Saving and Progressivism," 295.

121. Kounse, *Annotated Lawrence County Children's Home Register*, 147.

122. *Indiana Quarterly Bulletin of Charities and Corrections*, June 1907, 132.

123. Kleinberg, *Widows and Orphans First*, 124.

124. *Annual Report*, OBSC, 1884, 16. Not all counties stopped direct aid during the 1890s and 1900s. Trustees of the poor in Ohio, who also managed the poor farms, regularly distributed food and fuel, paid doctor and funeral expenses, and granted occasional payments.

125. Kleinberg, *Widows and Orphans First*, 2–3; White, "The History and Development of the Illinois Children's Home," 86. Sophonisba Breckinridge coined the phrase.

126. Ladd-Taylor, *Mother-Work*; Kleinberg, *Widows and Orphans First*, 104, 106.

127. Drew, "Child Labor and Child Welfare," 318.

128. *Pickaway*, September 1915, 56; Eckman, "Public Aid to Children in their Own Homes."

129. "Knox County Ranks Third," *The Democratic Banner*, March 20, 1917; Bessie A. McClenahan, "Social Service by a State University," *The Survey* (August 28, 1915): 485–487.

130. Interestingly, Knox County initially relied on a private institution to handle its dependent children, and in 1904 that institution was found lacking by the state; not until the 1910s did the county build its own children's home. 1902 Biographical History of Knox Co.; 1904 State Report.

131. *26th Annual Report*, Lucas County Children's Home, CAC-BGSU; Hewins and Webster, *The Work of Child Placing Agencies*, 48.

132. "Report of Juvenile Officer," *The Democratic Banner*, August 8, 1919; *Annual Report*, Lucas County Children's Home, 1915, CAC-BGSU.

133. *Annual Report*, IBSC, vol. 32, 1921, 156.

134. Eckman, *Public Aid to Children in their Own Homes*, 8–12.

135. Mintz, *Huck's Raft*, 180.

136. Ashby, *Endangered Children*, 97; Ladd-Taylor, *Mother-Work*, 156; Lindenmeyer, "A Right to Childhood," 154.

137. Agnew, *From Charity to Social Work*, 2, 4.

138. Skocpol, *Protecting Soldiers and Mothers*, 55.

139. *Ohio Bulletin of Charities and Corrections* 7, no. 2 (1901): 30.

140. *Proceedings of the Ohio State Conference on Dependent Children held at Dayton, Ohio*, 14–16.

141. *Annual Report*, IBSC, 1920, 175–179.

142. Katz, *In the Shadow of the Poorhouse*, 131; Hewins and Webster, *The Work of Child Placing Agencies*, 41.

143. Crenson, *Building the Invisible Orphanage*, 317.

144. A study of recent foster care practices indicates that foster parents believed that the intervention and supervision from state officials and social workers undermined their ability to parent and disrupted the traditional family structure. Swartz, "Mothering for the State."

145. Hewins and Webster, *The Work of Child Placing Agencies*, 54.

146. Hewins and Webster, *The Work of Child Placing Agencies*, 73–74.

147. *Annual Report*, IBSC, 1920, 181.

148. Cravens, "Child-Saving in the Age of Professionalism."

149. *Home Life for Childhood* (October 1923): 7, RJDL.

150. W. S. Reynolds, "Report of the State Agent," IBSC, 1911, 159.

151. *Annual Report*, IBSC, 1919, 164.

152. *Annual Report*, IBSC, 1919, 163.

153. *Home Life for Childhood*, no. 1 (1922): 19, RJDL.

Chapter 5. The Farm, the Federal Government, and the Decline of Placement

1. Slingerland, *Child Placing in Families*, 124.
2. Slingerland, *Child Placing in Families*, 130–131.
3. Slingerland, *Child Placing in Families*, 122.
4. Cmiel, *A Home of Another Kind*, 63. For placements in the 1940s, both the courts and caseworkers were involved in the placement and supervision. See Book 2, MCCH.
5. Bowers, *The Country Life Movement in America*, 24–25; Wunderlich, *American Country Life*; Peters and Morgan, "The Country Life Commission," 302.
6. Mapes, *Sweet Tyranny*, 168.
7. Zelizer, *Pricing the Priceless Child*, 3–6.
8. Lindenmeyer, "A Right to Childhood," 12; Hart, "A Nation's Need for Adoption," 144.
9. Agnew, *From Charity to Social Work*, 2.
10. L. A. Warner, "The Rural Social Problem," *Michigan Farmer*, October 22, 1904, 313.
11. Barron, *Mixed Harvest*, 243; Thompson, "Thomas Jefferson and Agrarian Philosophy," 48–49; Anderson, "The Metamorphosis of American Agrarian Idealism," 182–188.
12. Hagenstein, Gregg, and Donahoe, eds., *American Georgics*, 155.
13. Danbom, *Born in the Country*, 134.
14. Montmarque, "American Agrarianism," 59.
15. Barron, "Rural America on the Silent Screen," 407; Danbom, *Born in the Country*, 150.
16. Shideler, "'Flappers and Philosophers' and Farmers," 284.
17. Various explanations for the rejection of Populism in the agricultural states outside the Plains have been offered. Along with a wide variety of other local farm organizations to join and a more stable farm economy, farmers in states such as Ohio tried to use the competitive two-party system inside the state to advance reforms. Thus, the Populists did not represent their only chance for farm-friendly legislation or activism. See Postel, *The Populist Vision*; Pierce, "Farmers and the Failure of Populism in Ohio."
18. Nelson, *Farm and Factory*, 20. See also Scott, *The Agrarian Movement in Illinois*.
19. Burns, *Pastoral Inventions*, 237; Guth, "The National Board of Farm Organizations."
20. Warner, "The Rural Social Problem," *Michigan Farmer*, October 22, 1904, 313.
21. Robert Tontz, "Memberships of General Farmer's Organizations"; Hurt, *Problems of Plenty*, 21.
22. C. L. Northrup, "Another Explanation of Why Children Desert the Farm," *Michigan Farmer*, December 31, 1904, 522.
23. "Agriculture—Some of the Topics that Interest," *Cleveland Herald*, September 20, 1887.

24. "A Woman's Opinion on Farm Laborers Wages," *Cleveland Morning Herald*, April 22, 1872; "Rates of Wages and Cost of Living Among Farm Laborers," *InterOcean*, Chicago, August 26, 1879.

25. "More About Farm Labor," *Cleveland Morning Herald*, January 21, 1873.

26. Hatton and Williamson, "What Explains Wage Gaps between Farm and City?" 267.

27. "Our Boys," *Ohio Farmer*, December 22, 1877, 395.

28. "What May Be Done for the Bright, Ambitious Farmers Son," *Indianapolis Times*, August 31, 1884.

29. Riney-Kehrberg, unpublished notes and *Childhood on the Farm*, 168.

30. Burns, *Pastoral Inventions*, 58. Muir came of age during the 1840s and 1850s, but his description of work is representative of what many children continued to do decades later.

31. *Pantagraph*, McLean, Illinois, January 16, 1884, 4, Orphan Train Folder, MCML.

32. *Annual Report*, Cincinnati Children's Home, 1890, 15, CHLA.

33. *Annual Report*, Cincinnati Children's Home, 1890, 13, CHLA. See also Liberty Hyde Bailey, "Rural Development in Relation to Social Welfare," NCCC, 1908, 83–91.

34. Mapes, *Sweet Tyranny*, 73.

35. Reef, *Alone in the World*, 54.

36. Dodge, *American Farm Labor*, 84.

37. Riney-Kehrberg, *Childhood on the Farm*, 16. Children adopted by farm families would be listed as living with their parents. It is unclear at this time how many informal adoptions or name changes took place exclusively on farms.

38. Quote reprinted in Sonntag, "'Protect the children—protect the boys and girls'"; Zelizer, *Pricing the Priceless Child*, 77–79; Mapes, *Sweet Tyranny*, 73.

39. Pinkett, "Government Research Concerning Problems of American Rural Society."

40. Danbom, *The Resisted Revolution*, 175. See also Shaw, "No Place for Class Politics"; Lowry, "The Rise of Rural Sociology"; Ziegler, "'The Burdens and the Narrow Life of Farm Women.'"

41. Hurt, *Problems of Plenty*, 15–16.

42. Curry, *Modern Mothers in the Heartland*, 66–67.

43. Nelson, *Farm and Factory*, 14; Bowers, *The Country Life Movement in America*, 13.

44. Riney-Kehrberg, *Childhood on the Farm*, 209.

45. Eva Wardell Underhill, "The Farm Home, Why Desert It?" *Michigan Farmer*, March 26, 1904, 285.

46. Danbom, *Born in the Country*, 167; Peters, "Every Farmer Should be Awakened."

47. Liberty Hyde Bailey, "Rural Development in Relation to Social Welfare," NCCC, 1908, 87. See also Liberty Hyde Bailey, "Community Life in the Open Country," NCCC, 1909, 123–129.

48. Liberty Hyde Bailey, "Rural Development in Relation to Social Welfare," NCCC, 1908, 90.

49. Landis, *Rural Welfare Services*, 21.

50. Quoted in Martinez-Brawley, *Seven Decades of Rural Social Work*, 13.

51. Landis, *Rural Welfare Services*, 22.

52. Thompson and Warber, *Social and Economic Survey*, 64.

53. Hewins and Webster, *The Work of Child Placing Agencies*, 43.

54. Hurt, *Problems of Plenty*, 17; Taylor, "The Rise of the Rural Problem," 33; Peters and Morgan, "The Country Life Commission."

55. Katherine Piatt Bottorff, "Tragedies of Village Slums," *The Survey* (September 21, 1912): 767–769; J. J. Kelso, "Children in Rural Districts," *The Survey* (October 21, 1911): 1054–1055.

56. Taylor, "The Rise of the Rural Problem."

57. "Power in the Farm Home," *Indiana Farmer's Guide*, August 31, 1918, 26.

58. Thompson and Warber, *Social and Economic Survey*, 64.

59. W. S. Jennings, "Educating Farm Children World's Educational Business: What's the Matter with our Rural Schools?" *Indiana Farmer's Guide*, November 27, 1920, 5.

60. Steffes, "Solving the 'Rural School Problem,'" 188.

61. Thompson and Warber, *Social and Economic Survey*, 50–52.

62. Steffes, "Solving the 'Rural School Problem,'" 181.

63. Clement, "With Wise and Benevolent Purpose."

64. *Biennial Report*, MNSPS, 1910, 14–15.

65. Provasnik, "Judicial Activism and the Origins of Parental Choice."

66. *Children Indentured by the Wisconsin State School*, 74.

67. *Children Indentured by the Wisconsin State School*, 112.

68. "Truancy Law," *Marshall County Independent*, December 9, 1898, 1.

69. *Annual Report*, IBSC, 1920, 177.

70. Hindman, *Child Labor*, 285–286.

71. Folks, "Farm Labor and School Attendance," 16.

72. *Biennial Report*, MNSPS, 1900, 31.

73. *Biennial Report*, MNSPS, 1900, 29.

74. Letter to Ellis Kerr, November 10, 1906, Cincinnati General Protestant Orphan Home, vol. 70, CHLA.

75. Schindler, "Dependent Children and the State," 276.

76. Lyons-Barnett, "Child Labor in Commercialized Agriculture," 72, 149.

77. Supreme Court cases *Hammer v. Dagenhart* and *Bailey v. Drexel Furniture Co.* both denied the federal government the right to intercede on the state's power to control commerce. See Hawes, *Children Between the Wars*, 49–50.

78. Kohlstedt, "'A Better Crop of Boys and Girls,'" 75.

79. Brownwell, "The Agrarian and Urban Ideals," 580.

80. Larson and Zimmerman, "The USDA's Bureau of Agricultural Economics."

81. Griswold, *Farming and Democracy*, 129–130.

82. Curry, *Modern Mothers in the Heartland*, 78.

83. Lauck, *The Lost Region*, 75–76.

84. Dorn, "The Rural Ideal and Agrarian Realities," 52.

85. Dorn, "The Rural Ideal and Agrarian Realities," 52.

86. Hawes, *Children Between the Wars*, 54. Women's working hours and wages were also improved in most states. See, Skocpol, *Protecting Soldiers and Mothers*, 10.

87. Lindenmeyer, "A Right to Childhood," 19.

88. Homer Folks, "Unity of Child Helping Work," NCCC, 1909, 45. The change in wording, as reported by Folks, was proposed by Superintendent Crouse of the Cincinnati Children's Home.

89. Lindenmeyer, "A Right to Childhood," 21–23.

90. Wald operated one of the nation's leading settlement houses, Henry Street, and Kelly ran the National Consumers League.

91. Hasci, *Second Home*, 39; idem, "Orphanages as a National Institution," 240.

92. Zelizer, *Pricing the Priceless Child* .

93. Dulberger, "*Mother Donit for the Best*," 16; Riney-Kehrberg, *Childhood on the Farm*, 16. During and after World War I, farmers needing additional labor looked to migrant workers from outside the United States, with Mexico providing a large percentage of seasonal workers. See Lyons-Barnett, *Child Labor in Commercialized Agriculture*, 126–129.

94. Mapes, *Sweet Tyranny*, 171.

95. Mapes, *Sweet Tyranny*, 168. This connection between healthy labor for young people and the sugar beet industry continued into the 1950s, when Red River Valley farmers in the Dakotas tried to replace undesirable Mexican workers with local teenagers. See Norris, "Growing Up Growing Sugar."

96. Mapes, *Sweet Tyranny*, 170.

97. "The Child Labor Amendment," *Herald of Gospel Liberty*, September 11, 1924, 867.

98. Grace Abbot, "The Child Labor Amendment I," *The North American Review*, December 1924, 223.

99. Quoted in Effland, "Agrarianism and Child Labor Policy for Agriculture," 288, 290. Only about one-third of children younger than twelve worked in the fields in the same capacity.

100. Hindman, *Child Labor: An American History*, 250.

101. Hahamovitch, *Fruits of Their Labor*, 57.

102. Mapes, *Sweet Tyranny*, 170.

103. A. J. McKelway, "Child Labor and Citizenship," NCCC, 1908, 351–363.

104. Mapes, *Sweet Tyranny*, 125–126.

105. "Farm Boys Needed at Home," *Indiana Farmer's Guide*, May 3, 1919, 10.

106. Hahamovitch, *Fruits of Their Labor*, 108.

107. *Annual Report*, IBSC, 1918, 198.

108. Lyons-Barnett, *Child Labor in Commercialized Agriculture*, 111.

109. Ramey, *Childcare in Black and White*, 97.

110. *Biennial Report*, MNSPS, 1904, 14.

111. *Biennial Report*, MNSPS, 1912, 344; Clement, "With Wise and Benevolent Purpose," 11.

112. Higbie, "Rural Work," 67.

113. "Centennial Series: The Children's Year, 1918–1919," Online Digest, May 2012.

114. *Annual Report*, IBSC, 1913, 153. Health problems notwithstanding, the Allen County Children's Home also suffered from a flood during that year, resulting in property damage and the death of three children.

115. Lindenmeyer, "A Right to Childhood," 146.

116. *The Child Welfare Special*, 5.

117. *The Child Welfare Special*, 5.

118. *The Child Welfare Special*, 11.

119. Ladd-Taylor, "A Right to Work," 178–187. Congress allowed the Sheppard-Towner Act to expire in 1929, and state financial support for the act's measures varied widely when it was in effect.

120. Charles Moreau Harger, "What's the Matter with Rural Health?" *Outlook*, March 29, 1922, 507.

121. *The Child Welfare Special*, 17.

122. Lindenmeyer, "A Right to Childhood," 1.

123. Lindenmeyer, "A Right to Childhood," 95.

124. Kleinberg, *Widows and Orphans First*, 106.

125. "Children Indentured by the Wisconsin State School," 8.

126. "Children Indentured by the Wisconsin State School," 98–99.

127. *Biennial Report*, MNSPS, 1912, 334–335.

128. "Children Indentured by the Wisconsin State School," 4.

129. "Children Indentured by the Wisconsin State School," 51.

130. "Children Indentured by the Wisconsin State School," 58.

131. "Children Indentured by the Wisconsin State School," 59.

132. Anders, *The History of Child Welfare in Cincinnati*, 213. See Holt, *The Orphan Trains*, 179.

133. Longman, *Report of the Placing of Children in Family Homes*, 2.

134. Clement, "With Wise and Benevolent Purpose," 8.

135. "Children Indentured by the Wisconsin State School," 56–57.

136. Neva R. Deardorff, "Bound Out," *The Survey* 56 (July 1926): 458.

137. Hewins and Webster, *The Work of Child Placing Agencies*, 4.

138. Hewins and Webster, *The Work of Child Placing Agencies*, 30.

139. "Children Indentured by the Wisconsin State School," 74.

140. "Children Indentured by the Wisconsin State School," 112.

141. Hewins and Webster, *The Work of Child Placing Agencies*, 15.

142. "History of CAS Emigration Programs, including 'Family Emigration,' Employment, Adoption, and Foster Care," http://dlib.nyu.edu/findingaids/html/nyhs/childrensaidsociety_at.html.

143. Hewins and Webster, *The Work of Child Placing Agencies*, 22.

144. Hewins and Webster, *The Work of Child Placing Agencies*, 39.

145. "Children Indentured by the Wisconsin State School," 114. Included in the report was a response from the state board of control in Wisconsin. The letter claimed that many of the problems identified were in the process of being remedied, and employees from 1923 had since been replaced. However, changes had not been implemented in their entirety because of a lack of state funding.

146. McGill, *Children in Agriculture*.

147. Correspondence with author, Robert Beireis, August 22, 2013; Book 1, MCCH.

148. See Skocpol, *Protecting Soldiers and Mothers*, 10; Lindenmeyer, "A Right to Childhood."

Epilogue

1. *Annual Report*, IBSC, 1920, 179.
2. "Children Indentured by the Wisconsin State School," 108.
3. Griswold, *Farming and Democracy*, 148–150.
4. Griswold, *Farming and Democracy*, 46.
5. Zelizer, *Pricing the Priceless Child*, 196; Berebitsky, *Like Our Very Own*, 69.
6. Gillette, "The Drift to the City," 663.
7. Griswold, *Farming and Democracy*, 199.
8. Dave Jamieson, "Child Labor Farm Rules Scrapped by White House Under Political Pressure," *Huffington Post*, April 7, 2012, http://www.huffingtonpost.com/2012/04/27/white-house-child-labor-agriculture_n_1458701.html.
9. Kleinberg, *Widows and Orphans First*, 126.
10. Nadasen, Mittelstadt, and Chappell, *Welfare in the United States*, 15.
11. Nadasen, Mittelstadt, and Chappell, *Welfare in the United States*, 89–92. In 1931, the Children's Bureau calculated the average amount of monthly mother's aid payments in all the participating states. Midwestern states fell in the first two-thirds of payouts: Michigan paid on average $37.04, Illinois $26.11, Ohio $21.68, and Kansas $14.05.
12. Reef, *Alone in the World*, 108. During the 1880s, critics of the foster care system predicted this problem. They believed paying adults to care for dependent children would result in the expectation that all such relationships result in a payment. See "Should they be permanently sheltered in asylums?" *Logansport Daily Journal*, September 1, 1886.
13. Ashby, *Endangered Children*, 112–117.
14. Stuart, "The Early Years," 18–19; Nadasen, Mittelstadt, and Chappell, *Welfare in the United States*, 16–17; Gordon, *Pitied But Not Entitled*.
15. Swartz, "Mothering for the State," 585.
16. Carp, "Two Cheers for Orphanages."
17. *Laws Concerning Children*, 4. The Indiana Soldiers' Orphans' Home remained open until 2009 and closed after a 3-year-long investigation determined that it cost approximately $91,000 annually to educate each of the 185 children living there,

among other problems. See "Indiana Soldier's and Sailor's Children's Home," http://www.in.gov/isdh/23517.htm, accessed December 16, 2013. Ohio closed its state orphan home in 1997 and Illinois closed the home in Normal in 1979.

18. Lucas County Children's Home, CAC-BGSU.

19. This notation was written into the entry in the Perry County ledger of 1900 by the administrator in 1965. In 1900, the care for this boy and his sisters cost the county thirty-five cents per day. See Register, 1900, Perry County, Ohio, children's home, OHSL.

Bibliography

Archival Collections

Abraham Lincoln Presidential Library (ALPL)
    Massac County Poor Farm Records
    New York Juvenile Asylum Train Records
    Springfield Home for the Friendless
Ancestry.com (www.ancestry.com)
    United States Census Records (1850–1940), U.S. Census Collection
Center for Archival Collections-Bowling Green State University (CAC-BGSU)
    Defiance County, Local Government Records, Children's Services Board, County Home Minutes, 1868–1897
    Fulton County, Local Government Records, County Home Correspondence 1874–1939, Indenture Records 1875–1883
    Henry County, Local Government Records, County Recorder, Deed Records 1872–1885
    Huron County, Local Government Records, County Home Indenture Records 1850–1859
    Lucas County Children's Home Collection (restricted)
    Putnam County, Local Government Records, County Home Minutes, 1869–1907
    Van Wert County, Local Government Records, County Home Semi-Annual Reports 1876–1904
    Williams County, Local Government Records, County Home Minutes 1874–1900
    Wood County, Local Government Records, County Home Indenture Records, Cleveland Protestant Orphan Asylum 1870–1890
    Wyandot County, Local Government Records, Board of Commissioners Journals County Home 1883–1889

Bibliography

Cincinnati Museum Center, Cincinnati History Library and Archives (CHLA)
    Children's Home of Cincinnati, Mss 532
    General Protestant Orphan's Home Records Mss 1043 (formerly the German Protestant Orphan's Home Collection housed under the Convalescent Hospital for Children records)
    Proceedings of the Fifth Annual Conference of Charities and Corrections, 1880, Cincinnati, Ohio
Illinois Regional Archives Depository (IRAD)
    Delinquent and Dependent Children Records, Warren County, McComb
    Fulton County Almshouse Register, McComb
    Madison County Poor Farm Inmate Registers, Carbondale
    St. Clair County Poor Farm Register, Carbondale
    Woodford County Poor Farm Records, Normal
Indiana State Library (ISL)
    Annual Report of the Northern Indiana Orphan's Home (Children's Aid Society of Indiana)
    Annual Reports of the Orphans' Home Association of Logansport, Indiana
    Children's Home Finder, 1909
    Vigo County Board of Children's Guardians Report, 1896
McClean County Museum Library, Bloomington, Illinois (MCML)
    Orphan Train Folder
Ohio Historical Society Library (OHSL)
    Belmont County Inmate Register
    Brown County Indentures
    Champaign County Record of Inmates
    Green County Children's Home Ledger
    Miami County Record of Indentures, 1880–1904, State Archive Series 5816
    Montgomery County Children's Home Indenture Records
    Perry County Registers, Records of Admittance and Indenture
    Warren County Record of Inmates
Richard J. Dailey Library Special Collections and University Archives, University of Illinois at Chicago (RJDL)
    Children's Home and Aid Society of Illinois Records Series V
State Historical Society of Indiana (IHS)
    Blackford County Infirmary Records
    County Poor Asylums—Construction and Management: Reports of Visits by Secretary, Statistics of County Poor Expenses. Indianapolis: n.p., 1890.
    Marion County Board of Children's Guardians
Vigo County Public Library Community Archives (VCPL)
    Rose Orphan Home Collection (ROH)
    Vigo County Poor Asylum Ledger

Newspapers and Periodicals

Akron Daily
Christian Advocate
Christian Observer
Christian Union
Cleveland Daily Herald
Cleveland Morning Herald
Coleman's Rural World
Daily Ohio Statesman
Daily Tribune
Denver Daily News
Forum
Friend's Intelligencer
Herald of Gospel Liberty
Hocking Sentinel
Indiana Farmers' Guide
Indiana State Journal, Indianapolis
Indianapolis Times
InterOcean
Jasper Weekly Courier
Logansport Daily Journal, Logansport, Indiana
Mahoning Dispatch
Marietta Daily Leader
Marshall County Independent, Marshall, Indiana
Michigan Farmer
Ohio Democrat
Ohio Farmer
Omaha Daily Bee
Our Young Folks
Outlook
Pantagraph
Perrysburg Journal
Stark County Democrat
St. Louis Republic
The Daily Commonwealth
The Democratic Banner
The Huffington Post
The Independent, Plymouth, Indiana
The North American Review
The St. Paul Daily Globe
The Survey, Charity Organization Society of New York
Valentine Daily
Wichita Eagle
Youth's Companion

Published Primary Sources

Annual and Biennial Reports, Michigan State Public School (MSPS).
Annual Report of the Trustees of the Illinois Soldiers' Orphans' Home for the Year 1893. Springfield: State Journal Printing, 1893.
Annual Reports, Indiana Board of State Charities (IBSC).
Annual Reports, Ohio Board of State Charities (OBSC).
Benevolent Institutions 1904. Washington, D.C.: GPO, 1905.
Biennial Report, Illinois Board of Charities.
Biennial Reports, Minnesota State School for Dependent Children (MNSPS).
Board of Administration of the State of Illinois. *Sixth Annual Report of the Department of Visitation of Children Placed in Family Homes*. Springfield: Illinois State Journal Co. Printers, 1911.
Brace, Charles Loring. "What is the Best Method?" *Journal of Social Science* (May 1880).
Children Indentured by the Wisconsin State School. Children's Bureau Publication no. 150. Washington, D.C.: GPO, 1925.
Dodge, J. R. *American Farm Labor*. Washington, D.C.: GPO, 1901.
Eckman, Lulu. *Public Aid to Children in their Own Homes: A Tabular Summary of State Land in Effect*. November 1, 1922. Washington, D.C.: GPO, 1923.
Fifth Annual Ohio State Proceedings of Conference of Charities.
Folks, Gertrude. "Farm Labor and School Attendance." In *School Life*, Department of the Interior, Washington D.C., vol. IV, 1920.
Folks, Homer. "Some Developments of the Boarding Out System." *Charities Review* 2 (March 1893).
———. *The Care of Destitute, Neglected, and Delinquent Children*. New York: Macmillan, 1902.
———. "Why Should Dependent Children Be Reared in Families Rather than in Institutions." *Charities Review* 6 (1896).
Foster, John. "Preventative Work in Michigan." Coldwater, Mich., 1885.
Hall, Granville Stanley. *Youth: Its Education, Regimen, and Hygiene*. New York: D. Appleton and Co., 1908.
Hewins, Katherine, and L. Josephine Webster. *The Work of Child Placing Agencies*. Washington, D.C.: GPO, 1927.
Historical Sketches of the Higher Educational Institutions and also of Benevolent and Reformatory Institutions of the State of Ohio. Columbus: State Commissioner of Common Schools, 1876.
Indiana Department of Welfare. *The Development of Public Charities in Indiana*. Indianapolis: William Buford, 1905.
Indiana Quarterly Bulletin of Charities and Corrections. Indianapolis Board of State Charities, various years.
Johnson, Alexander. *The Almshouse, Construction and Management*. New York: Charities Publication Committee, 1911.
Laws Concerning Children, Indiana Department of Public Welfare.
Laws Related to Interstate Placement of Children. Children's Bureau Publication no. 139. Washington, D.C.: GPO, 1924.

Longman, R. A. *Report of the Placing of Children in Family Homes from the Children's Home of Cincinnati During a Period of Nine Years Beginning January 1, 1904 and Ending December 31, 1912*. Cincinnati: The Children's Home, 1912.

McGill, Nettie P., and Ella A. Merritt. *Children in Agriculture*. Children's Bureau Publication no. 187. Washington, D.C.: GPO, 1929.

Morris, Edmund. "Farming for Boys." *Our Young Folks*, n.p., 1868.

Ohio Bulletin of Charities and Corrections.

Proceedings of the Annual Convention of Trustees and Superintendents of the Children's Homes in Ohio.

Proceedings of the National Conference of Charities and Corrections (NCCC).

Proceedings of the Ohio State Conference on Dependent Children held at Dayton, Ohio. Cincinnati. N.p., 1915.

Records of Children admitted into the Miami County Children's Home (MCCH) 1879–1930, transcribed, Troy County Historical Society, http://www.thetroyhistoricalsociety.org/m-county/c-home/children.htm.

Sangamon County Poor Farm Inmate Records, Buffalo, Illinois. Springfield: Sangamon County Genealogical Society, 1994.

Schindler, Solomon. "Dependent Children and the State." *The Arena* (September 1905).

Slingerland, William Henry. *Child Placing in Families: A Manual for Students and Social Workers*. New York: Russell Sage Foundation, 1919.

Streeter, William. "The Care of Dependent Children in Indiana." *Forum* 32, no. 6 (February 1902).

Tenth Annual Convention of the Trustees and Superintendents of the Children's Homes in Ohio. N.p., 1891.

"The ABC's of Foster Care." Children's Bureau. Washington, D.C.: GPO, 1933.

"The Child Welfare Special, A Suggested Method of Reaching Rural Communities." U.S. Department of Labor, Children's Bureau, 1920.

U.S. Country Life Commission. *Report of the Commission on Country Life*. New York: Sturgis and Walton, 1911.

Wiggin, Kate Douglas. *Children's Rights: A Book of Nursery Logic*. Boston: Houghton Mifflin, 1893.

www.childrensaidsociety.org/about/history/orphan-trains.

www.hcgs.net, Early Deed Records, Henry County Genealogical Services, accessed January 31, 2008.

www.poetry-archive.com/r/little_orphan_annie.html, accessed March 13, 2012.

www.thetroyhistoricalsociety.org/m-county/c-home/children.htm. Transcription, Book 1, Miami County Children's Home, accessed June 5, 2013.

Secondary Sources

Agnew, Elizabeth. *From Charity to Social Work: Mary E. Richmond and the Creation of an American Profession*. Champaign: University of Illinois Press, 2004.

Anders, Steven. "The History of Child Welfare in Cincinnati, 1790–1930." Ph.D. diss., Miami University of Ohio, 1981.

Anderson, Clifford. "The Metamorphosis of American Agrarian Idealism in the 1920s and 1930s." *Agricultural History* 35, no. 4 (1961): 182–188.
Argersinger, Peter, and Joanne Argersinger. "The Machine Breakers: Farmworkers and Social Change in the Rural Midwest of the 1870s." *Agricultural History* 58, no. 3 (1984): 393–410.
Ashby, Leroy. *Endangered Children: Dependency, Neglect, and Abuse in American History*. New York: Twayne, 1997.
———. *Saving the Waifs: Reformers and Dependent Children, 1890–1917*. Philadelphia: Temple University Press, 1984.
Askeland, Lori. "'The Means of Draining the City of these Children': Domesticity and Romantic Individualism." *American Transcendental Quarterly* 12, no. 2 (1998): 145–163.
Atack, Jeremy, and Fred Bateman. *To Their Own Soil: Agriculture in the Antebellum North*. Ames: Iowa State University Press, 1987.
Babener, Liahna. "Bitter Nostalgia: Recollections of Childhood on the Midwestern Frontier." In *Small Worlds: Children and Adolescents in America, 1850–1950*, edited by Elliot West and Paula Petrik. Lawrence: University Press of Kansas, 1992.
Bacon, Jack. "Denver Historian Exposes Dark Side of Dispensing Justice in Colorado." *Denver Catholic Register*, November 27, 2002, http://www.archden.org/dcr/archive/20021127/2002112710ln.htm, accessed August 17, 2012.
Barillas, William. *The Midwestern Pastoral: Place and Landscape in Literature of the American Heartland*. Athens: University of Ohio Press, 2006.
Barron, Hal. *Mixed Harvest: The Second Great Transformation in the Rural North, 1870–1930*. Chapel Hill: University of North Carolina Press, 1997.
———. "Rural America on the Silent Screen." *Agricultural History* 80, no. 4 (2006): 383–410.
Baum, Rosalie Murphy. "The Burden of Myth: The Role of the Farmer in American Literature." *North Dakota Quarterly* 53, no. 4 (1985): 4–24.
Beito, David. "Mooseheart: 'The Child City.'" In *Home Away from Home: The Forgotten History of Orphanages*, edited by Richard B. McKenzie. New York: Encounter Books, 2009.
Bellingham, Bruce. "Institution and Family: An Alternative View of Nineteenth-Century Child Saving." *Social Problems* 33, no. 6 (1986): S33–S57.
Berebitsky, Julie. *Like Our Very Own: Adoption and the Changing Culture of Motherhood*. Lawrence: University Press of Kansas, 2000.
Bowen, C. E. *Abby Blake or Bound Out at Farm Service*. New York: Nelson and Sons, 1885.
Bowers, William L. *The Country Life Movement in America, 1900–1920*. Port Washington, N.Y.: Kennikat, 1974.
Brace, Emma, ed. *The Life of Charles Loring Brace*. New York: Arno, 1976.
Bradley, Martha Sonntag. "'Protect the Children—Protect the Boys and Girls': Child Welfare Work in Utah, 1888–1920." Ph.D. diss., University of Utah, 1987.
Brownwell, Blaine A. "The Agrarian and Urban Ideals: Environmental Images in Modern America." *Journal of Popular Culture* 5, no. 3 (1971): 576–587.

Brunner, Edmund de S., and J. H. Kolb. *Rural Social Trends*. New York: Greenwood, 1969.

Burns, Sarah. *Pastoral Inventions: Rural Life in Nineteenth Century American Art and Culture*. Philadelphia: Temple University Press, 1989.

Bush, William S. *Who Gets a Childhood? Race and Juvenile Justice in Twentieth-Century Texas*. Athens: University of Georgia Press, 2010.

Carp, E. Wayne. "Two Cheers for Orphanages." *Reviews in American History* 24, no. 2 (1996): 277–284.

Carp, E. Wayne, ed. *Adoption in America: Historical Perspectives*. Ann Arbor: University of Michigan Press, 2002.

Cayton, Andrew R. L. "The Anti-Region: Place and Identity in the American Midwest." In *The Identity of the American Midwest: Essays on Regional History*, edited by Andrew R. L. Cayton and Susan E. Gray. Bloomington: Indiana University Press, 2001.

Cayton, Andrew R. L., and Susan E. Gray, eds. *The Identity of the American Midwest: Essays on Regional History*. Bloomington: Indiana University Press, 2001.

"Centennial Series: The Children's Year, 1918–1919." Online Digest, May 2012, http://cbexpress.acf.hhs.gov. Accessed September 10, 2012.

Channing, Alice. "Illinois Soldiers' Orphans' Home." M.A. thesis, University of Chicago, 1926.

Clayton-Drew, John. "Child Labor and Child Welfare: The Origins of Uneven Development of the American Welfare State." Ph.D. diss., Cornell University, 1987.

Clement, Priscilla Ferguson. "Families and Foster Care: Philadelphia in the Late Nineteenth Century." *Social Service Review* 53 (1979): 406–420.

———. *Growing Pains: Children in the Industrial Age, 1850–1890*. New York: Twayne, 1997.

———. "With Wise and Benevolent Purpose: Poor Children and the State Public School at Owatonna, 1885–1915." *Minnesota History* 49, no. 1 (1984): 2–13.

Cmiel, Kenneth. *A Home of Another Kind: One Chicago Orphanage and the Tangle of Child Welfare*. Chicago: University of Chicago Press, 1995.

Cohen, Ronald D. "Child-Saving and Progressivism, 1885–1915." In *American Childhood: A Research Guide and Historical Handbook*, edited by Joseph Hawes and Ray D. Hine. Westport, Conn.: Greenwood, 1985.

Cook, Jeanne. "Experiences of Orphan Train Riders: Implications for Child Welfare Policy." Ph.D. diss., University of South Carolina, 1994.

Cornelius, Janet Duitsman, and Martha LaFrenz Kay. *Women of Conscience: Social Reform in Danville, Illinois, 1890–1930*. Columbia: University of South Carolina Press, 2008.

Coulter, John Lee. "Agricultural Laborers in the United States." *Annals of the American Academy of Political and Social Science* 40 (1912): 40–44.

Cowger, Thomas. "Custodians of Social Justice: The Indianapolis Asylum for Friendless Colored Children." *Indiana Magazine of History* 88, no. 2 (1992): 93–110.

Craig, Lee, and Thomas Weiss. "Hours at Work and Total Factor Productivity Growth in Nineteenth Century U.S. Agriculture." In *Advances in Agricultural Economic History*, edited by Kyle D. Kauffman. Stamford: JAI, 2000.

Cravens, Hamilton. "Child Saving in the Age of Professionalism, 1915–1930." In *American Childhood: A Historical Handbook and Research Guide*, edited by Joseph Hawes and Ray D. Hiner. Westport, Conn.: Greenwood, 1985.

Crenson, Matthew. *Building the Invisible Orphanage: A Prehistory of the American Welfare System*. Cambridge, Mass.: Harvard University Press, 2001.

Cronon, William. *Nature's Metropolis: Chicago and the Great West*. New York: W.W. Norton, 1991.

Cruse, Jennifer, and Larry Cruse. *History of the Children: Rose Orphan Home, Terre Haute, Indiana, Residents Admitted between 1884–1901*. N.p. Authors, 2006.

Curry, Lynne. *Modern Mothers in the Heartland: Gender, Health, and Progress in Illinois, 1900–1930*. Columbus: Ohio State University Press, 1999.

Curtis, Susan. *A Consuming Faith: The Social Gospel and Modern American Culture*. Columbia: University of Missouri Press, 2001.

Danbom, David. *Born in the Country: A History of Rural America*. Baltimore: Johns Hopkins University Press, 1995.

———. *The Resisted Revolution: Urban America and the Industrialization of Agriculture*. Ames: Iowa State University Press, 1979.

———. "Romantic Agrarianism in Twentieth Century America." *Agricultural History* 65, no. 4 (1991): 1–12.

Demos, John. *Past, Present, and Personal: The Family and the Life Course in American History*. New York: Oxford University Press, 1986.

Dorn, Jacob. "The Rural Ideal and Agrarian Realities: Arthur E. Holt and the Vision of a Decentralized America in the Interwar Years." *Church History* 52, no. 1 (1983): 50–65.

Drew, John Clayton. "Child Labor and Child Welfare: The Origins and Uneven Development of the American Welfare State." Ph.D. diss., Cornell University, 1987.

Dulberger, Judith. *"Mother Donit for the Best": Correspondence of a Nineteenth-Century Orphan Asylum*. Syracuse, N.Y.: Syracuse University Press, 1996.

Effland, Anne. "Agrarianism and Child Labor Policy for Agriculture." *Agricultural History* 79, no. 3 (2005): 281–297.

———. "When Rural Does Not Equal Agricultural." *Agricultural History* 74, no. 2 (2000): 489–501.

Elbaum, Bernard. "Why Apprenticeship Persisted in Britain but not in the United States." *Journal of Economic History* 49 (1989): 337–349.

Erisman, Fred. "Transcendentalism for American Youth: The Children's Books of Kate Douglas Wiggin." *New England Quarterly* 41, no. 2 (1968): 238–247.

Fitzgerald, Deborah. *Every Farm a Factory: The Industrial Ideal in American Agriculture*. New Haven, Conn.: Yale University Press, 2003.

Franklin, Benjamin. *The Autobiography of Benjamin Franklin*. New York: Cuneo, 1936.

Gelle, Richard J., and John Harrop. "The Risk of Abusive Violence Among Children with Nongenetic Caretakers." *Family Relations* 40, no. 1 (1991): 78–83.

Gillette, John. "The Drift to the City in Relation to the Rural Problem." *American Journal of Sociology* 16, no. 5 (1911): 645–667.

Gittens, Joan. *Poor Relations: The Children of the State in Illinois, 1818–1990*. Urbana: University of Illinois Press, 1994.

Gjerde, Jon. *The Minds of the West: Ethnocultural Evolution in the Middle West, 1830–1917*. Chapel Hill: University of North Carolina Press, 1997.

Gollaher, David. *Voice for the Mad: The Life of Dorthea Dix*. New York: The Free Press, 1995.

Gordon, Linda. *Heroes of Their Own Lives: The Politics and History of Family Violence*. Urbana: University of Illinois Press, 1988.

———. *The Great Arizona Orphan Abduction*. Cambridge, Mass.: Harvard University Press, 2001.

———. *Pitied But Not Entitled: Single Mothers and the History of Welfare, 1890–1935*. Cambridge, Mass.: Harvard University Press, 1998.

———. "The Politics of Sexual Child Abuse: Notes from American History." *Feminist Review* 28 (Spring 1988): 56–64.

Gratton, Brian, and Jon Moen. "Immigration, Culture, and Child Labor in the United States, 1880–1920." *Journal of Interdisciplinary History* 1 (2004): 355–391.

Griswold, Alfred W. *Farming and Democracy*. New York: Harcourt and Brace, 1948.

Guth, James. "The National Board of Farm Organizations: Experiments in Political Cooperation." *Agricultural History* 48, no. 3 (1974): 418–440.

Hagenstein, Edwin, Sara Gregg, and Brian Donahue, eds. *American Georgics: Writings on Farming, Culture, and the Land*. New Haven, Conn.: Yale University Press, 2011.

Hahamavitch, Cindy. *Fruits of Their Labor: Atlantic Coast Farm Workers and the Making of Migrant Poverty, 1870–1945*. Chapel Hill: University of North Carolina Press, 1997.

Hammack, David. *Making the Nonprofit Sector in the United States*. Bloomington: Indiana University Press, 1998.

Hart, Patricia S. *A Home for Every Child: The Washington Children's Home Society in the Progressive Era*. Seattle: University of Washington Press, 2010.

———. "A Nation's Need for Adoption and Competing Realities: The Washington Children's Home Society, 1895–1915." In *Adoption in America: Historical Perspectives*, edited by E. Wayne Carp, 140–159. Ann Arbor: University of Michigan Press, 2002.

Hasci, Timothy. "Orphanages as a National Institution: History and Its Lessons." In *Home Away from Home: The Forgotten History of Orphanages*, edited by Richard B. McKenzie. New York: Encounter Books, 2009.

———. *Second Home: Orphan Asylums and Poor Families in America*. Cambridge, Mass.: Harvard University Press, 1998.

Hatton, Timothy, and Jeffrey Williamson. "What Explains Wage Gaps Between Farm and City? Exploring the Todaro Model with American Evidence, 1890–1941." *Economic Development and Cultural Change* 40, no. 2 (1992): 267–294.

Hawes, Joseph. *Children Between the Wars: American Childhood, 1920–1940*. New York: Twayne, 1997.

———. *The Children's Rights Movement: A History of Advocacy and Protection*. Boston: Twayne, 1991.

Heller, Charles, and John Houdek. "Farm Tenants and Landlords in Nineteenth Century Southern Michigan: A Study of Two Townships." *Agricultural History* 70, no. 4 (1996): 598–625.

Herndon, Ruth Wallis, and John E. Murray, eds. *Children Bound to Labor: The Pauper Apprentice System in Early America*. Ithaca, N.Y.: Cornell University Press, 2009.

Higbie, Frank Tobias. "Rural Work, Household Subsistence, and the North American Working Class: A View from the Midwest." *International Labor and Working-Class History* 65 (Spring 2004): 50–76.

Hindman, Hugh D. *Child Labor: An American History*. Armonk, N.Y.: M. E. Sharp, 2002.

"History of CAS Emigration Programs including Family Emigration, Employment, Adoption, and Foster Care." http://dlib.nyu.edu/findingaids/html/nyhs/childrensaidsociety_at.html.

Hofstadter, Richard. *The Age of Reform*. London: Jonathan Cape, 1962.

Holloran, Peter C. *Boston's Wayward Children: Social Services for Homeless Children, 1830–1930*. Rutherford, N.J.: Fairleigh Dickinson University Press, 1989.

Holt, Marilyn Irvin. *Children of the Western Plains: The Nineteenth Century Experience*. Chicago: Ivan Dee, 2008.

———. *Indian Orphanages*. Lawrence: University Press of Kansas, 2001.

———. "The Orphan Trains as an Alternative to Orphanages." In *Home Away from Home: The Forgotten History of Orphanages*, edited by Richard B. McKenzie. New York: Encounter Books, 2009.

———. *The Orphan Trains: Placing Out in America*. Lincoln: University of Nebraska Press, 1992.

Hood, Laura. *Foster Home Care for Dependent Children*. Washington, D.C.: GPO, 1926.

Hurley, Daniel. *One Child at a Time: A History of the Children's Home of Cincinnati, 1864–1989*. Cincinnati, Ohio: The Children's Home, 1990.

Hurt, R. Douglas. *Agricultural Technology in the Twentieth Century*. Manhattan, Kans.: Sunflower, 1991.

———. *American Agriculture: A Brief History*. West Lafayette, Ind.: Purdue University Press, 2002.

———. *Problems of Plenty: The American Farmer in the Twentieth Century*. Chicago: Ivan Dee, 2002.

Hyde Bailey, Liberty. *The Country Life Movement in the United States*. New York: Macmillan, 1911.

Jeffers, Mildred. "The Development in Indiana of Public Resources for the Sick Poor, the Tuberculous, the Epileptic, and the Crippled, with Special Reference to the Care of the Sick and Crippled Children." M.A. thesis, Indiana University, 1951.

Katz, Michael. *In the Shadow of the Poorhouse: A Social History of Welfare in America*. New York: Basic Books, 1996.

Keppel, Ann M. "The Myth of Agrarianism in Rural Education Reform." *History of Education Quarterly* 2, no. 2 (1962): 100–112.

Kidder, Clark, and H. D. Clarke. *Orphan Trains and their Precious Cargo: The Life's Work of Reverend H. D. Clarke*. Bowie, Md.: Heritage Books, 2001.

Kindell, Alexandra. "Washingtonian Agrarianism: Antebellum Reformers and the Agrarian Image of George Washington." *American Nineteenth Century History* 13, no. 3 (2012): 347–370.

Klein, Philip. *From Philanthropy to Social Welfare: An American Cultural Perspective*. San Francisco: Jossey-Bass, 1971.

Kleinberg, S. J. *Widows and Orphans First: The Family Economy and Social Welfare Policy, 1880–1939*. Urbana: University of Illinois Press, 2006.

Kohlsted, Sally Gregory. "'A Better Crop of Boys and Girls': The School Gardening Movement, 1890–1920." *History of Education Quarterly* 48, no. 1 (2008): 58–93.

Kounse, Martha J. *Annotated Lawrence County Children's Home Register, 1874–1926*. Milford, Ohio: Little Miami Publishing, 2003.

Ladd-Taylor, Molly. *Mother-Work: Women, Child Welfare and the State, 1890–1930*. Urbana: University of Illinois Press, 1995.

Landis, Benson Y. *Rural Welfare Services*. New York: Columbia University Press, 1949.

Langsam, Miriam. *Children West: A History of the Placing Out System of the New York Children's Aid Society, 1853–1890*. Madison: Wisconsin Historical Society, 1964.

Larson, Olaf, and Julie Zimmerman. "The USDA's Bureau of Agricultural Economics." *Agricultural History* 74, no. 2 (2000): 227–240.

Lauck, Jon. *The Lost Region: Toward a Revival of Midwestern History*. Iowa City: University of Iowa Press, 2013.

Leiberman, Alice, and Kristine Nelson, eds. *Women & Children First: The Contribution of the Children's Bureau to Social Work Education*. Alexandria, Va.: Council on Social Work Education, 2013.

Lindenmeyer, Kristie. *"A Right to Childhood": The U.S. Children's Bureau and Child Welfare, 1912–1946*. Urbana: University of Illinois Press, 1997.

Loewen, James. *Sundown Towns: A Hidden Dimension of American Racism*. New York: New Press, 2005.

Lowry, Nelson. "The Rise of Rural Sociology: The Pre-Purnell Period." *Rural Sociology* 30, no. 4 (1965): 407–427.

Lyons-Barnett, Mary. "Child Labor in Commercialized Agriculture." Ph.D. diss., University of Nebraska, 2002.

Mangold, George. *Child Problems*. New York: Macmillan, 1910.

Mapes, Kathleen. *Sweet Tyranny: Migrant Labor, Industrial Agriculture, and Imperial Politics*. Urbana: University of Illinois Press, 2009.

Marshall, Joan E. "Parents and Foster Parents, Shapers of Progressive Era Child Saving Practices: A Case Study, Tippecanoe County, Indiana, 1887–1916." *Indiana Magazine of History* 90, no. 2 (1994): 147–173.

Marten, James, ed. *Children in Colonial America*. New York: New York University Press, 2007.

Martinez-Brawley, Emilia. *Seven Decades of Rural Social Work: From Country Life Commission to Rural Caucus*. New York: Praeger, 1981.

McConnell, Grant. *The Decline of American Democracy*. Berkeley: University of California Press, 1959.

McMath, Robert C. *American Populism: A Social History*. New York: Hill and Wang, 1993.

Mennel, Robert M. "The Family System of Common Farmers: The Early Years of Ohio's Reform Farm, 1858–1884." *Ohio History* 89, no. 2 (1980): 279–322.

Mintz, Steven. *Huck's Raft: A History of American Childhood*. Cambridge, Mass.: Belknap Press of Harvard University Press, 2004.

Montgomery, Lucy Maud. *Anne of Green Gables*. Electronic reproduction. Boulder, Colo.: NetLibrary, 2001.

Montmarque, James A. "American Agrarianism: The Living Tradition." In *The Agrarian Roots of Pragmatism*, edited by Hilde Thompson. Nashville: Vanderbilt University Press, 2006.

Morris, Edmund. *Farming For Boys*. Boston: Fields & Osgood, 1869.

Morton, Marian. "The Transformation of Catholic Orphanages: Cleveland, 1851–1996." In *Home Away from Home: The Forgotten History of Orphanages*, edited by Richard B. McKenzie. New York: Encounter Books, 2009.

Murray, John, and Ruth Wallis Herndon. "Markets for Children: The Political Economy of Pauper Apprenticeship." *Journal of Economic History* 62, no. 2 (2002): 356–382.

Nadasen, Premilla, Jennifer Mittelstadt, and Marisa Chappell. *Welfare in the United States: A History with Documents, 1935–1996*. New York: Routledge, 2009.

Nelson, Claudia. *Little Strangers: Portrayals of Adoption and Foster Care in America, 1850–1929*. Bloomington: Indiana University Press, 2003.

———. "The Orphan in American Children's Literature." In *Children and Youth in Adoption, Foster Care, and Orphanages: A Historical Handbook and Guide*, edited by Lori Askeland. Westport, Conn.: Greenwood, 2006.

Nelson, Daniel. *Farm and Factory: Workers in the Midwest, 1880–1990*. Bloomington: Indiana University Press, 1995.

Norris, James. "Growing Up Growing Sugar: Local Teenage Labor in the Sugar Beet Fields, 1958–1974." *Agricultural History* 79, no. 3 (2005): 298–320.

O'Conner, Stephen. *Orphan Trains: The Story of Charles Loring Brace and the Children He Saved and Failed*. Chicago: University of Chicago Press, 2004.

Orme, John T., and Cheryl Buehler. "Foster Family Characteristics and Behavioral and Emotional Problems of Foster Children: A Narrative Review." *Family Relations* 50, no. 1 (2001): 3–15.

Peters, Scott J. "Every Farmer Should be Awakened: Liberty Hyde Bailey's Vision of Agricultural Extension Work." *Agricultural History* 80, no. 2 (2006): 190–219.

Peters, Scott, and Paul Morgan. "The Country Life Commission: Reconsidering a Milestone in American Agricultural History." *Agricultural History* 78, no. 3 (2004): 289–316.

Pierce, Michael. "Farmers and the Failure of Populism in Ohio, 1890–1891." *Agricultural History* 74, no. 1 (2000): 58–85.

Pinkett, Harold. "Government Research Concerning Problems of American Rural Society." *Agricultural History* 58, no. 3 (1984): 365–372.

Pleck, Elizabeth. *Domestic Tyranny: The Making of Social Policy Against Family Violence from Colonial Times to the Present*. Oxford: Oxford University Press, 1987.

Postel, Charles. *The Populist Vision*. New York: Oxford University Press, 2009.

Provasnik, Stephen. "Judicial Activism and the Origins of Parental Choice: The Courts' Role in the Institutionalization of Compulsory Education in the United States, 1891–1925." *History of Education Quarterly* 46, no. 3 (2006): 311–347.

Ramey, Jessie B. *Childcare in Black and White: Working Parents and the History of Orphanages*. Urbana: University of Illinois Press, 2012.

Reef, Catherine. *Alone in the World: Orphans and Orphanages in America*. New York: Clarion, 2005.

Reid, Bill. "The Agrarian Tradition and Urban Problems." *Midwestern Quarterly* 6, no. 1 (1964): 75–86.

Riley, Glenda. *The Life and Legacy of Annie Oakley*. Norman: University of Oklahoma Press, 1994.

Riney-Kehrberg, Pamela. *Childhood on the Farm: Work, Play, and Coming of Age in the Midwest*. Lawrence: University Press of Kansas, 2005.

———. *The Nature of Childhood: An Environmental History of Growing Up In America Since 1865*. Lawrence: University Press of Kansas, 2014.

Rooke, Patricia, and R. L. Schnell. *Discarding the Asylum: From Child Rescue to the Welfare State in English Canada, 1800–1950*. Lanham, Md.: University Press of America, 1983.

Ross, Catherine. "Society Children: The Care of Indigent Youngsters in New York City, 1875–1903." Ph.D. diss., Yale University, 1977.

Ruswick, Brent. *Almost Worthy: The Poor, Paupers, and the Science of Charity in America*. Bloomington: Indiana University Press, 2013.

Ryan, Patrick J. "'Six Blacks from Home': Childhood, Motherhood, and Eugenics in America." *Journal of Policy History* 19, no. 3, (2007): 253–281.

Saksena, Marian E. "Out of Home Placements for Abused, Neglected, and Dependent Children in Minnesota, A Historical Perspective." *William Mitchell Law Review* 32, no. 3 (2006): 1007–1048.

Sanders, Elizabeth. *Roots of Reform: Farmers, Workers, and the American State, 1877–1917*. Chicago: University of Chicago Press, 1999.

Schob, David. *Hired Hands and Plowboys: Farm Labor in the Midwest, 1815–1860*. Urbana: University of Illinois Press, 1975.

Scott, Roy V. *The Agrarian Movement in Illinois*. Urbana: University of Illinois Press, 1962.

Sealander, Judith. *The Failed Century of the Child: Governing America's Young in the Twentieth Century*. New York: Cambridge University Press, 2003.

Shaw, Christopher. "No Place for Class Politics." *Agricultural History* 85, no. 4 (2011): 520–539.

Shideler, James. "'Flappers and Philosophers' and Farmers: Rural-Urban Tensions of the Twenties." *Agricultural History* 47, no. 4 (1973).

Shortridge, James. *The Middle West: Its Meaning in American Culture*. Lawrence: University Press of Kansas, 1989.

Shover, John L. *First Majority, Last Minority: The Transforming of Rural Life in America*. DeKalb: Northern Illinois University Press, 1976.

Skocpol, Theda. *Protecting Soldiers and Mothers: The Political Origins of Social Policy in the United States*. Cambridge, Mass.: Belknap Press of Harvard University Press, 1995.

Steffes, Tracy L. "Solving the 'Rural School Problem': New State Aid, Standards, and Supervision of Local Schools, 1900–1930." *History of Education Quarterly* 48, no. 2 (2008): 181–220.

Steinson, Barbara. "Rural Life in Indiana, 1800–1950." *Indiana Magazine of History* 90, no. 3 (September 1994).

Stuart, Paul H. "The Early Years: Research and Advocacy, 1912–1938." In *Women & Children First: The Contribution of the Children's Bureau to Social Work Education*, edited by Alice Lieberman and Kristine Nelson. Alexandria, Va.: Council on Social Work Education, 2013.

Swartz, Teresa Toguchi. "Mothering for the State: Foster Parenting and the Challenges of Government-Contracted Carework." *Gender and Society* 18, no. 5 (2004): 567–587.

Taylor, Carl. "The Rise of the Rural Problem." *Journal of Social Forces* 2, no. 1 (1923): 29–36.

Thompson, Carl William, and Gustav Paul Warber. *Social and Economic Survey of a Rural Township in Southern Minnesota*. Minneapolis: University of Minnesota, 1913.

Thompson, Paul B. "Thomas Jefferson and Agrarian Philosophy." In *The Agrarian Roots of Pragmatism*, edited by Paul B. Thompson and Thomas C. Hilde. Nashville: Vanderbilt University Press, 2000.

Tiffin, Susan. *In Whose Best Interest? Child Welfare Reform in the Progressive Era*. Westport, Conn.: Greenwood, 1982.

Tontz, Robert. "Memberships of General Farmer's Organizations, United States, 1874–1960." *Agricultural History* 38, no. 3 (1964): 143–156.

Trammell, Rebecca S. "Orphan Train Myths and Legal Realities." *The Modern American* 5, no. 2 (2009): 3–13.

Vandepol, Ann. "Dependent Children, Child Custody, and the Mother's Pensions: The Transformation of State-Family Relations in the Early Twentieth Century." *Social Problems* 29, no. 3 (1982): 221–235.

Wall, Helena M. "'My Constant Attension on My Sick Child': The Fragility of Family Life in the World of Elizabeth Drinker." In *Children in Colonial America*, edited by James Marten, 155–167. New York: New York University Press, 2007.

Welle, Dorinda. "'Things Which I Was Never Interested In': Labor, Moral Reform, and the Discipline of Community at the Berkshire Industrial Farm for Boys." *Research and Society* 5 (1992): 7–34.

Wells, Christopher. "The Changing Nature of Country Roads: Farmers, Reformers, and the Shifting Uses of Rural Space, 1880–1905." *Agricultural History* 80, no. 2 (2006): 143–166.

West, Elliot, and Paula Petrik, eds. *Small Worlds: Children and Adolescents in America, 1850–1950.* Lawrence: University Press of Kansas, 1992.

White, Elizabeth. "The History and Development of the Illinois Children's Home and Aid Society." M.A. thesis, University of Chicago, 1934.

Woodward, Rob. *19th Century Care of Orphan and Pauper Children in Wabash County.* Wabash, Ind.: Wabash County Genealogical Society, 2008.

Wunderlich, Gene. *American Country Life.* Lanham, Md.: University Press of America, 2003.

www.pbs.org. Transcript of American Experience, episode: Annie Oakley. Accessed March 16, 2012.

Zelizer, Viviana. *Pricing the Priceless Child: The Changing Social Value of Children.* New York: Basic Books, 1985.

Ziegler, Edith. "'The Burdens and the Narrow Life of Farm Women': Women, Gender, and Theodore Roosevelt's Commission on Country Life." *Agricultural History* 86, no. 3 (2012): 77–103.

Zipf, Karen. *Labor of Innocents: Forced Apprenticeship in North Carolina, 1715–1919.* Baton Rouge: Louisiana State University Press, 2005.

Index

Abbott, Grace, 163–64, 181
abuse: physical, 79–82, 88, 92–98, 201n120; sexual, 14, 95–96, 105
adoption, 87, 171–72; failures, 10, 84
Agricultural Adjustment Act, 179
Aid to Dependent Children, 181
Aid to Families with Dependent Children, 181
Alden, Ernest, 91, 198n22
Alden, Lyman, 4–5, 39–40, 53, 63, 66, 77, 95; placement correspondence, 35, 99; publications, 68; on supervision of children, 118–19; work in Michigan, 65, 115. *See also* "The Shady Side of Placing Out"
American Country Life Association. *See* Country Life Movement
American Farm Bureau Association. *See* Farm Bureau
Anne of Green Gables, 21
apprenticeship, 9, 59–60, 81, 96
Apprenticeship Act, 48

Bailey, Liberty Hyde, 30, 41, 153–54. *See also* Country Life Commission
Belmont County, Ohio, 54–55, 57, 73, 90
Berea College, 99
Beveridge, Albert, 151–52
Bicknell, Ernest, 111
binding out, 9, 48, 121, 174
biological parents: African American, 53, 61; contact with children, 53, 84, 101, 139; oversight of, 135–39; reclaiming children, 52–54, 134, 205n109; removal from, 103, 116, 134; surrendering children, 52
boarding, 9, 58, 139, 170, 174. *See also* boarding payments
boarding payments, 52–54, 130, 138–40; Massachusetts use of, 48, 138, 185n28; paid by parents, 130. *See also* foster care
Board of State Charities and Corrections. *See* state boards of charity
Boys Working Reserve, 165
Brace, Charles Loring, 4, 24–25, 42, 61; criticisms of, 87. *See also* Brace Farm; CASNY; orphan train
Brace Farm, 27. *See also* Brace, Charles Loring; farm training
Brinkerhoff, R., 110
Brown, J. A., 131
Brown County, Ohio, 86
Burbank, Luther, 22
Butler, Amos, 112–13, 120, 140
Butler County, Ohio, 136
Byers, A. G., 45–46, 110
Byers, J. P., 112

caseworkers. *See* social workers; visiting agents
CASNY, 2, 67, 70–72, 85, 87–88; agents for, 31; criticisms of, 56; decline of emigration, 173–74. *See also* Brace, Charles Loring; orphan trains
Cass County, Indiana, 75. *See also* Dykeman, Mary
Champaign County, Ohio, 83

charity boards. *See* state boards of charity
Charity Organization Society, 116, 123
Chicago Nursery and Half Orphans' Asylum, 28. *See also* urban institutions
child dependency. *See* dependency
child labor: boys, 23, 55, 149; chores, 37, 123, 150; cost, 37; criticism of, 23, 71, 121, 145; danger of, 40, 103, 149–50; with family, 7, 149; on farms, 6, 23, 60, 86, 89, 100, 145, 151, 163–65, 179–80; girls, 34, 37, 86; industrial, 39–40, 159, 162; legal restrictions, 150–51, 162–63; as punishment, 29; seasonal, 31; during World War I, 165–67. *See also* juvenile reformatory
children: African American, 98; arrested, 102; destroying property, 102; disobedient, 91, 100–101; earning wages, 91, 100, 165–66; idiotic and insane, 69; illegitimate, 48; pregnant, 96; runaways, 86, 91, 94, 98–100, 132; sexually active, 85, 95–96, 100; urban, 30
Children's Aid Society, 26, 49, 121–22, 124; Canada, 106; Michigan, 123, 136, 173–74
Children's Bureau, 129, 135, 139, 151, 155, 181; development of, 144–46, 162–63; health care initiatives, 166–68; publications, 95, 174–75; research, 16, 157–59, 163–69, 172–75, 201n11
Children's Home and Aid Society, 121–22, 131
Children's Home Finding Society, 121, 141; of Illinois, 49, 121–22. *See also* Children's Aid Society
Children's Home of Cincinnati, 27, 30, 65–67, 82, 170–71; farm institution of, 67, 73. *See also* Green, G. T.
Children's Home Society, 7, 122, 125, 128
Child Welfare League of America, 168
chores. *See* child labor
Cincinnati General Protestant Orphan Home, 94
Cleveland Protestant Orphans' Home, 62, 67
Clinton County, Ohio, 86
Collingsworth, Herbert, 21–22
Committee on Industrial Relations, 164
contracts. *See* indenture contracts
Cooperatives. *See* Grange
Country Life Commission, 15, 30, 41, 153–56, 175; findings of, 156, 160, 167; goals, 145, 152. *See also* Bailey, Liberty Hyde

Country Life Movement, 152, 154–57, 170
county agents. *See* volunteer boards
County Boards of Children's Guardians, 116–17, 136, 141
county boards of supervisors. *See* trustees of the poor
county children's homes, 13, 55, 130, 140; building of, 47, 50–51, 65; closures, 113, 130–31, 141; correspondence to, 183; costs, 54, 131; management of, 113–14; per diems to, 113, 141; placements from, 66, 105
county commissioners, 114
county infirmary. *See* poor farm
courts: involvement in placing, 132–33, 173
Crouse, Meigs V., 25, 66, 74, 170. *See also* Children's Home of Cincinnati
cruelty. *See* abuse

Darke County, Ohio: poor farm, 78–79
Davies, Mary Allen, 129, 158. *See also* visiting agent
Dawes Severalty Act, 19
deaths: accidental, 96; intentional, 96–98
Defiance County, Ohio, 60
Department of Welfare: Illinois, 135; Indiana, 120; Ohio, 129–30, 140, 178
dependency: causes of, 7, 137; court involvement in, 134; definition of, 185n21
direct aid, 115, 134, 136–38, 205n124; as part of the New Deal, 180. *See also* mother's aid
disabilities, 69, 143. *See also* children, idiotic and insane
Dix, Dorothea, 45
Dykeman, Mary, 75. *See also* Cass County, Indiana

elopement, 99
emigration. *See* orphan train
ethnicity: of children, 63, 71–72; of parents, 63; of placement parents, 32, 62

Fairmount Children's Home, 69, 72, 112. *See also* Stark County
family labor, 7, 32–33, 36–37, 39–40, 145, 151–52. *See also* child labor, with families
family preservation, 134, 137–39, 143–44, 168. *See also* biological parents
Farm Bureau, 148, 159, 163, 180
Farmers' Alliance, 147. *See also* Populists

MEGAN BIRK is an associate professor of history at the University of Texas Rio Grande Valley (formerly the University of Texas–Pan American).

The University of Illinois Press
is a founding member of the
Association of American University Presses.

———————————————

University of Illinois Press
1325 South Oak Street
Champaign, IL 61820-6903
www.press.uillinois.edu